JOHN HUME

JOHN HUME
Irish Peacemaker

Seán Farren & Denis Haughey
EDITORS

FOUR COURTS PRESS

Set in 10.5 on 13 point AGaramond for
FOUR COURTS PRESS LTD
7 Malpas Street, Dublin 8, Ireland
www.fourcourtspress.ie
and in North America by
FOUR COURTS PRESS
c/o ISBS, 920 N.E. 58th Avenue, Suite 300, Portland, OR 97213.

ISBN 978-1-84682-586-6

A catalogue record for this title
is available from the British Library.

Printed in England
by Antony Rowe Ltd, Chippenham, Wilts.

Contents

Illustrations

IMAGE CREDITS

7, 8, 9 Willie Carson archive; 1–4, 6, 10, 14, 15, 17, 20–3, 25 Hume family collection; 16 *Irish Times*; 5, 11–13, 19 SDLP archive

Abbreviations and Acronyms

APL	Anti-Partition League
CDU	Campaign for Democracy in Ulster
CSJ	Campaign for Social Justice
DCAC	Derry Citizens' Action Committee
DHA	Derry Housing Association
DHAC	Derry Housing Action Committee
EC	European Community
EEC	European Economic Community
EP	European Parliament
EU	European Union
GAA	Gaelic Athletic Association
HC	House of Commons
INCORE	Institute for Conflict Research
IRA	Irish Republican Army
NATO	North Atlantic Treaty Organization
NI	Northern Ireland
NICRA	Northern Ireland Civil Rights Association
NILP	Northern Ireland Labour Party
NIO	Northern Ireland Office
RUC	Royal Ulster Constabulary
SDLP	Social Democratic and Labour Party
UK	United Kingdom
US	United States
USC	Ulster Special Constabulary
UWC	Ulster Workers' Council

Significant Dates and Developments

1937   John Hume, eldest child of Annie and Sam Hume, born in Derry.

1941–58   Educated at St Eugene's Primary School and St Columb's College in Derry, and at St Patrick's College, Maynooth.

1960   Hume marries Pat Hone.

1960   Derry Credit Union established with John Hume a founding member.

1963   Terence O'Neill elected Prime Minister of Northern Ireland; Hume chairs the University for Derry committee.

1964   John Hume's seminal *Irish Times* articles published; Hume elected President of Credit Union League of Ireland.

1965   Hume chairs the Derry Housing Association committee.

1966   Hume becomes manager of Derry-based smoked salmon business *Atlantic Harvest*.

1967   Northern Ireland Civil Rights Association founded.

1968   October civil rights march in Derry baton charged by police; Hume elected vice-chair of Derry's Citizens' Action Committee.

1969   Hume elected MP to Northern Ireland Parliament; 'siege' of Derry's Bogside in August.

1970   SDLP founded with Gerry Fitt MP as Leader and John Hume Deputy Leader; IRA launches terror campaign.

1971   SDLP withdraws from parliament; internment without trial directed against IRA; Assembly of the Northern Ireland People established.

1972   Thirteen men shot dead by British Army in Derry on 'Bloody Sunday'; Northern Ireland Parliament prorogued and William Whitelaw appointed Secretary of State.

1973   Hume elected to new Northern Ireland Assembly; power-sharing executive and Council of Ireland agreed in the Sunningdale Agreement.

1974   Hume takes office as Minister of Commerce; power-sharing execu-
            tive collapses in face of unionist opposition, the Ulster Workers'
            strike and IRA violence.

1975   Hume elected to Northern Ireland Convention established to seek
            cross-community accord.

1976   Convention fails to reach agreement; Hume spends semester at the
            Harvard Centre for International Relations.

1978   Hume appointed a member of EC Commissioner Richard Burke's
            cabinet.

1979   Hume elected to the European Parliament; Hume's key article 'The
            Irish Question, a British Problem' published in *Foreign Affairs*.

1980   Secretary of State Atkins' inter-party talks fail; Taoiseach Charles
            Haughey and Prime Minister Margaret Thatcher initiate new round
            of inter-governmental talks.

1981   Republican paramilitary prisoners' hunger strikes result in the deaths
            of ten men at the Maze prison.

1982   SDLP rejects participation in proposed new assembly and opts to
            establish a Council for a New Ireland in conjunction with constitu-
            tional parties in the South.

1983   New Ireland Forum comprising representatives of SDLP, Fianna Fáil,
            Fine Gael and Labour convenes in Dublin; Hume elected MP at
            Westminster for Foyle constituency.

1984   New Ireland Forum issues report; forum's key constitutional propos-
            als rejected by Margaret Thatcher; Hume re-elected to European
            Parliament.

1985   Anglo-Irish Agreement signed at Hillsborough, Co. Down, gives Irish
            government consultative role in northern affairs.

1987   IRA bomb outrage at Enniskillen Remembrance Sunday ceremony;
            Hume-Adams talks commence.

1988   Hume-Adams dialogue expands into wider SDLP-Sinn Féin talks;
            killing of three IRA members in Gibraltar, followed by killing of
            mourners at their funeral, followed by killing of two British Army
            personnel at the mourners' funeral.

1989   Hume re-elected to European Parliament.

1990   Secretary of State Brooke launches new initiative aimed at inter-party
            negotiations.

1991–2	Inter-party and inter-governmental talks in Belfast, London and Dublin produce limited agreement.
1993	Hume-Adams dialogue intensifies; Downing Street Declaration in December.
1994	Hume re-elected to European Parliament; IRA declares ceasefire on 30 August; loyalist paramilitaries follow suit in October.
1995–6	Preparations for comprehensive negotiations; IRA breaks ceasefire; President Clinton visits Northern Ireland; International Commission on Decommissioning of Paramilitary Arms established by Irish and British governments; negotiations open in June 1996 in Belfast, chaired by US Senator George Mitchell; Sinn Féin excluded because of IRA's failure to renew ceasefire.
1997	Second IRA ceasefire in July; Sinn Féin enter negotiations in September.
1998	Good Friday Agreement; joint referenda North and South endorse agreement; new Northern Ireland Assembly elected; Hume and Trimble receive Nobel Peace Prize.
1999	Power-sharing executive appointed; North-South Ministerial Council established along with British-Irish Council. Hume re-elected to European Parliament for fifth time.
2001	Hume retires as Leader of the SDLP, and is succeeded by Mark Durkan.
2004	Hume retires from European Parliament.
2005	Hume retires from Westminster and is succeeded as MP for Foyle by Mark Durkan.

Foreword

PRESIDENT BILL CLINTON

When 'the Troubles' began in 1968, I was a young graduate student on a Rhodes Scholarship at Oxford University, enjoying my first trip abroad and the tremendous opportunity I had been given to study and travel. Until then, most people outside of Northern Ireland, including myself, were unaware of the growing discontent among the region's nationalist, largely Catholic, minority, and their frustration with housing, local elections, and jobs policies that favored the unionist, largely Protestant, political majority whose Ulster Unionist Party had dominated the Northern Ireland government at Stormont since Ireland's partition in 1921.

The civil rights march in Derry on 5 October 1968 forever changed that. Calling for greater equality, nationalists took to the streets demanding, among other things, fairer voting rights and an end to prejudicial policing. In the new era of mass media, the television coverage recorded every water cannon fired and every baton strike by the Royal Ulster Constabulary on the local protesters, and the world's eyes – and mine – were finally focused on the long-simmering tensions between nationalists and unionists that had erupted that day and would fester for the next thirty years – costing far too much in both lives and livelihoods.

1968 was a tumultuous year in the United States, as well, with Americans protesting the Vietnam War and continued racial and economic disparities at home, and the tragic assassinations of Martin Luther King, Jr and Senator Robert Kennedy. While Dr King was most well-known for his efforts to advance racial equality, he had also begun to address the related issues of joblessness and economic empowerment through his Poor People's Campaign, much as protestors were doing in Derry and Belfast in the late 1960s. Growing up in the segregated South, I had seen firsthand the corrosive effects of discrimination and the long-term damage caused by restricted job and educational opportunities. Though the history and the specifics were different, the parallels between Northern Ireland's civil rights movement and our own were unmistakable.

I recognized the frustrations of nationalists who felt marginalized in their own country and the fear among unionists that ceding ground to them would threaten the constitutional arrangement that tied them to Great Britain and formed the root of their political power and social identity. So, I remained interested in the Irish question after I came home to America. During my campaign for President in 1992, a number of prominent Irish-Americans began to push for a greater role for the United States in brokering peace, and after the election, I felt I finally might be in a position to help advance this effort.

In the interim, one remarkable man from Derry had been working tirelessly for a resolution, putting himself at great personal risk in the quest for peace between the two sides. Together with his wife, Pat, their five children, members of the community, and colleagues like Séamus Mallon who formed the core of the new, moderate Social Democratic and Labour Party, John Hume worked patiently for three decades to put in place a plan for non-violent reconciliation, at the heart of which was a vision for a power-sharing arrangement that would include Northern Ireland's primary political parties and draw upon the region's diversity as a source of strength rather than as a point of perennial division.

As the leader of the SDLP, Member of the European and British Parliaments, and the Northern Ireland Assembly, John stood at the forefront of Northern Ireland's non-violent civil rights movement, working patiently to gather support for a political solution, and reframing the debate surrounding Northern Ireland's future to make it possible. He helped both unionists and nationalists see that peace was not a zero-sum game and that the option for self-determination could help both sides advance the causes they cared about together. Moreover, John understood that peace built on a strong economic future would be more durable than one built on uncertainty and division, and he deserves credit for his efforts at home and abroad to prioritize job creation and encourage foreign investment – efforts that would be critical to sustaining an eventual peace. As John often said, 'We must learn to spill our sweat, not our blood.'

During the course of our long friendship, I saw in John what so many others had – a man of great conviction and infinite patience who believed deeply in the ultimate capacity of the other side to compromise given the right conditions and concessions. Perhaps as a result of his early years studying for the priesthood or establishing Northern Ireland's first credit union, John had one of the most highly developed senses for the potential of partnerships to effect positive change, and his unwavering belief in the possibility of unity helped everyone involved in the peace process – my administration included – weather the volatility and uncertainty of years of negotiations.

At the time I became involved in the peace process, John had already seen the Sunningdale and Anglo-Irish agreements, both of which he helped shape, come and go and the promise of power-sharing scuttled by unionist parties who weren't yet ready for the arrangement.

While neither agreement fulfilled its potential to end the conflict in Northern Ireland, both attempts improved cooperation between the Irish and British governments and provided important stepping stones for the Good Friday Agreement.

Critically, during the late 1980s, John had also begun talking secretly with Gerry Adams, whose Sinn Féin party formed the political arm of the Irish Republican Army. The IRA's aim to force the unification of Ireland was being driven by a campaign of violence both at home and throughout Great Britain. It was being returned in equal measure by unionist paramilitary groups and with several hundred people a year being killed, the violence was wreaking havoc on families, the local economy, and prospects for peace. Although Hume never wavered in his commitment to non-violence, he believed that, with strategic steps to meet the nationalist concerns, the IRA could be convinced to put aside its weapons and support politics over violence, and that engaging Adams was the best way to encourage this. He took some fierce criticism from within his own party for this, but those who trusted his intentions supported his methods. Indeed, what distinguished the SDLP during John's tenure was not so much its goals, but its means – most notably its commitment to non-violence.

Thanks to his growing rapport with Adams and his ability to read the climate of compromise within the IRA, John was instrumental in helping my administration identify a key opening in the road to a ceasefire. In early 1994, sensing Sinn Féin's genuine commitment to a political solution and Adams' willingness to press the IRA for a ceasefire, John encouraged me to extend a visa to Adams to bolster his influence at home, increase his leverage within his own party, and create a pathway for him to encourage key players in the United States to support a ceasefire.

It was a risky decision, with much of my administration against it, but with hopes of advancing a real and lasting peace in the balance, and great faith in John's counsel, it was too important an avenue not to try. Thankfully for everyone involved, we were rewarded for the risk. Within seven months, the IRA declared a ceasefire, and a few months after that, the loyalist paramilitaries followed suit. For the first time in decades, it was possible to imagine that Northern Ireland's future would be settled by inclusive talks and not by bombs or intimidation.

The road to the Good Friday Agreement was never smooth, and the 1994 ceasefire would break down a year-and-a-half later amid renewed violence. But we were on the right track, and the dialogue John had begun with Gerry Adams would continue with the addition of David Trimble and Sir Reg Empey, the leaders of the Ulster Unionist party, my special envoy, George Mitchell, and the governments of Ireland and Great Britain. And there were enough memorable moments full of hope along the way that helped us all remember why we needed to stay the course. I'll never forget hosting John and Gerry Adams at the annual White House St Patrick's Day celebration in 1995 and the impromptu duet they sang together after dinner.

Nor will I ever forget my first visit to Northern Ireland in the fall of 1995, where I visited with both unionists and nationalists, and walked the ancient walls of Derry with John, and felt the luck of the Irish turning our way.

When the Good Friday Agreement was signed in 1998, it was one of the happiest days of my Presidency. The end of sectarian violence was an extraordinary achievement for all those who had made it their life's work, and I was especially pleased to see John Hume and David Trimble recognized with the Nobel Peace Prize for their dogged efforts under difficult circumstances. John was instrumental both in getting the peace process launched, and in mainstreaming it, something that could only happen when Sinn Féin and the DUP took ownership. And while sticking points still remain, walking over the Peace Bridge in Derry with John and Pat on my most recent trip to Northern Ireland in 2014 was a powerful reminder of just how far we'd come. The agreement reached that day in 1998, and all the revisions since, represent the incredible trust placed in all parties and John's unwavering willingness to elevate principle and peace over person and party.

We all owe John a debt of gratitude for embracing the dividends of peace over the politics of constant conflict, and I'm delighted the remarkable account of his lifelong efforts is being detailed in this book. This is a true story that should inspire leaders everywhere.

Introduction

SEÁN FARREN & DENIS HAUGHEY

John Hume transformed the politics of Ireland North and South, and reshaped relationships between Ireland and Britain. He also changed perceptions of the Northern Ireland situation in the outside world, particularly in Britain and the United States, but also within the European Union, and much further afield as well. When he – and the generation of Northern Ireland civil rights leaders for whom he was a major strategist and spokesperson – took to the streets in 1968, to protest about long-standing abuses of power by successive unionist governments, an avalanche of change followed. Afterwards, the politics of this island could never be the same again.

Before the civil rights movement, the political elite in Dublin had largely forgotten about Northern Ireland, and knew very little about what was going on there. Before the civil rights movement, the nationalist political elite in the North had settled into a futile routine of protesting about partition, and sectarian discrimination, and hopelessly calling upon successive British governments to end their predicament. However, in the decades after partition, British governments resolutely refused to intervene in the politics of Northern Ireland, for fear of stirring up a hornets' nest that would intrude into the domestic politics of Britain. After 1968 it was clear that this approach could not be maintained. The world had been changed utterly by television; pictures of civil rights protests and police onslaughts on peaceful demonstrators were being beamed all over the world. British governments, which held ultimate responsibility for Northern Ireland, could not be seen to be completely inert in the face of legitimate demands for change, and the obvious deterioration of public order in part of the United Kingdom which followed unionist opposition to reform.

Television was the ideal medium for John Hume. He quickly developed an easy mastery of the mass media, projecting an articulate, personable and highly persuasive persona. He also developed a clear and compelling analysis of the Northern Ireland problem, and a compelling framework of democratic principles upon which a solution had to be based. His philosophy rested upon principles of tolerance, social justice, respect for and accommodation of difference, the complete rejection of violence, and the imperative of working for political progress by means of dialogue aimed at achieving consensus. He drew heavily on the inspiration of Mahatma Gandhi, and Dr Martin Luther King Jr, whom he quoted repeatedly. This approach was more than difficult to resist, in the late twentieth century, and almost impossible for the unionists and the British to rebut.

In the late 1960s, and throughout the 1970s and 1980s, Northern Ireland was constantly in the news, internationally. The person most frequently consulted by the international media about the ongoing crisis was John Hume. As a consequence, and because of his enormous influence in Irish-America and in the European Parliament, he became an internationally known and widely respected world figure. The word 'charisma' has almost been worn out by repetition and misuse, but what other word can be used to describe the qualities of someone who, by the force of his personality, the cogency of his logic, the visionary content of his message, and his mastery of the arts of communication through the mass media, won over to his point of view a whole generation of Irish political leaders, the elite of the Irish-American establishment, the overwhelming majority of European political leaders and a very significant section of British public opinion. It is difficult to imagine how the Northern Ireland problem might have been resolved, or the Good Friday Agreement achieved, were it not for the fact that John Hume had lined up such an enormously powerful international alliance in favour of a settlement based upon the principles he enunciated.

John's charisma derived from his absolute inner certainty that he had correctly analysed the problem, and had formulated the right answer. It was not an answer peculiar to him. His party colleagues were of like mind, and others who were initially sceptical came to share his analysis and solution. However, it was Hume's communication skills that convinced the initially sceptical, and so it was to him that people looked for guidance, analysis and leadership. Whenever challenged about his constant repetition of the same message (friends and opponents alike referred to it – mostly with good-humoured indulgence – as his 'single transferable speech') his response was that the problem hadn't changed and, therefore, neither did the answer. And so his message became an essential part of the vernacular in which the three-fold set of relationships he sought to resolve were discussed – relationships within Northern Ireland, between North and South and between Ireland and Britain. It was called 'Hume-speak'.

As this volume of essays reveals, John Hume was not lacking in critics, nor was he above criticism. Many people in the unionist community regarded him as, at best, an incessant peddler of clichés, or, at worst, a cunning, devious and unscrupulous manipulator of well-meaning people who wished to help, but didn't really understand the Northern Ireland problem. John is open to the criticism that he should have devoted more of his time and his formidable powers of persuasion to trying to change attitudes in the traditional unionist community. Possibly he

decided that the task of prising open the closed mindset of unionism, as he perceived it, was beyond his or anyone else's capacity, and that his time and his
powers were better used in pursuing objectives where the difficulties and obstacles
were less forbidding. But it remains a moot point.

On the other hand, some in the Irish national community, at home and
abroad, condemned and despised his non-violent politics. Such people insisted
that violence was the only means of making progress, and that Hume and his followers weakened and diminished the resolve of Irish nationalists to reunify the
country by armed force. Others in the Irish national community, especially some
Dublin-based commentators, regarded him as a dangerous agitator who threatened to precipitate a sectarian holocaust in the North, by stirring up old nationalist grievances and ambitions, and that the relatively stable southern state would
be dragged into the ensuing strife. Indeed, some of his Dublin-based critics
evinced much greater empathy with northern unionists, and one of the more
prominent of them, former Irish government minister Conor Cruise O'Brien,
actually joined a hard-line unionist fringe party and became, for a time, one of its
main spokespersons in the 1996–8 negotiations at Stormont.

However Hume is regarded, most commentators acknowledge that he was the
principal architect of the 1998 Good Friday/Belfast Agreement, the agreement that
has transformed constitutional and institutional arrangements for governing
Northern Ireland, and has also restructured relationships with the rest of Ireland,
as well as relationships between the whole of Ireland and Britain.

The contributions in this volume offer intriguing analyses of one of Ireland's
most important public figures. These analyses include;

- a description of the northern political context into which Hume was born,
  and from which he emerged to become a dominant figure in Irish political
  life from the late 1960s until he retired in 2005;
- his early forays into public affairs through the credit union movement, and
  the 'university for Derry campaign';
- his role in the civil rights movement;
- his first election as a representative of his native city;
- his relationships with the powerful figures in Irish, British, American and
  European politics;
- his involvement in the first power-sharing experiment in 1973–4;
- his later achievements in the European Parliament;
- and his efforts to end the violence and make possible a fully inclusive new
  dispensation in Northern Ireland.

There are also assessments of his leadership qualities, his place in the pantheon of
Irish political leaders, and a description by his indomitable wife, Pat, of life with
one of the great men of our time.

Éamon Phoenix's opening chapter traces the political and social background to John Hume's childhood and youth. His review spans the years from partition in 1920 to the early nineteen sixties, and highlights the disarray, the sense of betrayal and entrapment that had gripped many within the nationalist community in the North throughout that period. Nationalist attitudes and feelings were matched by equally negative unionist feelings of the need to dominate to 'ensure' against any possible loss of control. In the public domain, relationships between the two communities remained frozen for several decades following partition, and it was not until the late 1950s that any signs of a thaw in those relationships began to emerge. It was then that John Hume was taking his first steps onto the public stage.

Paul Arthur discusses Hume's apprenticeship to public life in the early 1960s, first in Derry where his strong belief in self-help sparked his interest in and commitment to the credit union movement as a vehicle to assist people and lift them out of poverty. There quickly followed his involvement in and leadership of the campaign to have the North's second university sited in Derry. When this campaign failed to achieve its objective, there followed his almost inevitable involvement in the civil rights movement and his entrée into a political career that would endure for the next thirty-five years.

Austin Currie, John Hume's close political colleague and co-founder of the SDLP, discusses the emergence of the civil rights movement, and the slow process of transforming nationalist politics from a loose, disorganized alliance of individuals into a properly structured modern political party in the SDLP. Currie stresses the non-violent nature of the civil rights movement, its success in winning extensive reform in public housing allocation, in local government, in the local franchise and even initial reforms in policing. Hume's influence was critical in articulating these demands and in shaping the early development of the SDLP.

Maurice Hayes offers a fascinating insight into the brief period of hope that surrounded the Sunningale Agreement of 1973, its precarious and short-lived implementation over the first five months of 1974 when it was threatened by militant loyalist and by unionist strikers, as well as by paramilitaries on all sides. As a senior civil servant Hayes worked closely with the power-sharing executive and particularly with Hume who, as the minister responsible for energy, was a particular target of the strikers who had assumed control of the North's main power stations. There followed the futile attempt to reach inter-party agreement in the Northern Ireland Convention, 1975–6, and the onset of a long, politically barren period for Hume and his SDLP colleagues.

The transformation of mainstream political thinking in the South on Northern Ireland was due to a considerable extent to John Hume and the SDLP. Seán Donlon, from his vantage point as a key member of the Department of Foreign Affairs' team charged with maintaining contact with leading public figures in the North throughout the 1970s and early 1980s, traces the development of Hume's influence, and in particular his relationships with southern political leaders Jack Lynch, Garret FitzGerald and Charles Haughey. Donlon's discussion includes Hume's initiatives in the United States and Europe. In each case he highlights Hume's effectiveness in building alliances and friendships that would eventually help achieve a comprehensive agreement in Northern Ireland.

David McKittrick reflects on perceptions of John Hume as he dealt with British prime ministers and secretaries of state over a period of thirty years. Prime ministers like Heath, Thatcher, Major and Blair were among those he regarded as willing to take bold steps towards a settlement, while Wilson and Callaghan were hesitant and acquiescent when confronted by unionism. Thatcher was the most surprising since she had refused concessions to the hunger strikers in 1981, had dismissed the recommendations in the New Ireland Forum's report in 1984, but then within a year had signed the Anglo-Irish Agreement, an agreement Hume had helped to shape. It was a watershed moment in that it gave the Irish government a formal consultative role in the affairs of Northern Ireland and reflected Hume's firm view that both governments needed to work together in the search for agreement. Of the many secretaries of state sent to Northern Ireland Hume had respect for only a few, notably Whitelaw and Brooke, both of whom also demonstrated a capacity for risk taking in the interest of peace and a political settlement.

Arthur Aughey discusses how John Hume was perceived and judged by many unionists, but whether by all is open to question. To many he was perceived in extremely negative terms as a leader of nationalism intent on deceiving unionists on to a path that would inevitably trap them into a united Ireland. Confirming this perception Marianne Elliott remarks in her chapter that, as a member of the Opsahl Commission, she was 'surprised to discover the level of animosity towards John Hume expressed by so many Protestants'. The chapter is extremely important in highlighting one reason – unionist apprehensions about what might be in store – why it took so long to reach the 1998 agreement.

From his unique position as assistant to and close confidant of John Hume, Mark Durkan's intriguing chapter discusses Hume's central role in persuading Sinn Féin to abandon support for the IRA's futile and violent campaign to extract a British declaration of intent to withdraw from Northern Ireland over the heads of the people of the North. Firmly opposed to violence as the means of effecting constitutional change in Ireland, Hume's appreciation of Irish history taught him that division in Ireland long pre-dated partition, and that unity could only be achieved by those who were convinced of its benefits convincing those who were not. Furthermore, he forcibly argued that violence only deepened existing division and inhibited any progress towards unity. Durkan carefully traces the background to Hume's dialogue with Sinn Féin Leader Gerry Adams, which commenced in 1987 following the Anglo-Irish Agreement, and the UK government's affirmation that it would facilitate unity if that were to be the wishes of a majority in the North. He then discusses the parallel process of inter-party discussions during the Brooke/Mayhew talks of 1991–2, and their contribution to the later negotiations leading to the Good Friday Agreement in 1998. The convergence of both processes was to be made possible with the 1994 IRA and loyalist ceasefires.

Seán O'Huiginn, a close colleague of Donlon's in the Department of Foreign Affairs, traces Hume's efforts to influence the republican movement away from its brutal and futile campaign of violence towards participation in mainstream politics through his highly controversial dialogue with Gerry Adams of Sinn Féin which extended over several years before eventually achieving the Provisional IRA's ceasefire in 1994. O'Huiginn's reference to Hume's scraps of 'papyrus', as he describes the many pieces of paper on which John would have noted drafts of possible statements for the Irish and British governments to make, highlights Hume's unorthodox manner of record keeping – everything was a work in progress and nothing was finalized until it was finalized *and* agreed.

In the European Union Hume found a stage and a model well suited to his style of politics. As a product of post-Second World War efforts by France, Germany and Italy in particular, to overcome the causes which had led to two world wars in forty years, and the subsequent legacy of bitterness, Hume was strongly influenced by the consensual approach adopted within its institutions, and by the recognition and respect afforded all its members. He had always wanted to develop the SDLP in the consensual tradition of European social democracy, rather than follow the confrontational model of the British labour movement. Likewise, as a model for conflict resolution in Northern Ireland, he pointed to the manner in which the European Parliament and the European Commission operated. Brigid Laffan examines Hume's role in Europe and how he used the opportunities he found there to develop relationships and take initiatives that would benefit Northern Ireland in the search for a negotiated agreement. It was another part of his strategy to seek a political solution in a wider context than on the narrow ground of the North itself and, as far as Hume was concerned, Europe offered the ideal context, and the institutional models for overcoming the effects of violent conflict.

Nancy Soderberg, a close aide, first to Senator Edward Kennedy, then to President Bill Clinton, outlines from the perspective of her very strategic position, the influence Hume was able to exercise over decision-makers in the US Congress and in the White House. As in Europe, the carefully nurtured relationships with key representatives like Hugh Carey, Edward Kennedy, Daniel Moynihan and Tip O'Neill helped Hume gain the ear of White House incumbents Jimmy Carter, Ronald Reagan, George Bush and above all Bill Clinton. Such relationships helped steer most Irish-Americans away from supporting the Provisional IRA and in favour of a peaceful resolution. A corollary was the support Hume won for US investment in the North and in the South's border regions through the International Fund for Ireland.

Marianne Elliott discusses John Hume against the background of Ireland's national struggle using Wolfe Tone's oft-quoted statement of his aims being to unite all of the people of Ireland and to abolish the memory of all past dissensions, as her departure point. Tone was not an historical figure that Hume himself would have sought inspiration from – Mahatma Gandhi, Martin Luther King and Nelson Mandela were more likely to feature in his discourse. However, abolishing the malign influence of 'past dissensions', if not the memory, was part of Hume's objectives, and the manner in which he set about transforming nationalist attitudes and challenging those of unionists, is central to her discussion. Elliott argues that Hume's articulation of the objectives adopted by the Dungannon-based Campaign for Social Justice, and by the broader based Northern Ireland Civil Rights Association, were 'a return to the essence of constitutional nationalism'. She sees Hume as urging, like successful constitutional leaders in the past, that nationalists could more effectively change the *status quo* from within than by attempting to overthrow it by force. His message that a united Ireland could only come about by the will of a northern majority and that it could only be achieved through a process of reconciliation, resonated with other voices that were being raised within the North's nationalist community in the early 1960s. But Hume's articulation of the message was to become the most forceful, the most clearly and persistently argued, hence the most influential.

Cathy Gormley-Heenan offers a critical assessment of Hume's leadership 'in terms of his role, capacity and effectiveness rather than … leadership in more personal terms'. She compares him to the salmon steadily swimming upstream, against the current of other opinions, and 'against the tide of his own party at times'. Despite the hazards, like the salmon he persists until he reaches the goal he had predetermined from the outset. On his hazardous journey she argues that 'Hume maintained continuity of thought and action throughout his time as leader of the SDLP [and …] His oft-repeated view was that the conflict was as a consequence of the division of the people on the island of Ireland and not the territory of the island of Ireland and he never wavered from a complete insistence on the non-violent approach'. These were the qualities that marked his leadership and in them he was vindicated by the Good Friday Agreement.

Finally, Pat Hume, John's wife, offers a very personal insight into John's public life, its effects on their family life as well as very acute perceptions on the general political scene. Her account of the toll that Northern Ireland's apparently unending tragedies took on her husband's health and well-being reminds readers of the impact of risks taken to achieve peace and, indeed, how much a politician like John Hume needed the support of a companion like Pat.

As editors we wish to express our deepest thanks and appreciation to all contributors for their painstaking research and analyses. We are especially grateful to President Bill Clinton for his Foreword. We also thank Four Courts Press for enthusiastically agreeing to publish this volume and a special word of thanks to Jim Fitzpatrick for generously assisting its publication.

July 2015

Before John

ÉAMON PHOENIX

John Hume's Ireland had been defined a decade and a half before his birth by the British Parliament's Government of Ireland Act (1920) and the Anglo-Irish Treaty of 1921.

This 1920 Partition Act represented the political response of Lloyd George's coalition government to the long-smouldering question of Irish self-government, challenged by the militarization of Ulster unionist and British conservative resistance during 1912–14, and now made more urgent by the 1916 rising, the Sinn Féin landslide in the 1918 general election and the outbreak of the Anglo-Irish War.

The task of finding a solution to the Irish issue was a daunting one for the British coalition whose members had been so bitterly divided on the issue of Home Rule only six years earlier. It was inevitable, however, given the shift in the balance of power at Westminster from the Home Rule Party to Ulster unionism after 1918 (thanks to Sinn Féin's 'blessed abstention'), that unionist leaders Carson and Craig were well placed to influence Britain's Irish policy, and it is no exaggeration to say that the fourth Home Rule Bill – the only bill to be even partially implemented – was drawn up in close collaboration with them.

But while partition was the major aim of the government, the Lloyd George cabinet was agreed that if American and Dominion opinion was to be satisfied, the bill should pave the way for an all-Ireland parliament when both North and South were willing to accept it. Another major problem that faced the drafting committee in late 1919 was the crucial question of the 'acreage' to be included in the new 'Ulster'. The government felt that the choice lay between the six-county *bloc,* accepted by Carson and northern members of the Irish Parliamentary Party (albeit as a 'temporary' expedient) in 1916, and the historic nine-county province. It was strongly urged in cabinet that if the ultimate aim of the bill was the unity of Ireland, it would be desirable to place the whole province, with its large Catholic minority (some 43 per cent), in the northern area. In the end, however, the cabinet acquiesced in James Craig's pragmatic view that a six-county *bloc* would provide a more 'homogeneous' and viable area for unionist control.[1]

On the principle that 'self-determination' for all Irishmen would best find favour with world opinion, the Government of Ireland Act (1920) divided Ireland politically into two jurisdictions, 'Northern Ireland' embracing the six counties, and 'Southern Ireland' covering the rest. Each area was to have its own local parliament and government. This marked a new offer to Ulster unionists who had never sought Home Rule, but Craig and his followers quickly grasped the value of a parliament of their own as a further bulwark against any threat to subject to them to a Dublin parliament.

The new northern legislature was subordinate to the British Parliament, and like its projected southern counterpart, was empowered to make laws for the peace, order and good government of its jurisdiction. Other matters, including tax-raising powers, were 'reserved' to the Imperial Parliament.[2]

In its second major provision, the bill seemed to foreshadow eventual Irish unity by providing 'a bond of union' in the shape of a low-powered Council of Ireland, to consist of twenty representatives elected by each Irish Parliament. A number of relatively minor matters, such as railways and fisheries, were placed under the remit of the council but the hope was firmly expressed at the time that this body might evolve into an all-Ireland parliament by mutual consent of North and South.

The 1920 act represented a major triumph for the Ulster unionists, much as they might declare their acceptance of it 'a supreme sacrifice in the interests of peace'. As one of their spokesmen, Captain Charles Craig, told the British House of Commons in March 1920: 'the Bill gives us practically everything we fought for, everything we armed ourselves for … in 1913 …' They would be 'in a position of absolute security' for the future.[3]

Sinn Féin, the motive force in nationalist Ireland with growing support among northern Catholics fearful of partition, remained intent on the achievement of an all-Ireland republic. On the nationalist side, only Joe Devlin, the leader of the northern Home Rulers and a solitary figure at Westminster, saw the dangers of the 'Partition Act' and inveighed against it as portending both 'permanent partition' and 'permanent minority status' for Ulster Catholics. Not without justification Devlin attacked the glaring lack of safeguards in the act for the minority. Apart from a clause forbidding discrimination and the retention of proportional representation for a three-year period, the act was deficient in this vital respect. To nationalist anger, the proposed northern senate was to be a mirror-image of the lower house rather than part of a system of checks and balances in a divided soci-

---

1 Michael Laffan, *The partition of Ireland, 1911–25* (Dublin, 1983), pp 62–3, 67. 2 Ian Colvin, *Life of Carson*, vol. iii (London, 1936), p. 381. 3 Laffan, *Partition of Ireland*, p. 65.

ety. Devlin's appeal for minority safeguards, however, was disregarded by the British government, which seemed to assume that majority rule would operate as satisfactorily in Northern Ireland as it did in Britain.[4]

The passage of the 1920 bill through Westminster coincided with the outbreak of serious sectarian and political violence in Ulster itself, as the tensions of the Anglo-Irish War and the spiralling IRA (Irish Republican Army) campaign spilled over into the province. The election of a nationalist-dominated corporation in the city of Derry under PR in June 1920 sparked a 'mini civil war' in which at least forty people were killed. The worst episode, however, occurred in Belfast that summer when the IRA assassination of a northern-born RIC (Royal Irish Constabulary) officer in the South resulted in the mass expulsion of some 8,000 Catholic workers from the shipyards and other industries. These events were a foretaste of the serious sectarian disturbances which were to polarize the two communities in the new state. Over 450 people, a majority of them Catholics (some 267), were killed during this period.[5]

The upsurge of violence had two important effects. First, it seemed to confirm nationalist fears of being subjected to the rule of the unionist majority in a separate state. The black days of 1920–2 made it certain that the new entity of Northern Ireland would find the politico-religious minority difficult to govern, let alone assimilate. Second, the mounting unrest in the Six Counties led the government to endorse Sir James Craig's plans for the enrolment of an auxiliary police force that might 'curb rebel influences'. Thus was born in October 1920 the sectarian 'Ulster Special Constabulary'(USC), commonly known as the 'B Specials', drawn from the ranks of the former exclusively Protestant UVF (Ulster Volunteer Force). In nationalist eyes, this force was perceived 'with a bitterness exceeding that which the Black and Tans inspired in the South',[6] and, was to become a permanent feature of the state. By June 1921, Northern Ireland had been established as a self-governing entity within the United Kingdom with its own unionist government and Craig as prime minister.

With British pledges to unionism now fulfilled, negotiations began between the British government and the Sinn Féin leadership for a settlement. The resulting treaty of 6 December 1921, with its grant of dominion status for the South, came as a bitter shock to the northern government, however. Under its terms, Northern Ireland was automatically included in the new Irish Free State and although its right to 'opt out' was carefully guarded, Article 12 provided that the North must purchase such immunity at the expense of a revision of her frontiers

4 Patrick Buckland, *A history of Northern Ireland* (Dublin, 1981), p. 23; *Hansard, House of Commons Debates*, 5 series, v. 136, cols 882–7.   5 Michael Farrell, *Northern Ireland: the Orange State* (London, 1976), p. 6; Éamon Phoenix, *Northern nationalism: nationalist politics, partition and the Catholic minority in Northern Ireland, 1890–1940* (Belfast, 1994), p. 251.   6 Michael Farrell, *Arming the Protestants: the formation of the Ulster Special Constabulary and the Royal Ulster Constabulary, 1920–27* (Brandon, 1983), p. 15.

by a boundary commission. This formula, invented by Lloyd George to prevent a breakdown of the negotiations, seemed to hold out the prospect of the subtraction from Northern Ireland of such nationalist majority areas as Fermanagh, Tyrone and Derry City. Indeed, many nationalists hoped that this might produce Irish unity by a process of 'contraction'. To Craig, however, the proposal to tamper with the North's 1920 frontiers was a perfidious breach of faith on the part of the British government and he signalled his government's intention to ignore the commission. Thus, it is impossible to underestimate the de-stabilizing effect of the Boundary Commission on the northern state during its early formative years.

Despite the attraction of the Boundary Commission, the sense of betrayal of northern nationalists at the Dáil's failure to remove the hated border, or at least secure cast-iron safeguards for the minority, was encapsulated by the nationalist mayor of Derry, Hugh C. O'Doherty, at a meeting with Dáil Ministers in the wake of the treaty: 'Our representatives have given away what we have fought for, for the last 750 years. It is camouflaged …We are no longer a united nation … If Belfast contracts out [under the Treaty] you are handing over manacled the lives and liberties of the Catholics who live in that area …We will be ostracised on account of our creed'.[7]

The treaty was accepted by the Dáil in January 1922, but the subsequent drift towards civil war had a profound effect on the already unstable situation in the North. Two major problems confronted Craig's administration in 1922: the attitude of the minority towards the state and its institutions, and the continuing problem of IRA and sectarian violence, especially in Belfast. Northern nationalists had refused to recognize the new state since 1921 and were now supported in this policy by the pro-treaty government of Michael Collins who confronted partition with a confusing blend of non-recognition, diplomacy and coercion. 'Non-recognition' meant that, for ten months, many Catholic teachers refused to accept their salaries from the Craig government and were paid by Dublin; nationalist councils pledged their allegiance to the Dáil and were promptly dissolved; and nationalist and Sinn Féin MPs enforced a strict boycott of the new parliament.

Second, the IRA, now secretly assisted by Collins, continued its campaign of burning and disruption within the Six Counties in an effort to undermine the unionist government's authority. The unionist government's response to this concerted threat to its existence was the draconian Civil Authorities (Special Powers) Act, passed in 1922 and subsequently made permanent, and the introduction of internment and the strengthening of the USC.

It was against this background that two agreements were signed by Craig and Collins in 1922. Both men had much to gain from the restoration of settled conditions, North and South, while Craig recognized the need to conciliate his own

7 Phoenix, *Northern nationalism*, p. 157.

resentful minority. Their prospects of success were blighted by the violent activities of the anti-treaty IRA in the South and the unconcealed hostility of the
Northern Ireland Ministry of Home Affairs towards the nationalist community.
Its reactionary minister, Dawson Bates, and the policing authorities showed no
urgency or imagination in implementing the detailed pact of 30 March 1922 and
scuppered efforts by nationalists and the Catholic Church to enlist Catholics in
the 32,000-strong special police. It was not until the outbreak of open civil war in
the Free State and the adoption of a 'peace policy' towards 'North-East Ulster' by
the new Irish government of William T. Cosgrave in the summer of 1922 that the
violence which had plagued the North for two years finally ended.[8]

It was during these years that the basic local government and educational
framework of Northern Ireland was laid down. Moreover, the strict nationalist
boycott ensured that policy was determined without any constructive criticism
from the minority population. Notwithstanding this factor, however, the fact
remains that on all matters over which the regional parliament had real control –
especially education, representation and law and order – policy 'was determined
by the majority with scant regard for the interests and susceptibilities of the
minority'.[9]

The 1923 Education Act, steered through the Belfast Parliament by Lord
Londonderry, the Minister for Education, provided for a state system of non-
denominational primary schools, based on a series of regional education committees. Under it, there were to be three classes of school. The ministry undertook to
pay teachers' salaries in all three classes of school but while the first group – 'transferred schools' – received the full cost of building and maintenance from public
funds, the 'voluntary' schools – those schools, mainly Catholic, which for religious
reasons stood outside the system – got no building or maintenance grants. The
new act, however, provoked a vigorous campaign by the Protestant churches and
Orange Order to have 'Bible teaching' and 'Protestant teachers for Protestant
pupils' included in the educational code. The government's surrender found lasting expression in the 1930 Education Act. This amounted to the 'virtual endorsement of Protestantism' by the state and was thus contrary to the religious
safeguard in the Government of Ireland Act. It required a Catholic threat to ask
Westminster to rule on the validity of the legislation to force the unionist government to make fifty per cent grants available to voluntary schools.[10]

At local government level, the regional government by an act of 1922 abolished
proportional representation for local elections and set in train the re-drawing of
electoral wards. This decision, taken under pressure from the border unionist

8 Ronan Fanning, *Independent Ireland* (Dublin, 1983), p. 36.   **9** Buckland, *A history of Northern Ireland*, pp
50–1.   **10** Patrick Buckland, *The factory of grievances: devolved government in Northern Ireland, 1921–39*
(Dublin, 1979), p. 263.

grass-roots, was bitterly resented by the nationalist population who saw PR as a safeguard and rightly feared an attempt to paint the nationalist border counties with 'a deep Orange tint' (in Collins' phrase) in anticipation of the Boundary Commission. These measures, together with the nationalist boycott of the inquiry, ensured the effective domination of local government by unionism and underlined the indifference of the Craig government to minority interests. The overhaul of local government provoked angry nationalist charges of gerrymandering, charges which were to be upheld by the Cameron Commission almost fifty years later. By 1924, only two major councils were controlled by nationalists compared to twenty-two before partition.[11]

Nationalist resentment was also sharpened by the adoption of 'a sectarian security policy' during the troubles of the early 1920s; internment and floggings, for example, tended to be directed only at the 'disaffected and disloyal' section of the population, convincing many that they could not expect impartial treatment from the new regime.[12]

By 1925 one major constitutional threat still faced Northern Ireland. Owing largely to the civil war in the South and the recalcitrance of Craig, it was not possible to constitute the Boundary Commission until 1924. Early in 1925, the three commissioners – the chairman, Judge Richard Feetham of the South African Supreme Court, Professor Eoin MacNeill, representing the Free State, and Joseph Fisher, appointed by the British government to uphold the interests of Northern Ireland – perambulated the frontier, taking evidence from nationalists and unionists. Craig seized the opportunity to hold a 'border' election which faithfully reflected unionist feeling on the issue. It soon became clear that the chairman was committed to 'mere rectification' of the boundary line rather than large-scale changes. The leak of the commission's report in November 1925 revealed that only a few uneconomic areas of Northern Ireland were to go to the South whereas an important area of east Donegal was to be transferred to the North, thus dashing nationalist hopes of Derry's transfer to the Free State.

The result was the Tripartite Agreement of December 1925, signed by Craig, Cosgrave and Prime Minister Stanley Baldwin for the British government. The Free State government finally recognized the 1920 border in return for financial concessions. Craig rejected the suggestion of safeguards for northern nationalists but succeeded in having the 1920 Council of Ireland – the last formal bridge between the two Irelands – dissolved by general consent. His novel suggestion of joint cabinet meetings was never implemented and forty years would pass before a Northern Ireland prime minister again met his Dublin counterpart. Craig had

11 David Harkness, *Northern Ireland since 1920* (Dublin, 1983), pp 28–9; Michael Collins to Winston Churchill, 31 July 1922, University College Dublin, H. Kennedy papers, P4/V/10. 12 Buckland, *A history of Northern Ireland*, p. 51; *The factory of grievances*, p. 206.

won a notable victory, a fact recognized by the Northern Ireland Parliament, which presented him with a silver cup with the memorable phrase 'Not an Inch' inscribed on it.[13]

The 1925 pact came as a bitter disappointment to the border nationalists – mostly former supporters of Sinn Féin led by Cahir Healy – and by 1928 this section had joined with Devlin and the constitutional nationalists in a new united movement, the 'National League of the North', dedicated to pursue Irish unity by peaceful means. Devlin, a seasoned parliamentarian, was now leading a party of ten MPs in the Belfast House of Commons. But his appeals for the redress of nationalist grievances were repeatedly rejected by the unionist majority. His hopes that stability would bring about a new political alignment in Northern Ireland along class lines were finally dashed by the abolition of PR for parliamentary elections in 1929. In championing this measure, Lord Craigavon (Craig had become a viscount in 1927) signalled his determination to eliminate the various 'deviationists' who had embarrassed unionism under PR, as well as the prospects of the fledgling Labour Party. In Craig's words, there was room only for two political parties in Northern Ireland, 'men who are for the Union, on the one hand, or who are against it and want to go into a Dublin Parliament, on the other'.[14] The unionist monopoly of power was now complete and politics became so predictable that many parliamentary seats ceased to be contested.[15] Thus, after 1929, the unionists usually held 36–9 seats and the nationalists 9–11 seats. Finally, in 1932, Devlin, dispirited and ill, led his followers out of the northern parliament, declaring that the unionist government was determined to 'rivet sectarianism'[16] to the political system for the future.

Devlin died in 1934 and for the next decade his followers abstained for the most part from parliament, allowing the league to atrophy and preferring instead to enlist the support of the anti-treaty leader, Éamon de Valera – now returned to power in the South – in their efforts to end partition. This policy, however, merely entrenched the unionist government in its lack of generosity to the minority.

Thus 'Stormont', where parliament buildings were opened in 1932, became the symbol, for unionists as well as nationalists, of 'a Protestant Parliament for a Protestant State' in Craigavon's telling phrase. There was no sign of a rapprochement between the two communities or between North and South. Instead, the divisive pattern of government and politics sketched out in the violent early months was confirmed.[17] The government became the instrument of the Unionist Party, which drew its strength from the Orange lodges and never produced a Catholic MP in the fifty years of unionist rule that followed. Above all, the use of government patronage to reward its supporters meant that discrimination, long a

13 St John Irvine, *Craigavon, Ulsterman* (London, 1949), p. 507. 14 Buckland, *History of Northern Ireland*, p. 62. 15 Ibid., pp 67–8. 16 *Irish News*, 7 Nov. 1932. 17 Buckland, *History of Northern Ireland*, p. 55.

feature of northern life, 'became built into the processes of government and administration as the government pandered to unionist whims, large or small' in such diverse fields as local government, employment, education and civil service recruitment. To unionists, of course, this policy was easily justified by the claim that 'proven loyalty' was a prerequisite for government employment. Political considerations contributed to the minority's reluctance to serve a 'foreign' government in the early decades, but the tendency of government ministers like the Home Affairs Minister Dawson Bates to regard 'all Catholics as nationalists and all nationalists as enemies' was also a factor.[18]

The minority, on the other hand, equipped with its own social infrastructure of the Catholic Church, its schools, hospitals, sporting activities, newspapers, businesses, Gaelic culture and the sectarian Ancient Order of Hibernians, virtually opted out of the state, forming a kind of 'state within a state'. Unlike unionism, however, nationalism did not form a solid monolith, and there was constant rivalry between the constitutional advocates of Irish unity and an intractable republican element that favoured abstentionism and physical force.

One of the first casualties of the bitter divisions in Northern Ireland was the Labour Party. Despite the existence of a large unionized workforce, and the social and economic difficulties of the inter-war years, it could never command more than three or four seats at Stormont. A major factor here in the early decades was Labour's irresolute attitude towards partition, which alienated unionist voters, while nationalists and Catholics distrusted its socialism and largely Protestant leadership.

The inter-war period and the 1930s, in particular, were years of depression and persistently high unemployment in Northern Ireland. Unemployment affected on average nineteen per cent of the insured labour force between 1923 and 1930, and in the thirties the figure was twenty-seven per cent; of all the United Kingdom regions, only Wales had a worse record. The high unemployment rate in the North stemmed largely from the inexorable decline of the region's three staple industries: shipbuilding, linen and agriculture, which during the period accounted for over 40 per cent of the working population. All three fell victim, after a brief post-war boom, to worldwide economic trends which neither local industrialists nor government could control.

Social conditions also lagged behind the rest of the United Kingdom. Housing conditions were particularly poor. Only 7,500 public-sector houses were built before 1939, while a government report of 1937 characterized the poorer classes as 'mostly residing in homes more or less unfit for habitation'.[19] In unionist-controlled areas, especially west of the Bann, sectarian considerations invariably influenced the allocation of labourers' cottages and even unskilled council posts.

18 Ibid., p. 63.   19 D.S. Johnson, 'The Northern Ireland economy, 1914–39' in Liam Kennedy and Philip Ollerenshaw (eds), *An economic history of Ulster, 1820–1939* (Manchester, 1985), p. 213; Buckland, *A history of Northern Ireland*, p. 76.

But the high unemployment of the 1930s did not produce any sense of working-class solidarity apart from a brief moment in 1932 when Protestant and Catholic workers rioted in unison against inadequate unemployment relief. In general, sectarian rioting and sectarian rhetoric were more diagnostic hallmarks of the 'hungry thirties'. 1932 saw attacks on Catholic pilgrims travelling to the Eucharistic Congress in Dublin and the rise of the avowedly sectarian 'Ulster Protestant League'. But the worst outbreak of violence since the 1920s occurred in July 1935 when eleven people were killed and over 300 families, mostly Catholic, were expelled from their homes in an orgy of rioting, sniping and arson. Nationalist and Catholic Church leaders demanded a British inquiry into the disturbances but Prime Minister Baldwin refused this on the grounds that the matter was one which came solely within the jurisdiction of the Northern Ireland government. This state of affairs stoked minority resentment and led the British-based National Council for Civil Liberties to publish a scathing indictment of the Special Powers Act.

Nor were inter-communal tensions eased by the gratuitously offensive speeches of politicians and churchmen. In this regard, the public exhortation of Sir Basil Brooke, a future Prime Minister, to Protestants not to employ Roman Catholics, 'who were really out to cut their throats', was particularly unfortunate.[20] Similarly, Cardinal MacRory's remark that the Protestant churches were 'not even a part of the church of Christ' offended many Protestants.[21] There was much force in the words of the Belfast Coroner at the inquest on the victims of the 1935 disturbances: 'The poor people who commit these riots … are influenced almost entirely by the public speeches of men in high and responsible positions …'[22]

The British government, of course, retained ultimate responsibility for affairs in Northern Ireland, but while concern was expressed in official circles in the 1930s about minority grievances there, the Imperial Parliament took the steady view that events in Northern Ireland were 'no business of ours'.[23] Until 1968, Westminster's attitude remained one of strict non-intervention in view of the oft-cited 'rights and privileges of the Parliament of Northern Ireland'. The rise of de Valera in the South after 1932, his success in dismantling the 1921 treaty, his 1937 Constitution with its territorial claim over Northern Ireland (Article 2) and his renewed pressure on London for an end to partition tended to heighten unionist defensiveness while raising false hopes among northern nationalists.

During the 1930s, northern nationalism remained divided between remnants of the old Home Rule Party, the pro-de Valera 'ruralista' along the border and a revived IRA. In an attempt to regain the initiative, the leading border nationalist MP, Cahir Healy (a founder of the original 'non-violent Sinn Féin' party of 1905),

---

20 A.C. Hepburn, *The conflict of nationality in modern Ireland* (London, 1980), p. 164. **21** *Irish News*, 18 Dec. 1931. **22** Andrew Boyd, *Holy war in Belfast* (Belfast, 1987), p. 229. **23** Hepburn, *Conflict of nationality*, pp 169–70, citing the British Labour Home Secretary, Chuter Ede in 1949.

launched the 'Irish Union Association' in 1936. However, the new organization failed to attract either the younger generation or the Devlinite camp in Belfast which retained its own political machine under the moderate barrister and MP, T.J. Campbell. Nationalist disunity was compounded in 1937 with the formation of the Northern Council for Unity, committed to the application of de Valera's 1937 constitution to all Ireland.[24]

In an incisive survey of northern nationalist attitudes in 1937, a 'special correspondent' writing in the *Irish News* detected 'almost as many brands of nationalism in the Six Counties today as there are nationalists'. However, he identified two broad groups: 'a No Truck with Stormont' group and a 'Peace with Stormont' group, of which the peace group would be the smaller, even in Belfast, and would be quite insignificant in such border areas as South Armagh, Fermanagh and Tyrone. In the border counties, he added, 'the wound of partition is just as raw as on the morrow of the Anglo-Irish Treaty which cast six counties out of the Irish nation ...' In nationalist-majority areas such as Fermanagh and Derry inter-communal wounds had been inflamed by the gerrymandering of local councils and 'the practical re-enactment of the Penal Laws with regard to public appointments' by the local unionists 'with the approval of their Stormont leaders'.

In Belfast, on the other hand, where nationalists had a limited share in public appointments, some took a more pragmatic view: 'Stormont is here to stay for our generation. We must recognize it for the sake of our schools and social services'. In the view of this section, the nationalists should become the official opposition at Stormont and show a willingness to improve social problems such as housing and unemployment.[25] Ironically, John Hume, at the outset of his political career, would make a similar appeal for nationalist engagement in the early 1960s.

De Valera's failure to win concessions on either partition or the treatment of the northern minority in his Anglo-Irish negotiations with Neville Chamberlain in 1938 disappointed northern nationalists yet again. As Healy confided to a political colleague in 1939: 'de Valera made a civil war about the differences between Documents 1 and 2 [during the Treaty debates of 1922] but he is not prepared to say "boo" to Chamberlain over the loss of the Six Counties!' The veteran MP's disillusionment was partly relieved a year later when the Taoiseach joined all shades of northern nationalism and the Catholic hierarchy in a successful campaign against the extension of conscription to the north.

During the Second World War de Valera made it clear to northern nationalists that Irish neutrality remained his priority and that the survival of the independent Irish state 'could not be risked in any effort to reintegrate the country'. In the event, the North's key strategic role in the war did much to strengthen her con-

24 The new Irish constitution, drawn by Éamon de Valera, claimed Dublin's jurisdiction over the whole island. 25 *Irish News*, 24 Apr. 1937.

stitutional position and win British and US political support for the unionist position after 1945.[26]

The return of a Labour government at Westminster in 1945 had a catalytic effect
on politics in Northern Ireland. Labour was generally perceived as being friendly
towards Irish unity and this factor, plus the fear of 'creeping socialism', led the
Brooke cabinet briefly to consider Dominion status for the North before it finally
decided to work in harness with Attlee and his colleagues. For the nationalists, the
revival of Labour was the signal for a major upsurge of anti-partitionist activity as
the various strands of nationalism coalesced in a new mass movement, the Anti-
Partition League (APL). Supported by all the major parties in Dublin and a vocal
element in the British Labour Party, the APL waged a world-wide campaign against
'the evil of partition' in the late 1940s and early 1950s. But the movement's single
focus on the constitutional issue, rather than on well-founded grievances, drew no
encouragement from a Labour government indebted to unionism's wartime support. The accession to power of a coalition government in the South in 1948, which
included Seán MacBride's republican party, Clann na Poblachta, assisted the nationalist campaign, though the decision of the Costello ministry to 'take the gun out of
Irish politics' by declaring a republic in 1949 was to rebound to the unionists'
advantage. Following a further unionist triumph in the 1949 Northern Ireland election, the British Parliament passed the controversial Ireland Act (1949). This
strengthened partition by stipulating that the North's constitutional status could
not be changed without the consent of the Parliament of Northern Ireland.[27]

But if the old issues were rekindled after 1945, the immediate post-war period
witnessed a veritable revolution in the North. These years saw the coming of the
modern welfare state and major educational reform, changes which were to bind
Northern Ireland even more closely to Britain and to give unionists a 'bread and
butter' incentive for opposing Irish unity. In the sphere of social services, a series
of financial agreements (1945–51) enabled the 'step-by-step' policy to be maintained while resolving the financial problems that had dogged earlier Belfast governments. In return for the region's acceptance of more rigorous financial scrutiny
by the UK Treasury, Britain agreed to finance the massive increase in expenditure
required to enable Northern Ireland to enjoy the full range of cash social services
'from the cradle to the grave'. A Health Services Act of 1948 followed the British
Act in establishing the National Health Service in the North.

In education, the Stormont Act of 1947 implemented the revolutionary changes
wrought across the water by the 1944 'Butler Act'. This provided for free post-primary education for all children and a new system of primary, secondary and further

26 Report of interview between an Taoiseach and a northern nationalist deputation [n.d. 1940] (Armagh
Archdiocesan Archives, MacRory papers).   27 John A. Murphy, *Ireland in the twentieth century* (Dublin,
1975), pp 126–7; Harkness, *Northern Ireland since 1920*, p. 123.

education, while generous university grants put real equality of opportunity within the grasp of all pupils, regardless of social background. The dramatic expansion of third-level education was fraught with great significance for the future since it was to throw open the universities and the professions to a whole generation of Catholics, previously excluded from such opportunities for socio-economic reasons.[28]

These strides were not taken without friction, however, and sectarian controversy obtruded itself both in educational reform and in the health services, where the Catholic-controlled Mater Hospital, a respected acute and teaching hospital, remained for conscientious reasons outside the National Health Service. Incredibly, this issue festered until 1972 when, in a rather altered political climate, the Mater finally came in as 'a member of a bright constellation'.[29] Another controversial measure of these years was a politically loaded Safeguarding of Employment Act (1947), passed by Stormont to prevent large-scale immigration of workers from the South. Also in the same year, the regional government sowed the seeds of much future discord by its blatant refusal to follow the British example of 'one man, one vote' for Stormont and local government elections; the retention of government control in border areas was the chief determinant here. Nationalist and Labour protests were brushed aside by Brookeborough.

In the 1950s industrial expansion was promoted by generous inducements for new firms. However, this policy tended to neglect the less-favoured (and predominantly nationalist) districts in the south and west. To nationalists, it seemed that 'the government's policy was clearly to denude the west and enrich the east', a view confirmed by the partisan decision in 1965 to site the state's new university not in Catholic Derry, with its long tradition of higher education, but in unionist Coleraine. By 1966, only 16 of the 111 advance factories built by the Ministry of Commerce were sited west of the Bann, a predominantly nationalist area.

Notwithstanding the 'welfare revolution' and increased urbanization, Northern Ireland passed through the 1950s as the most divided as well as the poorest region of the United Kingdom. The Roman Catholic proportion of the population showed a slight rise during these years – from 33.5 per cent in 1926 to 34.9 per cent in 1961 – but Catholics continued to account for a disproportionate number of those leaving the North. Brookeborough's policy of ignoring the minority, and opposing every proposal for broadening the basis of unionism to include Catholics, tended to drive many nationalists into the arms of a revived republican movement by the mid-1950s. This was also a reflection of the failure of the APL to impact partition while its keynote policy of gaining 'a right of audience' for nationalists in the Dáil was thwarted by de Valera. Privately, Healy was sceptical

28 P. Jupp, 'County Down Elections 1783–1831', *Irish Historical Studies*, 18:70 (Sept. 1972), pp 177–206. 29 Speech by Northern Ireland Minister of Health, W.K. Fitzsimmons, as reported in *Belfast Telegraph*, 1 Dec. 1971.

of this policy, regarding it as an empty gesture.[30] In the Westminster election of 1955, the Nationalist Party stood aside, enabling Sinn Féin, with its emphasis on armed force, to win a record 152,000 votes and two seats. This was largely a protest gesture by a frustrated community, but it was seen by the IRA as providing the moral sanction for a renewed campaign of violence.

The resulting border campaign of 1956–62, aimed at expelling a 'British Army of Occupation' from the Six Counties, had never any prospect of success. By the time it was finally abandoned in 1962 it had cost sixteen lives and considerable material damage. Its failure was due to a combination of factors, amongst them the use of internment by both Irish governments, the strong condemnation of the Catholic Church, and, perhaps most importantly (the factor stressed by the IRA itself) the lack of any sizeable support from the nationalist population.

This was partly related to the impact of the 1947 Education Act on middle-class Catholics. A new group of graduates and professionals, articulate and unwilling to settle for a position of second-class citizenship, and affected to some degree by liberalizing influences within Catholicism, now preferred 'to use their own efforts to achieve a tolerable present rather than wait behind the barricades for a heavenly nationalist hereafter'.[31] 'Ulster Catholics', declared Dr G.B. Newe, a leading lay Catholic in 1958, had a duty 'to cooperate with the de facto authority' (the Northern Ireland state) 'and must forsake the traditional policy of passivity and abstentionism in political and social life'.[32]

By the early 1960s the old rural-based Nationalist Party was being challenged by a rising Catholic middle class – some of them beneficiaries of the transformative 1947 Education Act – to abandon the old policies of abstentionism and immediate Irish unity in favour of a recognition of constitutional realities and meaningful engagement with the state as it existed. In 1959 'National Unity', a group of young professionals, advocated reunification with a commitment to seek reforms within the Northern state. The fresh thinking of this ginger group and the Campaign for Social Justice, formed by the McCluskeys in 1964 to highlight discrimination in public housing and in public and private sector employment practices, chimed with key political changes in both parts of Ireland: the more pragmatic northern policy of the new Taoiseach, Seán Lemass, and the more conciliatory approach to the nationalist population of the new Northern Ireland Prime Minister, Terence O'Neill, after 1963. Lemass, though a veteran of the 1916 uprising, was focused on a new economic relationship with Britain and the European Economic Community (EEC), while his abandonment of both protectionism and his party's irredentist northern policy was greatly influenced by the Co. Down-born public servant and secretary of the Department of Finance in Dublin, T.K. Whitaker.[33]

30 Healy to Canon T. Maguire, 5 Nov. 1950 (PRONI D/2991/B/4/11B). 31 Desmond Fennell, *The Northern Catholic: an inquiry* (Dublin, 1958), pp 22–3. 32 Ian McAllister, *The Northern Ireland Social Democratic and Labour Party* (London, 1977), pp 9–10. 33 T.K. Whitaker, *Retrospect 2006–1916* (Dublin, 2006), pp 14–19.

Stung by its growing array of critics, the Nationalist Party successfully sought a meeting in March 1962 with the British Home Secretary, Rab Butler, to discuss the vexed issue of anti-Catholic discrimination in local government. The ten-strong delegation of MPs and Senators highlighted the situation in Derry Corporation where no Catholics were employed in such key departments as the Town Clerk's office or the welfare and rating or electricity sections, while of the twenty-five Corporation drivers, only four were Catholics. (This was in a city with a very large Catholic majority.) The meeting in Belfast was the first between a nationalist delegation and a British minister since 1922 but Butler declined to intervene, telling the delegation bluntly: 'I am not responsible for the detailed administration of Northern Ireland'.[34] Clearly, new tactics were necessary if equality in employment and housing were to be achieved.

In April 1964 National Unity called a meeting of all anti-partition groups at Maghery, Co. Armagh. It criticized the old Nationalist Party for its lack of policies and accountable party structure.[35] At the same time John Hume, then a twenty-seven year-old-school-teacher, penned a series of articles in the *Irish Times*. If he was critical of unionists for their neglect and undemocratic practices, he castigated the nationalists for 'sulking in their tents and failing to give positive leadership'.[36] Hume was concerned with Northern Ireland's urgent social and economic problems. While laying much of the blame with the forty-year-old unionist regime he did not spare the Nationalist Party of Healy and Eddie McAteer: 'Weak opposition leads to corrupt government', he wrote. 'Nationalists in opposition have been in no way constructive'. The young Derry man charged the nationalists with failing to make a constructive contribution 'on either the social and economic plane to the development of Northern Ireland'. He attacked the 'dangerous equation of Catholicism and nationalism' which had postponed the emergence of 'normal politics in the area' and had 'made the task of the unionist ascendancy easier'. Echoing his docker father's contempt for 'the comfortable leadership of flags and slogans', Hume called for a new, non-sectarian political approach by nationalists, adding: 'If one wishes to create a united Ireland by constitutional means, then one must accept the constitutional position'.[37]

The eleventh-hour attempt to modernize the Nationalist Party would fail and O'Neill would shatter nationalist expectations, but Hume's critique and the inexorable impact of the 1947 act on nationalist politics and society would foreshadow the rise of the civil rights movement and a new politics of engagement for nationalists in Northern Ireland. What few anticipated in those years of peaceful protest and mobilization, however, was the sudden, tragic onset of the Northern Troubles – the most sustained period of violence in modern Irish histoy and a maelstrom that would push John Hume, the emerging politician, centre stage.

34 Brendan Lynn, *Holding the ground: the Nationalist Party in Northern Ireland, 1945–72* (Farnham, Surrey, 1997), pp 152–3. 35 McAllister, op. cit., pp 18–21; Conn McCluskey, *Up off their knees* (Galway, 1989), pp 60–71. 36 Barry White, *John Hume: statesman of the Troubles* (Belfast, 1984), pp 43–5. 37 Ibid., pp 42–5.

Political Apprenticeship

PAUL ARTHUR

Famously, John Hume never kept a diary. In essence his public life was his diary so that there is an abundance of material to enable us to trace his political career. And this is reflected in several biographies beginning with Barry White's *John Hume: statesman of the Troubles* (1984). For his political opponents the very title smacked of hagiography and the epithet 'Saint John' followed him throughout his career. The nearest we come to personal reflection is his *Personal views: politics, peace and reconciliation in Ireland* (1996) but these are broad brush. Nowhere is there the equivalent of *Stepping Stones*, Dennis O'Driscoll's intimate and detailed conversation with Hume's friend, near-contemporary and fellow Nobel Laureate, Seamus Heaney.

Or is the dilemma solved by falling back on the memoirs of his fellow founding members of the SDLP? Three committed themselves to paper – Paddy O'Hanlon, Paddy Devlin and Austin Currie. O'Hanlon dropped out of party politics, Devlin was expelled from the party, and the exigencies of public life in Northern Ireland forced Currie to follow a successful political career in the Dáil. What they do reveal (sometimes inadvertently) is the constant force and consistency of Hume's political *persona*. He was the 'Big Beast' and big beasts attract animosity. This was particularly so with Devlin who felt that 'from the outset of our relationship I had misgivings about his motives and doubted the strength of his loyalty to the group'.[1] Second, they reveal the fissiparous nature of northern nationalist politics nourished, as it had been, on a sense of helplessness and a lack of discipline and organization.

Of course there is an array of academic commentaries on Hume, his party and anti-partitionist politics generally, but most of them fall into the 'culture' wars that

---

1 Paddy Devlin, *Straight left: an autobiography* (Belfast, 1993), p. 137. Devlin's title is (deliberately) revealing with its emphasis on his socialism and a pugnacious political style. For a broader consideration of these and other memoirs see 'Northern nationalists and memoir-writing' in Stephen Hopkins, *The politics of memoir and the Northern Ireland conflict* (Liverpool, 2013), pp 94–113

accompanied the Troubles and its outplaying in the post-1998 period. They veer from the sympathetic – Murray and McLoughlin – to downright hostility: writing in response to the Anglo-Irish Agreement, for example, Aughey describes Hume as 'a persistent and tireless hawker of platitudes' whose role in Anglo-Irish cooperation 'is ultimately a peripheral and expendable figure in that relationship'.[2] So we have a paradox. There is a burgeoning literature on John Hume and his times. His public life is (too) well known. But little is known about the inner man and the personal resources he employed to sustain the successes and overcome the adversities he encountered in a long political career. This chapter cannot overcome this hurdle. All that it can offer is a discussion on the milieu that drove Hume into politics and on the issues that shaped him during his political apprenticeship.

The thrust of the chapter will be concerned with his political apprenticeship; with the fact that his political world view began and ended in his home town – often to the chagrin of colleagues in the SDLP; that Derry was his moral and political compass and that the world (insofar as it suited his political project) was his hinterland; that he was consumed by what politics could achieve and, in that respect, that it was a practical exercise that entailed establishing relations of recognition and reciprocity; and that in a divided society the concept of 'community' was a contested one.

CONTEXT

In the barren years that stretched from 1921 until virtually the collapse of the Northern Ireland Parliament at Stormont in 1972 the life of a northern nationalist public representative was unenviable. It may not have been totally Hobbesian – solitary, poor, nasty, brutish and short – but it did not fulfil the enduring American myth of from the log cabin to the White House. There was to be no seat of ultimate power and the singular achievement of getting the Wild Birds Act through Stormont in 1931 was itself symbolic: it was as if one endangered species was attempting to protect the other. Nor did they enjoy the afterglow of the revolutionary elite in Dublin where dynastic politics could carry people to the top of the political tree. They were largely redundant and, with the passing of time, they felt a sense of abandonment. Consequently their political activity was furtive, fatalistic and schizophrenic veering from the doctrine of manifest destiny to a belief in the efficacy of the armed struggle. This was illustrated within one political household where Hugh McAteer had been Chief of Staff in the IRA and his brother Eddie would become Leader of the Nationalist Party

---

2 See Arthur Aughey, *Under siege: Ulster Unionism and the Anglo-Irish Agreement* (Belfast, 1989), p. 115. See too Gerry Murray, *John Hume and the SDLP: impact and survival in Northern Ireland* (Dublin, 1998) and Peter McLoughlin, *John Hume and the revision of Irish nationalism* (Manchester, 2012).

This was the political milieu into which John Hume was born in 1937. Since one of his mantras has been that one's identity has been shaped by the accident of where we are born, it is worthwhile dwelling on this aspect of his development. Like Seamus Heaney – 'we had a subsistence sort of living' – the social and economic conditions were to be less important than the opportunities they took to overcome modest beginnings. This is borne out in his maiden speech to the House of Commons when he dwelt on the fact that his constituency had 'the unenviable distinction of having the highest unemployment rate of any constituency represented in this House'. In particular he concentrated on youth unemployment in a society in which 'they have always seen security forces and violence on the streets, in which they have been continuously searched because they are young people.' Hence, if the government 'make a sensible and determined attack on the problems of youth unemployment, they would also be making a determined attack on the problems of extremism'.[3]

These were to be two recurring themes throughout his political career – a challenge to the extremist tradition in Irish politics, and to the cause of self-help. Married to the first was a critical analysis of the simplistic approach of the nationalist tradition which he considered to be 'sectional' based as it was on the Gaelic and Catholic strands of Irish nationalism to the exclusion of Protestants. In that respect he was setting out to remould constitutional nationalism, a journey that he had begun with two articles in the *Irish Times* entitled 'The Northern Catholic' in May 1964; and which he was to expand throughout his political career. In particular, the creation of the New Ireland Forum in May 1983 extended the self-analysis among the major constitutional nationalist parties on the island when he argued that 'flag-waving will no longer do'. When the Forum reported on 30 April 1984 many of the major shibboleths in Irish nationalism had been challenged, ranging from Church-State relations to the economic costs of Irish unity, and to the political and psychological costs induced by the demography of violence initiated by the IRA and like-minded groups. It might be said that the Forum assisted Irish nationalism in escaping from its insularity and that Hume was its chief architect.

Derry was a microcosm of all of these problems: 'Derry is a city of mirrors, the two sides of the community, the two sides of the Foyle, the two sides of the border, the inside and the outside of the walls. [Derry has had] a long preoccupation with duality, with images that mirror each other and yet reflect a difference perceived to be so extreme as to provoke murderous hatred and violence'.[4] Derry and its hinterland represented the challenges of borders and boundaries – the physical border that divided the island politically; and the psychological bound-

3 HC, *Debates* 28 June 1983, cols 507–8. 4 Susan McKay, '"And so they are ever returning to us, the dead": Willie Doherty in Derry' in Willie Doherty, *Unseen* (Derry, 2013), p. 12.

aries that existed in the peculiar electoral arrangements for the city. A means had to be found to break this binary conundrum.

For the Protestant minority (but political majority) the foundation myth was that of the siege of 1689 whose basic themes were defiance, solidarity, sacrifice and deliverance, a schizophrenic combination of fear of betrayal *and* the triumph of liberation, a sense of siege that they carried into contemporary events.[5] It was the Maiden City – wooed but never won by the Jacobite forces in 1689. Nevertheless, as McBride reveals, the Protestant community was deeply divided along lines of ideology, religious denomination and class. This provided a potent mix that made the Derry/Londonderry issue more fraught than most. Indeed Prime Minister Captain Terence O'Neill warned his cabinet (following a meeting with Harold Wilson on 4 November 1968) that in order to divert direct British intervention they might have to make a bitter choice between losing Londonderry and losing Ulster.[6] Catholic memories were longer. Their sense of place went back to Colmcille's monastic settlement of the sixth century and their culture of grievance was reinforced by twentieth century partition. For them this was a quintessentially Irish city situated on the border with the Irish Republic – in effect, they believed, the capital of north west Ireland.

Partition had cut off its natural hinterland; and the necessity to secure it in unionist hands led to allegations of discrimination and gerrymandering. By the 1930s there was a worry among unionists that they might lose control, so steps were taken in 1936 to redraw the local boundaries when the city's five wards were reduced to three. The result was that there was no symmetry in rateable valuations and no equity in the number of electors in each ward. The consequence was that in a city with a clear nationalist voting majority the North and Waterside wards returned 12 unionists – 8 and 4 respectively – and the South ward 8 nationalists. The events around Bloody Sunday in January 1972 concentrated in the South Ward. It might be said that the 1936 decision laid the first foundation stone for the civil rights revolt in the city more than thirty years later.

The three wards also symbolized the extent to which Derry was a divided society. There was the natural geographic boundary of the river which cut off the Waterside (with its small Protestant majority and eight unionist councillors) from the rest of the city. This natural boundary may be one reason why the sectarian tensions never reached the heights those of Belfast and elsewhere; and it and the wider rural environs acted as an escape route to Protestant families fleeing from the IRA's murderous campaign. The west bank was less a monolith and more a series of interconnecting urban spaces. Hume had been born in Rosemount –

5 See Ian McBride, *The Siege of Derry in Ulster Protestant mythology* (Dublin, 1997), passim. Its potency for contemporary loyalism should not be underestimated. The present First Minister, Peter Robinson, produced a book – *Their cry was no surrender* (Belfast, 1988) – dedicated to 'All Those Whose Answer To Ulster's Enemies Is Still – No Surrender'. See, too, Jonathan Burgess, *The Exodus* (2011), passim. 6 Cited by Éamon Phoenix in his survey of the Stormont cabinet papers, in *Irish News*, 1 Jan. 1999.

known colloquially as 'the village'. Before it entered international consciousness the Bogside was a single street. Those middle-class residents of the South Ward did not embrace it as a badge of pride until civil resistance became popular and the Bogside became a concept. Along with the Creggan estate it composed the bulk of the population of the South ward. So it is 'easy to see Derry as a city of enclaves or as a palimpsest of certain events from history, including recent history'.[7]

What united all of them was a deep sense of grievance. How that grievance was to be nurtured into a positive force was one of the tasks which Hume set himself. The image of Derry from that time onwards was of the linkage between socio-economic grievances and political violence, encapsulated in the opening lines of Seamus Deane's poem 'Derry':

> The unemployment in our bones
> Erupting in our hands like stones
> The thought of violence a relief
> The act of violence a grief;
> Our bitterness and love
> Hand in glove ...

Politically the city had been largely quiescent in the post-war period. There had been minor clashes between nationalist demonstrators and the police on St Patrick's Day in 1951 and 1952 and there had been a number of incidents during the IRA border campaign (1956–62). Derry was a (constitutional) nationalist constituency, held since 1953 by Eddie McAteer who went on to become leader of the Nationalist Party. As a young man he had published a pamphlet, *Irish Action*, on non-violent direct action – shades of the civil rights movement to come and, indeed, of Hume's own political philosophy. But as party leader he had urged caution in the early days of the civil rights campaign. McAteer (and most of his party) had been swept aside by the fervour of that campaign when he lost his seat to John Hume in the February 1969 Northern Ireland general election.

Catholics had consistently voted for McAteer because he personified traditional values. After the civil rights march in Derry on 5 October 1968 those values no longer pertained. Hume, who had flirted with the Nationalist Party for a short period after his *Irish Times* articles in 1964, decided that the time was ripe to challenge the old order. At its annual party conference in July 1968 the nationalists had rejected a call from Austin Currie to support a motion inviting it to commit itself to a campaign of civil disobedience. The gap between the old and the new was evident during the election campaign when the party highlighted 'the degree of discomfort felt by traditional nationalists within the civil rights movement and their

7 Colm Tóibín, *Bad blood: a walk among the Irish border* (London, 2010), p. 16.

belief that the Hume line was too Six-County orientated, and that the importance of the border issue was being downgraded'.[8]

That indeed was one of the fissures in the contemporary debate. Hume and his civil rights comrades believed firmly in Irish unity but one that could be attained only through the doctrine of consent. It was at the heart of the SDLP constitution. Another mantra that he had adapted from the outset was that the real unity that mattered was that of *people* rather than *territory*. But just as vital was the need to get on with the quotidian and that meant dealing with issues such as housing and jobs. The slogans at the heart of the civil rights campaign encapsulated the problem. 'One Man One Vote' referred directly to the lack of fit between Northern Ireland and the rest of the UK in the matter of voting at local government level; and indirectly to the issue of gerrymandering. But 'One Family One House' and 'One Man One Job' – the gender discrimination was redolent of the times and had a particular irony in Derry where so many of the bread winners were women who worked in the shirt factories – illustrated the deep underlying socio-economic grievances.

The Cameron Commission (established by the O'Neill government after the initial violence) found an extraordinary situation in the electoral arrangement of Londonderry County Borough in 1967. It amounted to gerrymandering. An equally bleak picture emerged in terms of local government appointments. The housing stock during the post war years was so bad that 300 homeless families squatted in abandoned temporary wartime structures until the 'Springtown camp' was closed down in 1967. Labour's victory in the 1945 British general election led to the creation of the Welfare State. Social policy in Northern Ireland had to reflect that change and the unionist government initiated a major public housing programme to build 100,000 new houses. This was to create problems for them in terms of controlling local electoral boundaries, more so in Londonderry Borough Council. Cameron admitted frankly that 'Council housing policy has also been distorted for political ends'.[9]

The response in Derry was twofold. One was a series of public protests led by the left. This local activism had benefited from the move from private renting to public housing and was to be 'central to the increasing political mobilization of Derry's Catholic community in the late 1960s'[10] and to the establishment of the radical republican Derry Housing Action Committee (DHAC) late in 1967. The other was to rely on self-help through the creation of the Derry Housing Association (DHA) early in 1965 with John Hume as its first chairman. By 1967

8 Cited in Brendan Lynn, 'Nationalist politics in Derry 1945–69' in Gerry O'Brien (ed.), *Derry – history and society* (Dublin, 1999), p. 619.   **9** *Disturbances in Northern Ireland. Report of the Commission appointed by the Governor of Northern Ireland* (Cmd. 532), September 1969, paras. 134, 1138, 139 respectively.   **10** Niall Ó Dochartaigh, 'Housing and conflict: social change and collective action in Derry in the 1960s' in O'Brien (ed.), *Derry*, p. 628. See, too, Eamonn McCann, *War and an Irish town* (London, 1974), passim. McCann was the most prominent leader of social agitation at the time.

the DHA had constructed a 27-house estate in the North Ward. But when it proposed building 500 houses at a nearby site in the same ward the unionist-controlled council rejected the proposal because they recognized that that would upset the local electoral balance and that in the longer run they would lose control of the council. The difference between the DHA and the DHAC was more than an upper-case initial. It represented two different world views that were to play out for the entire period of the conflict. And that calls attention to another of Hume's qualities: the constant search for consensus building, both within the SDLP and in the wider community generally.

A long-standing joke explained the enigmatic skeleton on the city's coat-of-arms as symbolic of a Derry Catholic waiting for a house (and a job). Unemployment created by the loss of work in war-time industries – Hume's father, Sam, an active trade unionist, was one such victim – led to massive emigration: in the decade after 1951 the official estimate was that almost thirteen per cent of the city's population had emigrated. The problem was compounded by demographics:

> we were a very fertile people … The 1961 census revealed that the natural annual increase in the population of Derry was 21.2 per 1,000, against 11.5 for Northern Ireland as a whole and 5.7 for England and Wales. The same census showed that two-fifths of the residents of the South Ward were under fifteen years. Eighty per cent of births in the city were Catholic. The population 'pyramid' for the area resembled that of a tropical 'third world' rather than a western metropolitan country. It corresponded to that for Britain in the middle of the nineteenth, not the twentieth, century.[11]

The unemployment figures deserve closer scrutiny for what they intimate about *perception* and *motivation*. In February 1967 unemployment in the city stood at an astronomical twenty per cent when the British average was only slightly more than two per cent and Northern Ireland's was eight per cent. A reason for the sudden hike in unemployment numbers was the closure of three Monarch Electric factories in January 1967. At one stage they had employed 1,800 people and they were virtually the sole industry employing males in the Bogside.

When Terence O'Neill became prime minister in 1963 he was intent on modernizing Northern Ireland – hence a series of commissions to enquire into means to improve the infrastructure. The Matthew Commission reported in 1963 and, *inter alia*, recommended the creation of the new city of Craigavon. Shortly thereafter the Benson Report advised on streamlining the railway system. And in 1965 the Lockwood Report recommended the building of a new university in Coleraine. The implication of all three reports was that modernization was cen-

---

11 McCann, *War and an Irish town,* pp 24–5.

tred on the industrial infrastructure east of the Bann. Given that Derry had lost its rail link to Donegal in 1963 and to Dublin in 1965 a growing sense of the further isolation of the Derry region was inevitable. Borders and boundaries were becoming more constricted.

There were deep-rooted social and historical considerations as well. The city's emblematic importance to Protestant and Catholic alike has already been mentioned. Add to that its strategic importance during the Second World War when Northern Ireland was seen as the most important geopolitical bulwark on Britain's western flank; and by 1943 Derry had evolved into the most important escort base in the UK. That was carried on into the cold war when it was used for NATO exercises until 1968.[12] In addition there was the presence of a major US naval communications base, and of HMS *Sea Eagle*. That presented a paradox. Nationalist Ireland resented a (British) military presence in the city. On the other hand it represented employment opportunities and *colour*. It overcame some of the drabness of the mundane. It enabled many to raise their heads above the parapet and to look outwards, none more so than Hume.

The port also served as a major point of emigration to the United States in the nineteenth century. Hume reflected on this when he wrote that it was hardly surprising that Derry people looked outwards: 'It was from Derry that many of our ancestors sailed into exile whether it was to the nearer island Britain, or west to the United States – we referred to Boston as "the next parish". When our first emigrants left these shores there was what we called "an American wake". In a sense, the person was as good as dead to the family …'[13] It was this diaspora that was to play such a vital part in reshaping the nature of the British-Irish conflict through the 1998 Belfast Agreement.

A geographer considered that high fertility was the most significant demographic feature in Derry. During this period fifty-eight per cent of the Derry population supported forty-two per cent either too young or too old to be gainfully employed. The result was high youth dependency, overcrowded living conditions, a low standard of living, high unemployment and migration. Since high fertility affected the Catholic community more than the Protestant it encouraged segregation.[14] All of these grievances produced a funeral pyre that was exploited in the civil rights campaign. And it was the legacy of these grievances to which Hume devoted his burgeoning political career.

---

12 G.R. Sloan, *The geopolitics of Anglo-Irish relations in the twentieth century* (London, 1997), pp 219, 248, 259.   13 John Hume, 'Transforming the Union: an evolving dynamic', British Council, *Britain and Ireland: lives entwined III*. n.d., p. 15.   14 A. Robinson, 'Social and economic geography of Londonderry' (MA thesis, Queen's University Belfast 1968), passim. These were issues that had a bearing on John Hume's political, economic and intellectual development. His MA thesis (1964), 'Social and economic aspects of the growth of Derry, 1825–50', was published later as a book. In 1964 he produced a BBC documentary, *A city solitary*, as another lasting impression of his city's evolution and expectations; and he was to produce

ISSUES

It might be said that Hume was 'lucky' in his timing in entering public life, a span that stretched from 1959 to 2004. We shall see that the nature of political discourse was changing as were the modes of communication. By 1969, when he was elected to Stormont, he had demonstrated his mettle in conveying his message to a wider audience through such as the *Irish Times* articles in 1964 and a television documentary *John Hume's Derry*, a copy of which he brought to the United States in 1969 when he visited Boston. The mass media was to be his *métier*. He had a decisive and incisive delivery that ran counter to what passed as (hot-headed) debate. The era of the monster public rally was coming to an end. The intimacy of the television studio mattered more. The skills of the lobbyist and of the 'committee man' were coming into their own. I witnessed the former in the US in November 1980. I was speaking at a conference in Connecticut. Afterwards I 'shadowed' Hume in New York and Washington when he attended meetings hosted by Senators Edward Kennedy, Daniel Moynihan, Governor Hugh Carey and Speaker Tip O'Neill, collectively known as the Four Horsemen. He was extraordinarily effective in selling his message of non-violence and of seeking to put pressure on the British government. The date was important because Ronald Reagan had just been elected President and Congressional Democrats were in retreat. It was out of these dire circumstances that the Horsemen morphed into the Friends of Ireland and the base of Irish-American pressure had been broadened.

Paddy Doherty gives a compelling account of his first encounter with John Hume in 1959 when the latter called at his house to discuss social, political and economic issues in an attempt to understand the widespread apathy that governed the area: 'I had never come across anyone so young with such confidence in his own ability'.[15] By this stage Hume had given up studying for the priesthood at the national seminary in Maynooth and had become a teacher of French and History at his *alma mater*, St Columb's College. One of his 'accidents' of birth was that his was the first generation who had been able to take advantage of the 1947 Education Act because it opened the way for entry into secondary and third level education for those with academic ability. This was the generation that was to play such a key role in the civil rights movement. Doherty's age didn't give him that advantage but he worked closely with Hume on establishing the credit union in Derry and in tackling the housing shortage. Like Paddy Devlin he had some mis-

---

two further documentaries, one on the role of the local psychiatric hospital, and the second, *Two hours from London*, to encourage tourism and industrial investment in the north-west, all of them a testament to his energy and a single-minded commitment to his city and region.   **15** Paddy Doherty, *Paddy Bogside* (Derry, 2001), p. 27. Doherty also believed passionately in self-help and was a huge influence in the creation of inner-city development as a way out of apathy and youth unemployment. He was closer than Hume to the more strident voices of Irish nationalism/republicanism like Sean Keenan and Neil Blaney.

givings: 'Hume's idea of "enlightened leadership" tended towards the premise that John Hume would lead'. Nonetheless he backed him because he considered him 'to be the best leader the Catholic people had'.[16]

That ran contrary to Hume's inclusive outlook, but what he could not be expected to overcome was his educational upbringing, and McCann is surely correct when he writes that St Columb's was 'quite a successful school by "ordinary" educational standards but that in the end we had been involved in an intellectual package deal and had been given a complete set of ideas, attitudes and pieces of knowledge and urged to understand that these were adequate to equip one for any human situation in which it was proper ever to find oneself'.[17] It was how one used those ideas, attitudes and knowledge that set Hume apart. Again he may have been lucky in the times that were in it. His political maturing was happening at a time of great flux in the western world. For the first time a Catholic of Irish-American stock had become US President; there was (positive) upheaval in the Catholic Church with the papacy of John XXIII that was to undermine the concept of Roman Catholicism as being monolithic; social movements were beginning to exert themselves in an era of democratization and decolonization; and racial inequality was being challenged in the US.

The last was to have a profound impact on Hume's political development. Martin Luther King Jr's 'Letter from Birmingham Jail' – *Why We Can't Wait* (16 April 1963) – introduced four basic steps into the concept of non-violent civil resistance: the collection of the facts to determine whether an injustice exists; negotiations; self-purification and direct action. The first was already under way with the work of the Campaign for Social Justice (CSJ). The second had some tentative beginnings with representations to the British government by such as the CSJ and the Northern Ireland Labour Party (NILP). The third had never ever been really part of the Irish political tradition; and, consequently, the fourth was conducted in less-than-ideal circumstances. Like King, Hume realized that non-violence 'is a powerful demand for reason and justice. If it is rudely rebuked, it is not transformed into resignation and passivity'. The politics of non-violence presents a theory of power specifying that rulers depend on the consent or acquiescence of the ruled. The challenge for like-minded people was how to ensure that a non-violent campaign did not become a harbinger for violence, but remained a steady and responsible quarrel with the establishment.

That was to be the rationale that guided his political activism. It is what distinguished him from earlier generations of Irish nationalists. His was not one of 'sneaking regard' for the men of violence. Instead he concentrated on the practi-

---

16 Ibid., p. 30.   17 McCann, *War and an Irish town*, pp 17–18. See, too, Maurice Fitzpatrick, *The boys of St Columb's* (Dublin, 2010), passim. The book is based around a series of interviews with former students who have been highly successful in life (including the two Nobel Laureates, Hume and Heaney). The school, a junior seminary, played a very important role in shaping values.

cal issues that had to be addressed. We have noted already his attitude to public housing through the creation of the DHA. But one enterprise that had a profound impact on his community was the creation of the credit union movement in Derry in 1960. It was as if he had been influenced by one of the key books of the nineteenth century, *Self help* published by Samuel Smiles in 1859, the same year as Darwin's *Origin of the species* and John Stuart Mill's *On liberty*. All three had a profound impact on how individuals shaped their lives. Given the different context the Irish response to self-help was more rural in constitution with the establishment of the Irish Agricultural Organization Society in 1894 led by Horace Plunkett and the poet, mystic and artist George Russell (Æ). The same year saw the foundation of the first experiment in cooperative banking in Co. Cork. By 1914 in excess of 800 cooperative societies, of which 232 were credit societies, had been established.

The one exception to this rule was the Belfast Cooperative Society, a child of the British cooperative movement and, obviously, an urban phenomenon. The credit union movement that spread throughout Ireland from the 1950s onwards helped to break a vicious cycle in working-class communities where the poor had relied on church organizations, 'tick' men, pawnbrokers and friendly societies. Even with the safety net of the welfare state many in the ghettoes lived in a precarious state. The credit union movement was to be a point of liberation based on the notion of the common bond – especially community, occupational and associational. By the second decade of this century the Irish League of Credit Unions had total assets of 14.3 billion euros.

The Derry Credit Union started with £7.50 (the combined savings of its founding members – Michael Canavan, Paddy Doherty, Hume himself and two fellow teachers). One commentary suggests that it gave Hume 'his first brush with politics'. The non-profit making organization catered primarily to the city's lowest paid and by enabling such citizens to manage their financial affairs collectively, gave them self-confidence to tackle other problems together. It transformed the personal finances of thousands of people in Derry.[18] It also enabled Hume to move up the credit union ladder where he established an international profile. But that was before he had illustrated his own commitment to self-help by resigning his teaching job and creating a small smoked salmon processing business. The outcome was two-fold. He demonstrated that people could control their own (economic) destinies and he released himself into a position whereby he could contemplate a career in politics.

The creation of the credit union movement was profound, positive but slow burning. The same could not be said of the decision by the Lockwood Committee to open up a second university for Northern Ireland in Coleraine – a decision that

18 George Drower, *John Hume: man of peace* (London, 1995), p. 30.

seems to have been based solely on its capacity to provide student accommodation and on the academic criterion that it could provide facilities for marine biology while it acknowledged that 'it had no cultural amenities'; that decision galvanized the city's population. It was a rare example of an issue that crossed party lines. Lockwood's ruminations that the city was unlikely to develop further industrially and that it was a 'frontier town' that would never lose its 'siege mentality' seemed to compound all the prejudices that officialdom held about the city. It was what brought Hume into the full glare of public life and it was one of those rare moments when his efforts had a wholly inclusive community thrust. On 18 February 1965, a 200-vehicle motorcade from Derry to Stormont led by Eddie McAteer and the unionist mayor demonstrated the depth of anger felt in the city.[19] It was the University for Derry campaign that thrust Hume into the limelight. Hereinafter he was public property.

When the SDLP was launched on 21 August 1970 in Belfast after several false starts it was the culmination of a journey that had begun in the struggles of the 1960s and in a culture that had resisted party discipline. When two Stormont MPs, Gerry Fitt and Harry Diamond, combined their two one-man parties into a single two-man party, the Republican Labour Party, they started a trend – that of breaking from the pietistic conservatism and individualism of northern nationalism. But progress for the SDLP was not to be a smooth journey. Problems about the party name, about personality clashes among its leaders, about its attitude towards its role of opposition in Stormont and many other issues, conspired to guarantee that the journey would be eventful. The dismissal of Paddy Devlin in 1977 and the resignation of Gerry Fitt in 1979 highlighted personality clashes and ideological differences. Political setbacks in the 1970s including the collapse of power-sharing, a wavering relationship with the Republic's political establishment and the continuation of the IRA's campaign (and loyalist counter-violence) highlighted the challenges confronting constitutional nationalism. Those were the circumstances that John Hume inherited when he became leader in 1979. By the end of the tenure of his leadership Northern Ireland and the historic Irish conflict were in a different, more secure place. All of the progress bears testimony to his constant refrain (repeated in his Nobel lecture) 'We shall overcome'.

CONCLUSION

For a man who devoted his public life to bringing the two traditions together it might be said that his apprenticeship yielded poor returns. With the exception of

---

19 See Gerry O'Brien, '"Our Magee problem": Stormont and the second university' in O'Brien (ed.), *Derry*, pp 647–96.

the University for Derry campaign there is little evidence that both communities embraced *Kumbaya*. Indeed, as many commentaries reveal, Hume was a divisive figure. He lacked the 'hail fellow well met' touch of Gerry Fitt and yet he achieved a resolution to the marching problem in Derry by patient negotiations with the Apprentice Boys, a sharp contrast to the deadlock in Belfast and elsewhere. His quintessential 'Derryness' did not always travel well. His undoubted intelligence did not fit the stereotype of someone raised in the ghetto. His single-minded pursuit of his political goals did not always lend itself to collegiality. To counter all of that there is the enormous contribution he made to his constituents both in terms of material well-being and in self-esteem.

The fact is that Hume was an incredibly complex political actor who understood too well the complexity of intractable conflict. In his seminal work *Key Words* Raymond Williams wrote that community, unlike other terms of social organization (state, nation, society etc.), 'seems never to have been used unfavourably'. But there are societies in which communities choose to maintain their traditions and customs by necessarily excluding others. Northern Ireland was one such society. Hume's life work was to challenge these asymmetries. The three-stranded approach of the 1998 Agreement addressed such asymmetry by creating institutions with relationships within the North, between North and South and between the two islands.

One of his political opponents summed up John Hume thus: 'He's not a man of ideas. He's a man of moderate action with great political acumen, judgment and luck'.[20] That is almost accurate. His luck arose out of the accident of the date of his birth. His political acumen and judgment were qualities he acquired and nurtured from a long political apprenticeship and a commitment to what the Romans called *virtu*, a dedication to public life. His moderation was a deeply held philosophical conviction born out of a close reading of Irish history. It was his tenacity, his moderation and his communication skills – quiet diplomacy and personal conversation – that set him apart from the historic nationalist political leader. The historian, Joe Lee, once commented that the 'heroic' in Irish history was denoted by resistance to the enemy rather than any positive quality that would enhance community. Hume, along with Seán Lemass, belonged to the latter.

Perhaps the greatest flaw in the McCann analysis is a misunderstanding of politics as an activity. It was the conservative political philosopher, Edmund Burke – not someone whom McCann would readily consult – in his essay *On the Present Discontents*, published in 1770, who made the important distinction: 'It is the business of the speculative philosopher to mark the proper ends of government. It is the business of the politician, who is the philosopher in action, to find out the proper means towards those ends and to employ them with effect'. That was pre-

20 Eamonn McCann cited in Drower, *John Hume*, p. 15.

cisely what Hume was about from the day he had his conversation with Paddy Doherty. His was a conceptual mind and his aims were narrow and clear sighted. In his often-cited 1953 essay on 'The Hedgehog and the Fox' Isaiah Berlin opens with a line from the Greek poet, Archilochus, which says: 'The fox knows many things, but the hedgehog knows one big thing'. Hume was a hedgehog, but, in keeping with his complex personality, he acquired the skills of a fox.

Civil Rights Movement

AUSTIN CURRIE

On 18 February 1965 a motorcade of many hundreds of cars arrived outside Northern Ireland's Parliament at Stormont, their occupants rallying to protest against what appeared, once again, to be a serious act of discrimination against their city – the decision of the unionist government at Stormont that the planned new university for Northern Ireland would be sited in Coleraine, rather than Derry. It was an impressive scene, showing the strong determination, and the apparently united demand, of the people of Derry/Londonderry, that the new university should rightfully be sited in their city.

Gerry Fitt and I, MPs respectively for Belfast Dock, and East Tyrone, watched from the first floor of the Parliament Building, as did the great majority of the members of the unionist government, and MPs and senators from all sides of the House. We looked down on this great demonstration of Derry power and apparent unity, as the three leaders of the motorcade began the long ascent of the steps up to the entrance. They were Senator Albert Anderson, unionist Mayor of Londonderry, and Eddie McAteer, nationalist MP for the Foyle constituency (who only ten days earlier agreed to accept the role of Official Leader of the Opposition in the Stormont House of Commons, in a significant gesture of rapprochement with the Northern Ireland state); these two men had never previously been seen together on the same platform in support of any cause; the third person was a younger man, a teacher, chairman of the University for Derry campaign and the main leader of the motorcade – John Hume. Fitt, who throughout his long career had acutely sensitive political antennae, particularly for political competition, nudged me and whispered 'I was in Derry last week, and Big Eddie will keep an eye on that boy'.

It was on that occasion that John Hume became a public persona, but for some time Derry people had known him as a talent in their midst. He was only twenty-eight years of age, but he already had a history of public service as a promoter of self-help schemes, initially in housing and later particularly as the initiator, in Derry, of the largest credit union in the world. Remarkably – given his youth – he had been elected President of the Credit Union League of Ireland. He had written some well-regarded press articles, and made a small number of speeches and television appearances. However, his biggest prominence was on the platform of Derry's Guildhall on 8 February 1965, at a public meeting on the controversy over the location of the new university.

The unionist government had, in 1963, established the Lockwood Committee to make recommendations about the creation of a second university for Northern Ireland, and the unionist dominated Londonderry Corporation – rather belatedly but unanimously – decided to make a submission. Confidence was high, because of Derry's history, culture, geographical position and size; and the small but long-established Magee University College appeared to be the obvious nucleus for the new university. Political aspirations of both traditions could also be satisfied by claiming the new university for Derry, since nationalists could prosper their city while creating educational opportunity, and unionists could protect and enhance the future of Magee, which they had always looked on as one of the major props of the Presbyterian tradition in the city.

The public meeting in the Guildhall was a triumph of hope. The enthusiastic audience did not really believe the rumours which suggested that Lockwood would recommend locating the university at the small market town of Coleraine, thirty miles away from Derry. A University for Derry campaign was established. It was cross-community in its composition and included three Magee College professors co-opted as advisers. Hume was the star of the occasion. He was proposed and elected as chairman of the campaign. As Barry White in his book recorded about his speech:

> His theme was the need to unite the two traditions, not just for the duration of the University campaign but for the good of the city in the long term. Derry stood for two traditions, he said. There was the Protestant siege tradition, followed by the sacrifices in two world wars, and the native Irish tradition of St Columcille. For one tradition it was the place where the battle had been fought and, for the other, the place where the battle was being fought. The university issue could provide a marriage of both traditions and both points of view. It was a unifying speech which caught perfectly the mood of the meeting and brought the crowd to its feet in recognition of this new ideal, so powerfully expressed by someone who was unmistakably a Derry man and yet could not be slotted into any of the existing pigeon-holes.

Notwithstanding the hope, the apparent confidence on all sides, and the organizing capacity of Hume and his committee, they never really had a chance. The government had already decided on Coleraine – and a group of powerful Derry unionists, the so-called 'faceless men', had secreted themselves in a political Trojan horse, and had been conniving with the unionist bosses at Stormont to assassinate their own city.

Despite the fact that Taoiseach Seán Lemass and Prime Minister Terence O'Neill had recently met in Stormont and in Dublin, and that the Nationalist Party had taken up the position of the official opposition, all in an atmosphere of optimism and hope for a shared future, 'No Surrender' and 'Not an Inch' intransigence still prevailed among many unionists in relation to Derry on this and every other issue. Hume had hoped that some unionist politicians would have common sense, and some appreciation of the fairness of the claims of Derry, but he was bitterly disappointed. O'Neill insisted on the Coleraine decision because he feared a parliamentary vote of no confidence from his own party members. Ultimately only a Derry man on the government benches, Desmond Boal, unionist MP for Shankill, voted in favour of his home city. A former unionist Attorney General, Edmond Warnock, MP for St Anne's, Belfast, later described the Coleraine decision as 'political madness' and added 'we have left on the front of Northern Ireland a tremendous ulcer which will give us nothing but trouble and danger ...'

Boal insisted that Lockwood had been got at; 'from a dispassionate and objective view of this matter, and when one looks at these reasons (environment, education, etc.) can one be forced to turn away – can one be forced to turn away if one is going to exercise one's intellect on this – from Londonderry? I suggest that one cannot and yet, oddly enough, the committee did. I leave it like that'. Later, Boal was to observe: 'We have made a mistake. We have jumped too rashly and that is a matter which is going to affect us for many years to come'.

Boal was only too prescient of the consequences, as bitter anger was felt strongly, even by moderates in the Derry community. For many, the betrayal of Derry was the ultimate humiliation. In a few short years, all in the sixties and at a time when new hopes for community relationships in Northern Ireland were on the rise, Derry had lost its train line to Portadown and to Dublin, the unionist government's planned new city was to be located at Craigavon, thirty miles from Belfast, and now the new university was to be established at Coleraine. Derry Catholics like John Hume saw their city being isolated and abandoned, because of deliberate, sectarian-motivated government policy.

Hume had expressed the hope, in his Guildhall speech, and in many television and radio appearances, that co-operation and unity on the university campaign would create a new spirit of common endeavour, engaging both traditions of the city. He hoped that it would bring about a partnership between the two traditions that might foster progress, and tackle the massive political, social and economic afflictions of Derry. It was not to be. Derry continued to experience gross inequality based on discrimination and an outrageous gerrymander by which a minority held power in city government over a majority of the citizens.

Surprisingly perhaps, in view of all this, it was in the smaller town of Dungannon – one sixth of the size of Derry, and with a Catholic majority of only fifty-one percent – that the civil rights movement took its initial shape. In Dungannon Urban Council, and similarly in Dungannon Rural District Council, there had always been an obdurate group of unionist councillors, who, in spite of the demographics, and as a consequence of another outrageous gerrymander, made up the majority of both councils. Since the creation of the Northern Ireland state, both had blatantly mis-allocated public authority housing in an out-rageously sectarian way.

In the early 1960s a Dungannon GP became increasingly concerned about the obvious relationship between the ill-health of many of his patients and the inade-quacy of their housing. In 1963 Dr Conn McCluskey, with his intrepid and very able wife Patricia, launched the Homeless Citizens League, along with many of Conn's homeless patients. From then onwards there was, in the Dungannon area, persistent agitation over housing issues, with activists squatting in houses that had been unjustly allocated and noisy protests at council meetings. The resulting pub-licity and propaganda were deliberately and specifically directed at Britain, to inform and influence opinion makers there so that they might exert pressure on the British government and the Northern Ireland government to end these injustices.

In January 1964 Conn and Patricia McCluskey, along with similarly motivated and public-spirited people from all around Northern Ireland, extended their activ-ities beyond Dungannon, by launching the Campaign for Social Justice in Northern Ireland (CSJ). Their objective was 'to collect comprehensive and accu-rate data on all injustices done against all political creeds and political opinions, including details of discrimination in jobs and houses, and bring them to the attention of as many socially minded people as possible'. One of the first publica-tions the CSJ produced – a pamphlet entitled *Plain Truth* – was targeted particu-larly at British opinion makers. It documented the facts about inequalities and injustices in employment practices, in public authority housing allocation, in appointments to public boards, and in employment patterns in the medical pro-fession, the police, the justice system, educational institutions, the post office, pri-vate business and the trade unions, as well as voting and electoral irregularities. It documented and pinpointed the neglect of the western areas of Northern Ireland where the majority of Catholics/nationalists lived, and it published statistics show-ing how gerrymandering had enabled unionist minorities to completely control local government in majority nationalist towns like Omagh, Armagh, Lurgan and Dungannon. All this information was thoroughly researched, published and cir-culated to audiences, particularly in Britain, which had been ignorant of the scale and extent of inequality and discrimination in Northern Ireland.

Plain Truth records that in Dungannon 'in 1963 there were upwards of 300 families on the housing list, some for as long as 12 years, and not one new Catholic family had been allocated a permanent house for 34 years. Council houses had been allocated to a pharmaceutical chemist, the council's own engineers and several other comfortably off Protestant people. Other Protestants had sold good villa residences to move into council houses'. By recording statistics such as this, the McCluskeys became the parents of the civil rights struggle in Northern Ireland; John Hume and I, and the other civil rights leaders, were their children.

However, the special case, the classic example of discrimination and gerrymander, was Derry/Londonderry. Because of its gerrymandered ward system, 10,274 unionist voters elected twelve unionist councillors, whereas 20,102 nationalist voters elected only eight councillors. This outrageous situation was buttressed by a restricted franchise; only householders could vote, and therefore control of housing allocation equalled control of voting numbers. The old Derry Corporation quite deliberately denied adequate housing to its nationalist population for this reason. Houses were votes, and with a franchise based on a property vote, human misery and degradation were simply tools to maintain electoral control.

The work of the McCluskeys prompted many others to become involved in the struggle against injustice and discrimination. When the Northern Ireland Civil Rights Association (NICRA) was formed in 1967 in Belfast it had five objectives:

1   to defend the basic freedom of all citizens
2   to protect the rights of the individual
3   to highlight all abuses of power
4   to demand guarantees for freedom of speech, assembly and association, and
5   to inform the public of their lawful rights.

The objectives were wide enough to cover those matters which were at the heart of the unjust system which unionists had built up since 1920 – discrimination in public authority housing allocation, discriminatory employment practices in both the public and private sectors, the gerrymandering of electoral boundaries, the absence of 'one person one vote' and the permanent presence on the statute book of the Special Powers Act, which was the envy of the apartheid government in South Africa. But possibly most significant of all, there was no reference, direct or indirect, to the re-unification of Ireland. NICRA was not to be based on the 1916 Proclamation of Independence or the programme of the first Dáil, but upon the aims and objectives of the British National Council for Civil Liberties, an organization that had been in existence for decades. NICRA was not aiming to end partition, but rather aimed to end inequality and injustice within Northern Ireland itself.

Largely due to the work of the McCluskeys, a group of British MPs established at Westminster the Campaign for Democracy in Ulster (CDU), led by Paul Rose, Stan Orme and Kevin McNamara. They based their case on the 1920 Government of Ireland Act, which provided for the ultimate sovereignty of the Westminster Parliament in Northern Ireland. Section 75 of the act made it clear that – 'Notwithstanding the establishment of the Parliament of Northern Ireland – or anything contained in the Act, the supreme authority of the Parliament of the U.K. shall remain unaffected and undiminished over all persons, matters and things in Northern Ireland and every part thereof'.

Despite the clarity of the act, however, a speaker's convention had evolved at Westminster that ruled out raising any matter there which was within the responsibility of the devolved parliament and government of Northern Ireland. The convention was, of course, convenient for successive British governments which, having got rid of the troublesome Irish in 1921, didn't wish to be dragged back into the Irish political bog. However, the convention was the cause of angry frustration for the members of the CDU. It was particularly galling for the mainly Labour members of the CDU when, during the first Wilson government 1964–6 (which had only a three vote majority in the House of Commons), the eleven Northern Ireland unionist MPs persisted in putting the government in peril by voting contrarily on matters which only concerned constituents of Labour members of the CDU in England, Scotland and Wales. Ending the convention became the primary aim of the CDU, which gathered a new momentum when Gerry Fitt was elected Westminster MP for West Belfast in 1966.

As a consequence of developments such as the CSJ, the foundation of NICRA, and the formation of the CDU, a new strategy was gradually being worked out – one which found the Achilles heel of unionism. It became clear when Fitt brought a group of British MPs to Coalisland, Dungannon, Newry, Strabane and Derry (where they met Hume). When the CDU came to my constituency, we held a public meeting for them in Coalisland. At that meeting I expressed the new formula as follows: 'If we are British, and the unionists say we are, then I demand the same rights for my constituents in Coalisland as for British citizens in Coventry, the exact same rights for the people of Belfast as for the people of Birmingham, and the same rights for the people of Derry as for the people of Doncaster'. It was simple and logical, but in terms of traditional Irish nationalism it was revolutionary.

In January 1968 I met with members of the CDU at the House of Commons. Paul Rose MP as chairman of the group had confirmed what I had come to suspect in the previous year or so. He bluntly stated, 'Austin, I have lost hope that this or any other British government will put pressure on the unionists unless it is forced to do so. Unless you and others like you can create a situation where this government will be forced to intervene in Northern Ireland, nothing will happen and the position will remain unchanged'.

Central to the civil rights campaign was the belief that the Northern Ireland government would not introduce the necessary reforms unless pressurized by

Westminster and that the British government would not intervene unless it had no alternative. Creating the circumstances that would compel the British to exercise its sovereign control was the motivating force behind those who planned and organized the campaign. Accordingly, the allocation of a council house in Caledon, Co. Tyrone, to a single Protestant girl in preference to 169 other applicants in far greater need (mostly needy families with several children), led to a squatting protest, organized by myself and other local activists, in which we took over the house, and called for its reallocation. This action generated considerable publicity and led directly to the first civil rights march between Coalisland and Dungannon on 24 August 1968. The model proposed was that of civil rights demonstrations in the United States, and it was put to the executive of NICRA by Councillor Michael McLoughlin of Dungannon and myself. NICRA agreed to sponsor the march.

Following the march, the majority of the executive of the NICRA, and the local organizers from the Coalisland / Dungannon area, met in Dr McCluskey's nearby house for a post-mortem. There was a general consensus that the march had been a very successful exercise, and that we should hold the next one in the city of Derry as soon as possible. It turned out that a march in Derry would not be as easily organized as we had thought. We soon found that nationalist/Catholic opinion there was divided by personal animosities. Previous protests in Derry had been dominated almost entirely by leftist agitators. The Derry Housing Action Committee (DHAC), a left wing organization headed chiefly by Eamonn McCann, Finbar O'Doherty and Eamonn Melaugh, had very recently conducted a successful demonstration by obstructing the opening of a new carriageway on the Craigavon Bridge linking both parts of the city across the Foyle. The DHAC had already announced, after the Coalisland-Dungannon march, that they would organize a similar march. When members of the NICRA executive and representatives of the Coalisland-Dungannon march organizers (Dr Conn McCluskey, Councillors Michael McLoughlin and John Donaghy, and myself) met with the various interested parties in Derry we encountered bickering and suspicion among the participants.

We thought it was vitally important to have the sponsorship of NICRA for a Derry march, as we had at Coalisland, because the civil rights cause transcended and avoided all other causes, such as anti-partitionism, or socialism or any other 'ism'. Eventually it was agreed that NICRA would be the sponsor, and that the civil rights banner from Coalisland would be carried. However, just before the march, at a meeting between NICRA and local organizers, there was a long discussion about whether to break the banning order (which had just been imposed by Bill Craig, the unionist Minister for Home Affairs) and to confront the police, or to stop the march at the police barrier as we had done in Dungannon. The moderates won, but the radicals were still opposed and determined to hijack the march as they had intended from the start.

NICRA had originally invited John Hume and James Doherty, a senior figure in the Nationalist Party, to form a branch of NICRA in Derry, but both refused, apparently fearful of extreme left infiltration. In fact Hume had not attended the Coalisland-Dungannon march, though quite a large contingent from Derry did, including James Doherty and Eddie McAteer. McAteer had not only attended the march from Coalisland, but had spoken on the platform at Dungannon. On this occasion, even though Hume too had reservations about the local Derry organizers, he allowed himself to be encouraged into the front line of the march along Duke Street, along with Fitt and myself.

Contrary to the reputation which he later acquired among many unionists, John Hume was always ultra-cautious about taking people out into the streets, for fear it would lead to violence. It has been alleged in some quarters that he had not been at the march in Derry. However the Cameron Report recorded: 'more significantly for the future in Londonderry there was also present Mr John Hume who had been active in organizing a credit union and a housing association in the city, and had been prominent in the agitation for the establishment of a second university there'. Also, with total credibility, John's wife Pat has said that John had returned home from the March, soaked to the skin by the water cannons.

The 5 October march changed the course of history. Conn McCluskey expressed the opinion

> I now have to admit that the militants could claim a success, since at that time every Westminster politician had been carefully briefed again and again by our Campaign for Social Justice, as to the true situation in Ulster, and were showing every sign of doing absolutely nothing about it. It seemed therefore to have required a brutal orgy to secure world attention which might lead to reforms. It began to dawn on me that, if the Northern Ireland Catholics had been waiting for statistics to influence events, they might have waited for a further 50 years.

However, Conn was being very unfair to himself, his wife Patricia and their CSJ colleagues. His carefully collected statistics were essential for the arguments of those like Hume and me; and the great triumph of Duke Street was not an achievement for violence on the part of the marchers, but derived from the use of police violence against non-violent protestors in front of television cameras.

John Hume won his title as a civil rights leader in the aftermath of the 5 October confrontation. Four days later, at a meeting in the City Hotel, moderates ousted the radicals from the leadership of the civil rights struggle in Derry with the creation of the Derry Citizen's Action Committee, chaired by Ivan Cooper, a Protestant and former Unionist Party member, and Hume as vice-chairman. Eamonn McCann refused a place on the sixteen member committee, and derided it as 'middle class, middle aged and middle of the road'. (It should be noted that Ivan Cooper was – at that point in his life – in his middle twenties, and John Hume was thirty-one and both were from very modest working-class Derry backgrounds.)

The report of the Cameron Commission on 'disturbances in Northern Ireland' referred not only to 5 October but also to violent events in Derry on 3–9 January, and on 15 January. Hume was praised for his efforts to maintain peace and for his leadership: 'the situation in Londonderry after 6 October was stabilized mainly by the activities of Mr John Hume'. Again the commission states, 'Mr Hume took the view that a "sit-down" was a very peaceful form of demonstration and, in the event, 19 October passed off quietly'. On 16 November, at an illegal march of 15,000 people, 'violence was only narrowly avoided … in accordance with the plea of the organizing committee, the procession being halted short of the barrier, a token breach of the barriers was made by a few chosen members of the parade, while the remainder of the crowd were advised by Mr Hume to make their way individually to the Diamond. This they did without further incident and a sit-down meeting took place in the Diamond. Thereafter the crowd were advised to and did disperse'. After 16 November the control of the committee 'showed signs of crumbling … There were several spontaneous marches and threats of marches, and had it not been for the ingenuity of the Derry Citizens Action Committee (DCAC), and in particular of Mr. Hume, there would almost certainly have been serious social and communal violence'. And finally in paragraph 211, the Cameron Commission had this judgment: 'for this, much, if not most, of the credit must go to Mr John Hume, who from the beginning has taken the lead and shown himself both responsible and capable. He himself was formerly a teacher and thereafter in business and is now dedicated to the political work which he has undertaken'.

Lord Cameron, Professor Sir John Biggart and J.J. Campbell, the members of the commission, rightly praised Hume, for he had provided leadership, judgment, initiative and courage. But there were others who were not given their fair share of the credit. Ivan Cooper, as chair of the DCAC, was a better orator than Hume; and moreover, Cooper's Protestant and unionist background validated his claim in the eyes of many observers and commentators to completely unsullied, non-sectarian civil rights objectives. Michael Canavan and James Doherty, as secretary and treasurer of the DCAC, provided calmness and farsightedness in periods of tension and crisis. And another DCAC member, a local GP Dr Raymond McClean, not only set up a field hospital but also created a body of stewards, which provided crowd discipline in periods of danger. Their work, their courage and the integrity of their purpose should have been better acknowledged.

The impact of Derry's civil rights agitation spread throughout Northern Ireland, and those who had planned the campaign to draw the attention of people outside Northern Ireland, particularly in Britain, to the serious injustices inside

Northern Ireland, had their hopes realized. TV exposure destroyed the carefully hidden reality of the gross abuse of power by unionist authorities. John Hume, and others like myself, seized the chance to further expose these abuses, and we revelled in it. Civil rights spokespersons spread the message and became almost as common on news programmes, particularly on local tv and radio, as David Frost, William Hardcastle and other commentators were on the London channels; unionist spokespersons failed to answer the deadly question – if you are British, why do you not accept British standards, like one person, one vote?

The civil rights movement had to win over national and international opinion-makers, and especially politicians in the sovereign parliaments at Westminster and in Dublin. John Hume's impact on television, and his mastery of the arts of mass media communication, made him the chief spokesperson for the civil rights cause. By means of articulate, logical, reasonable and factual presentations he influenced opinion throughout these islands. His media leadership was particularly required when NICRA was later split between factions. It might be said that Hume has to bear some responsibility for the fact that NICRA had never become a centrally organized movement. If he had devoted his formidable organizational skills to democratizing the civil rights movement, it would have been less vulnerable to infiltration by more extreme groups who were prepared to risk serious inter-communal violence by promoting more and more militant forms of protest. However, we all must bear some of the responsibility for that shortcoming. The lightning pace of events during that period is our only defence.

When Councillor Michael McLouglin and I initially proposed to the NICRA executive that civil rights marches be organized, our central suggestion was that the civil rights movement in the United States would be the model, and its anthem, 'We Shall Overcome', was sung at the conclusion of the Coalisland-Dungannon march. John Hume also knew his US history and politics, and was equally taken by the example of the civil rights movement in the southern American states. Throughout his career he regularly quoted Martin Luther King and, indeed, Mahatma Gandhi, another apostle of non-violent protest on behalf of civil rights.

Some commentators were surprised that the US civil rights movement had such a strong formative influence on the movement in Northern Ireland. Michael Farrell, a civil rights activist, commented:

> the civil rights movement took much of its inspiration, strategy and tactics from the movement in the United States. And it is a matter of some pride that a white, largely working class community in a political backwater 5,000 miles from Mississippi and Alabama, identified so strongly with their black sisters and brothers in the US. It is an interesting footnote as well that a religiously quite conservative Catholic community embraced a black Baptist preacher called after the father of the Protestant reformation as one

of its great heroes. Particularly so, when most of their cousins in Boston, the Bronx or Chicago were anything but supporters of black civil rights.

The civil rights campaign was a major success story; in particular, it demonstrated how quickly injustices that had humiliated and disadvantaged the Irish national population of Northern Ireland for fifty years could be remedied by intelligent, non-violent political action. Following Caledon in June, Coalisland and Dungannon in August, and then Derry on 5 October, Terence O'Neill and his ministers Brian Faulkner and Bill Craig were summoned by the British Prime Minister Harold Wilson and his Home Secretary James Callaghan to Downing Street, and a reform package was subsequently produced. The five points included an ombudsman, the abolition of the company vote in local elections, a review of the emergency Special Powers Act, a new Derry development commission to replace the gerrymandered corporation, and a points system for council housing allocation. 'One person, one vote' in council elections was soon to follow. Had O'Neill been able to make those changes, the civil rights movement would probably not have been originated!

When the civil rights agitation began, Northern Ireland had been under one party rule for forty-eight years. Unionist rule was absolute at all levels of power – political, economic and judicial – their hegemony based on a sectarian headcount and buttressed by gerrymandering and discrimination. Neither constitutional nor violent republicanism had created the slightest dent in unionist control and the sovereign government at Westminster remained content to allow the devolved government to rule in its own sectarian interest

Yet, within six months of the beginning of the movement, nearly all of its demands had been conceded; in just over a year the British government had been forced to intervene with its military and accompanying political presence; within four years the Northern Ireland Parliament and government had been suspended, and within another two years a government and institutions had been established through the Sunningdale Agreement, which provided for power-sharing in the North, and partnership institutions between North and South.

And all of this was achieved because we perceived and focused on the Achilles heel of unionism, which was that while unionists claimed they were British, they were not prepared to accept British standards of democracy. The success of the civil rights campaign was built on prioritizing these basic human rights demands over the traditional objective of national unity, and by the substitution of non-violent means for violence, which the unionists had always known how to deal with. The elaboration of a new strategy, the use of the head and not just the heart, created a revolution to which they had no answer.

The issue now for Hume and other civil rights leaders was the necessity to consolidate achievements and to make further gains, and to complete the transition from street agitation to more conventional politics. The challenge came quickly when in February 1969 Terence O'Neill declared an election in an effort to shake off the right wing of his party which was trying to thwart any liberal movement.

Demonstrating a sharp political interest at an early stage in his life, Hume had written two articles in the *Irish Times* on 18 and 19 May 1964 in response to Michael Viney's prior article in that paper, *Journey North*. Hume excoriated the Nationalist Party saying

> Weak opposition leads to corrupt government. Nationalists in opposition have been in no way constructive ... In 40 years of opposition they have not produced one constructive contribution on the social or economic plane to the development of Northern Ireland ... The only constructive suggestion from the nationalist side would appear to be that a removal of discrimination will be the panacea for all our ills ... leadership has been the comfortable leadership of flags and slogan. [And further:] If one wishes to create a united Ireland by constitutional means, then one must accept the constitutional position ... such an attitude too admits the realistic fact that a united Ireland, if it is to come, and if violence rightly is to be discounted, then it must come about by evolution, by the will of the northern majority. It is clear that is the only way in which a truly united Ireland, with the Northern Protestants integrated, can be achieved.

Hume's strong criticism of the Nationalist Party was neither controversial nor new. Organizations such as Tuairim (opinion), the New Ireland Society, National Unity and the very recently established National Political Front had attempted to furrow the frozen ground of nationalism with increasing frustration and disillusionment. In his *Irish Times* article Hume expressed the hope 'that the new National Political Front will create such an organization ... an organized democratic party'

So he was obviously very aware of the meeting at Maghery, Co. Armagh, on 19 April 1964, just one month before his *Irish Times* articles, and which surprisingly he had not attended. For someone with such an acute political interest, this is puzzling. About 300 activists including most of the nationalist politicians and large numbers of activists from a wide variety of nationally-minded organizations had attended that meeting, and the frustrations of the latter were so clearly and vociferously in favour of an organized political party, that even those MPs and senators who were less than enthusiastic about such a project trimmed their sails. A resolution was passed setting up a 'National Political Front' – 'to stimulate the growth of nationalist constituency organizations, to facilitate nationalist candidates being selected and to secure adequate representation in all public bodies, to decide in conjunction with other nationalist parliamentary representatives and other MPs who support the national ideal, to take immediate steps to create the democratic machinery of a normal political party'.

Maghery was an important development in the move towards the creation of an organized, card carrying, left of centre political party. Had the Nationalist Party embraced fully the proposals made at Maghery, and harnessed the enthusiasm and commitment of the majority of those present, it could have been the future SDLP. Instead vested interests had too firm a grip, and wanted no change that might affect their control of nationalist politics. Eddie McAteer did his best, and his constituency organization was probably the most effective in terms of open membership and democratic organization. John Hume did not apply for membership however. Possibly he perceived that an entirely new political project was called for.

Incidentally, in that same month of May 1964, I published in the *Dungannon Observer*, a manifesto asking for support in my bid for the Nationalist Party's nomination for the East Tyrone constituency, whose MP Joe Stewart had just died. I claimed that the

> Nationalist Party must be organized like any full-scale political party. Only if this is done can we hope to fight the unionist machine or keep the nationally minded people of the six counties united. It must have a branch in every area of the constituency. It must be an organization which permits men and women of talent and ability to rise through the ranks, which gives youth a chance to come forward, and which will enable a fresh approach to be made and new thinking to be done on the national and social problems of the present time.

So, if one aspect of John's *Irish Times* articles was not entirely novel, there was however one argument which was much more controversial.

John argued that Catholics could and should wholly participate in the solution of northern problems without fear of recrimination. Traditional nationalism had steadfastly refused to accept that any section of the Irish people had a right to secede from the nation, and that any display of consent to that separation should not be acceptable or tolerable. Indeed, the integrity of the 'national territory', and of the nation itself, took precedence over the separatist inclinations of a section of northern unionists, misguided and coerced by Britain, as they obviously were in the nationalist view. It had always been taken for granted that the unionists had no right to opt out of a united Ireland. Therefore, total participation in the unionist state had previously been seen as a dangerous acceptance of partition. However, thinking towards a more participative approach began to develop rapidly during the 1960s. Truly, 'the times they were a-changing'.

When the original foundation document of the SDLP was produced six years later and signed by the six founding MPs, it had the following aim – 'to promote co-operation, friendship and understanding between North and South with a view to the eventual re-unification of Ireland through the consent of the majority of the people in the North and in the South'. By that time the great majority of nationalists had accepted the necessity of consent, though a minority of so-called 'republicans' believed that unionists could be forced into a united Ireland by the use of the bomb and gun; they were to bear a heavy responsibility for the death and destruction which followed in the seventies and eighties, as they bloodily pursued their misguided objective. John Hume's contention in 1964, that majority consent was necessary for constitutional change underpinned the later formation of the SDLP. It was validated by developments like the O'Neill-Lemass meetings, and encouraged a number of other initiatives to normalize politics in the North. The experiences of the civil rights campaign and the subsequent eruption of republican and loyalist violence simply confirmed the correctness of Hume's judgment.

The organized, card-bearing, democratic and left-of-centre political party, which had been long desired by John Hume, myself, and many others, was eventually formed in 1970. The Social Democratic and Labour Party was the hoped-for vehicle to promote equality in Northern Ireland and the eventual re-unification of the country. The main problem over the years had been the nationalist dilemma caused by partition – the need for strong representation to fight discrimination versus the fear of buttressing partition by active participation in the institutions of the unionist state. That dilemma was compounded by personality politics and the lack of effective leadership.

John Hume had sought and received a mandate in the February 1969 election, to set about the creation of a new political party, and so also had the two other 'civil rights' independent MPs, Ivan Cooper and Paddy O'Hanlon. I had also sought such a mandate, and committed myself to that goal at my election five years earlier in 1964. The four of us could have formed a new party, but it would have had a serious, indeed fatal, deficiency without the involvement of Belfast politicians. The Nationalist Party had for many years, almost since the demise of its legendary leader 'Wee Joe' Devlin, been effectively obliterated in Belfast, and labour groupings of different varieties had succeeded it.

Now, after the 1969 election, the Belfast MPs who were essential to the new proposed party were Gerry Fitt of Republican Labour, and Paddy Devlin of the Northern Ireland Labour Party (NILP). On the positive side, both MPs were clearly committed to the civil rights cause and the winning of political, social and economic reform. Another persuasive factor for Fitt was the pressure he felt from his Labour Party friends at Westminster, who had urged that the Northern Ireland minority could greatly increase the possibility of reform if it spoke with one voice.

The development of good personal relationships between these six MPs was essential to the ultimate success of the project, and it was suggested by John, who regularly took his holidays in Bunbeg in Co. Donegal, that the six MPs, along with wives, girlfriends and children, gather there for discussions about the formation of the new party. From those early days the group that was to become the SDLP took seriously the parody of the rosary crusade slogan ('the family that prays together stays together'), replacing it with 'the party that drinks together stays together'! The six had strong personalities, but we respected each other in spite of strongly held differences of opinion. At meetings Gerry Fitt (who as a Westminster MP was the obvious choice for leader) was certainly non-authoritarian, and we all considered ourselves as equal. John did not at that stage have the position of dominance that he was later to acquire in the party.

In his maiden speech in the Stormont Parliament on 5 March 1969 the new member for Foyle had said; 'The real question that hangs over this house today and indeed over the whole community is: are politics going to remain on the streets, or are they going to be fought out in this chamber'. Making clear his own view, he nevertheless warned the government: 'if politics are to become in any way normalized, or if this House is to be the place where the essential issues and problems of the people are to be debated, then the voices of the elected representatives on this side of the House must be listened to'.

The transition from street politics to parliamentary democracy was his commitment, and it was paramount for him. In his final speech in the old Northern Ireland Parliament – the SDLP withdrew from Parliament in 1971 when the government refused an enquiry into the shooting dead by the RUC of two young men on a Derry street – while he again denounced violence and pleaded for reconciliation, he also warned of the threat of unionist leaders like Ian Paisley and Bill Craig – 'Let it be very clear that we are witnessing among these people the growth of Hitlerism in this community, and these are the people who must be stopped … There will be no solution until these people are confronted and the only people who can confront them are the British government. When they do that, they will clear the way for discussing a solution to the problems not only of Northern Ireland but of this whole island'. It was his belief at that point that the situation had gone beyond civil rights, and now required fundamental changes not only in Northern Ireland but between North and South, and between Britain and Ireland.

The road to political progress had dangerous and deep potholes. Martin Luther King expressed it aptly: 'The line of progress is never straight. For a period of time a movement may follow a straight line and then it encounters obstacles, and the path bends. It is like curving around a mountain when approaching a city. Often it feels as though you were moving backward and you lose sight of your goal but in fact you are looking ahead and soon you will see the city again close by'.

There were many obstacles in the months and years ahead – murder, death and destruction, the pogroms in Belfast in August 1969, the Falls Road curfew, internment, Bloody Friday and Bloody Sunday, and so many atrocities motivated by sectarian hatreds. But there were also some glimpses of Dr King's city. The

Hunt Report on policing followed by the disarming of the RUC, the abolition of the police reserve known as the B Specials; the British Army taking charge of security, and the accompanying British political involvement; the formation and leadership and courage of the SDLP; the creation of the Housing Executive to end housing discrimination; direct rule and the appointment of Willie Whitelaw as Secretary of State. And then we thought we had arrived at the city with the Sunningdale Agreement and the power-sharing executive. It was way beyond the original aims and hopes of the civil rights movement. Equality in government as of right appeared to have triumphed.

The collapse of the Sunningdale Agreement, brought down by loyalists and the IRA, was a disaster for Hume and for us all. However, as I pledged at the time, there would be no 'Flight of the Earls' – a reference to the Irish nobles who went into exile following their defeat by Queen Elizabeth's army in 1601. The SDLP held its nerve through the bleak years that lay ahead in the later seventies and the eighties, and began to elaborate new strategies for making progress. John Hume, and the rest of us who had set out upon this journey so many years previously, were to see Dr King's city again, in the Good Friday Agreement, and in the support for that agreement by the overwhelming majority of Irish voters in simultaneous referenda held in Northern Ireland and in the Republic.

That achievement was the result of the work of a great many people; but first and foremost it was the result of the commitment, leadership, vision and courage of John Hume. He undoubtedly stands in the company of the greatest Irish leaders – in the company of O'Connell and Parnell.

No! Minister

MAURICE HAYES

On 1 January 1974 John Hume was sworn in as Minister of Commerce in Northern Ireland's new power-sharing executive. It was the best of times and the worst of times. For the nationalist population, for whom he had emerged as a strong and confident voice, it was a new dawn. For the SDLP, newly emerging as a political force, it was a considerable achievement, less than four years after the formation of the party, to have secured so many of their primary objectives in the structures and programme for government, with six of their leaders as members of the administration, four as full members of the executive.

Elsewhere the outlook was less bright. Unionist leader and new Northern Ireland Prime Minister Brian Faulkner had already lost the support of most of his backbenchers and was to be rejected by his party's ruling council within the week. Secretary of State Willie Whitelaw, the principal midwife of the new arrangements, had already been called home to face the miners who were threatening industrial mayhem across Britain. British Prime Minister Edward Heath, the most forceful advocate of the settlement, was replaced by Labour's highly equivocal Harold Wilson and Secretary of State Merlyn Rees, whose commitment to the scheme engineered by their predecessors was never more than lukewarm, and for which they were not prepared to die, not even in the first ditch.

There was too the growing sense of loss in the Protestant and unionist working class, a virus of doubt and disaffection which soon lodged in the wider population, centred on the arrangements agreed at Sunningdale between the parties and the two governments for power-sharing in Northern Ireland and a Council of Ireland. So what had been in many ways the SDLP's greatest triumph was seen by many to have carried the seeds of destruction that were to bring down the whole edifice.

John Hume enjoyed only 148 days as a minister, the only time he was to hold office in a long and distinguished career – if indeed enjoyment is even in retrospect the dominant feature of the period. On the plus side there was access to the levers of power that had been denied to members of his community, the opportunity to implement the ideas he had been incubating, the ability to contribute to building a new society and a new consensual approach to politics. On the other hand there was the lack of time to do anything before the roof fell in, and a departmental machine which, while not unwelcoming or unco-operative, had its own policy framework of decisions already taken by the previous administration and partly implemented, and which, while supporting the minister, discovered its own set of priorities when the chips were down. Even at the best of times there was the hostility of the Protestant workers, especially in the skilled engineering industries, which were the backbone of employment, who, along with the majority of unionists, saw him as the main author of their problems, the initiator of the campaign of protest which had brought people out on the streets and had resulted in their loss of power, privilege and influence, and in having forced the withdrawal of SDLP from Stormont after two shootings in Derry in July 1971, had precipitated the prorogation of the Northern Ireland Parliament and government. Then, as the culmination of a concerted campaign of opposition to the Sunningdale arrangements, there was a virtual *coup d'état* in which the storm troopers of the loyalist paramilitaries were recruited and deployed in the energy industries, all of which fell within Hume's field of responsibility as a minister, with which he had to struggle with increasing difficulty and diminishing support, and to which, even as he struggled, others capitulated. And so ended the great experiment: not with a bang, but a whimper.

The pity is that John Hume had been well-groomed for the post. The SDLP ministers came into office with a firm sense of purpose and a clear idea of what they wanted to do. They had largely dictated the executive manifesto, *Steps to a Better Tomorrow*; they were accustomed to drafting documents, unlike the unionists who had relied on civil servants for drafts and for policies largely designed to sustain the status quo.

I remember John Hume telling me once (in fact, sitting in the dark during a power cut engineered by the loyalist Ulster Workers' Council) how he had been motivated to go into politics by the sight of an old Nationalist Party MP throwing in the towel during a discussion on housing on TV with Brian Faulkner, with the plaintive cry that he was in no position to refute the figures which Faulkner was throwing at him. I remembered that occasion too as really cringe-making, the antithesis of representation and the nadir of the policy of abstention. John said he had resolved that nationalist people deserved a better class of representative, one who would be well informed and sufficiently self-confident to take on opponents on their own ground. John, too, had a good background for a Minister of Commerce. His MA dissertation on social and economic development in Derry, a leading role in the development of the credit union movement in Ireland, and experience of business in the food processing and marketing were all relevant. He had developed his organizational and negotiating skills in the Derry university protest and the civil rights movement, in the formation of the SDLP and in hard bargaining with the British government and unionists in the lead up to the formation of the executive and the Sunningdale Agreement.

Despite the refusal of the SDLP to attend the Darlington conference, an early attempt by Whitelaw to promote dialogue between the political parties, while people, all of them from a nationalist background, were still interned without trial, it was their agenda on power-sharing and an Irish dimension which was carried forward into the green paper. *The Future of Northern Ireland,* and the subsequent white paper formed the basis for all further discussions and determined the parameters of debate up to the Good Friday Agreement.

The outcome was an agreement to form a shadow administration in which the SDLP would have four ministers in key posts and two junior ministers. John Hume, it must be assumed, chose to be Minister of Commerce. There was some surprise at the time that the SDLP had not opted for Finance, traditionally the senior and most influential post (after that of Prime Minister) in any administration, the expectation being that the post would have gone to John Hume as the man who was generally seen to be on top of his game. However, the SDLP had clearly targeted the spending departments where they could have an immediate impact on social conditions, disadvantage, housing and the repair of historic discrimination. Given Hume's interest in economic development west of the Bann, in job-creation as an antidote to conflict and in reducing unemployment in places like Derry and Strabane, it should come as no surprise that he should choose a post where he could tackle these problems with the energy they demanded. And, since no person's motives are ever entirely pure, it is possible that he made the shrewd political calculation that there was nothing very attractive to voters in the work of the Ministry of Finance, that it was better for a politician to be seen on television opening factories and bringing jobs to deprived areas than lurking in the background policing the spending of other colleagues.

Formation of the executive was quickly followed by the Sunningdale conference which was intended to flesh out the skeletal Irish dimension referred to in Whitelaw's white paper, in particular to agree the composition, format, functions and ambit of the proposed Council of Ireland. It was clear from the start that there was a deep conflict of interest between the SDLP and the Ulster Unionists. Faulkner, hoping to persuade his followers to accept power-sharing, wished the Council to be kept as vestigial as possible, symbolic rather than executive in its expression of an Irish identity, while SDLP policies required a body exercising executive authority over a broad range of activities, harmonizing laws and services, North and South, and capable of morphing into an all-Ireland parliament. In this they were supported by the Irish government, particularly by Foreign Affairs Minister Garret FitzGerald, and both based their negotiating stance on the assumption that Heath would similarly back Faulkner, which he signally failed to do.

It is generally accepted that the outcome saddled Faulkner with more weight than he could successfully carry. Faulkner, ever the salesman, was confident of his ability to do so, and in forcing him to accept, the Irish parties presented his opponents within unionism with a convenient stick with which to beat him. In the popular narrative of events, they are seen to have overbid their hand, a misjudgment shared by Garret FitzGerald and John Hume, both portrayed as hard-line nationalists.

If that were the case, it would not fit easily with what Hume had to say before and since, about Irish unity. He was not in the least like the traditional Irish nationalist, emphasizing the imperative of uniting people rather than territory, and the importance of bread and butter issues and social justice rather than rhetorical gestures and flag-wagging. Gerry Murray has described him as post-nationalist and there is little doubt that his vision was of a polity in which local conflicts were contained and resolved in a wider European consensus.

The hard graft of negotiation was not Gerry Fitt's forte, and it soon became clear, as Garret FitzGerald notes, that Hume had effectively taken over leadership of the SDLP delegation. It was his apparent hard line on the powers of the Council of Ireland, backed by the Irish government, which was to prevail. The result was, as Barry White has put it, that Sunningdale was both a great personal triumph for John Hume and a failure. One aspect of the failure was the lack of sensitivity on the Irish side (except by Paddy Devlin and Conor Cruise O'Brien) to the impact on unionists who were still reeling from the loss of 'their' parliament, and the difficulties this would cause Faulkner. Those who criticize Hume fail to appreciate the strength of the demand among SDLP party members for a strong and visible manifestation of the Irish dimension, with strong executive, harmonizing and supervisory powers. Less widely appreciated was Hume's concern to find a supra-national legitimization for policing, in the belief that policing and the administration of justice in Northern Ireland had been fatally corrupted by internment (which was still in force and which exposed the SDLP flank to republican attack) and the need to find a form of policing to which nationalists could give support. (This was to remain a problem until the Patten Report a quarter of a century later.) What was clear was that neither side in the negotiations had a clear appraisal of the pressures the other was under.

The problem with Sunningdale was that it had to be sold in two marketplaces. Faulkner told a sceptical and increasingly hostile unionist community that it was the bulwark which would prevent their being absorbed into an Irish republic, while Assembly Member Hugh Logue, in a rush of SDLP euphoria, hailed it as the vehicle that would trundle them into a united Ireland. The trouble was that republicans, Sinn Féin and the IRA, believed Faulkner and the unionists believed Hugh Logue. In either event it provided opponents to power-sharing with the gable-end slogan 'Dublin is just a Sunningdale away'.

The narrative of John Hume's career as Minister of Commerce falls very clearly into two parts, the first of relative normality (despite the campaigns of violence and murder being waged by terrorists (not yet gentrified into paramilitaries) on both sides), the second descending into chaos and anarchy and ultimate dissolution. The watershed came on 15 May, the first day of the protest action orchestrated by the Ulster Workers' Council.

The SDLP ministers fitted into their new posts very quickly, and were generally well received by civil servants. They were young, bright and energetic, they had a programme and a sense of purpose and they knew what they wanted to do. What civil servants want of a minister is to have a focused set of objectives, the ability to articulate them in public and to attract political support, the ability to absorb a brief and to make decisions, and the political weight to represent them in cabinet and to secure the necessary finance. Contrary to popular belief, civil servants prefer strong ministers who know their own minds, have resolute policies and the drive to achieve them.

On most of these criteria John Hume would have scored high – given the time to do so. In some ways the new men were less radical than many might have expected of them. I remember asking a senior man in Commerce, of a strong unionist background, I would assume, what he thought of his new minister. He confessed to being disappointed: 'I thought he would be different from the last guy and he was just the same'. Which reflected the fact that on most social and economic issues, John was a natural conservative, a social democrat, if you like, rather than a socialist, but he was obviously committed to the implementation in his area of responsibility of the aims of the manifesto to prepare a comprehensive social and economic plan with a central planning unit, to provide for local development, to maximize employment and to review energy policies. (It is interesting, in the light of later discussions, that the executive anticipated the need for the transfer of additional powers over taxation to Northern Ireland.)

My experience of John at this time was not as a minister in a department but as a member of the executive and at meetings of that body. In that company he was a towering figure, matched only by Brian Faulkner in his capacity for work, his command of his brief and the ability to grasp the wider significance of issues raised by colleagues. A more symmetrical allocation of responsibilities would have seen him, rather than the party leader and Deputy Prime Minister, Gerry Fitt, 'marking' Faulkner on behalf of the SDLP. Gerry had many wonderful attributes, but an appetite for administration and attention to detail were not among them. Many thought Hume could have done it in addition to his departmental duties, but that would have put other noses as well as Gerry's out of joint. Nevertheless, it was clear that he was de facto the strong man in the group.

The executive was a wonderful experience – for most of those engaged in the process, the highlight of their political or civil service careers – to see people like

Faulkner and Hume, who had been sworn enemies, sitting down together with a common purpose; to see mutual suspicion replaced by growing trust as people worked together was a candle lighted in dark times, and one that was to flicker fitfully in even darker times in the years ahead.

I never remember a vote in the executive as decisions were reached invariably by consensus. Unlike the current executive, the members committed themselves to a common programme of government and to the principle of collective responsibility.

I remember one amusing occasion when John Hume was reporting on yet another programme to rescue Belfast's Harland & Wolff shipyard from closure, called something like P300. This required the yard to process 300,000 tonnes of steel a year and turn it into ships to remain viable. It was John's sad task to report that after months of effort, they had only reached a level of productivity which equated to 70,000 tonnes a year. Faulkner misheard this as 270,000 tonnes a year and his natural optimism took over. You could almost see him do the mental arithmetic and conclude that they were within ten per cent of target. One more push would do it – congratulations all around! It was left to the Permanent Secretary, Ewart Bell (another Derry man), to bring him back to reality.

Another odd occurrence at the time was when John Hume went to the United States towards the end of April to address an audience of congressmen, senators and business leaders in Washington. For some reason the Ministry of Commerce refused to provide a draft speech on the grounds that it was political and not a proper task for departmental civil servants. This seemed an odd stance since the ultimate objective was to reassure influential Americans that Northern Ireland was emerging from conflict, that state institutions being built on a cross-community consensus would provide stability, and to secure the support of an important constituency for investment there – which I would have thought was no more than a proper role for a Minister of Commerce.

In the event, Ken Bloomfield, secretary to the executive, at short notice, asked me to draft the speech – which I did on the basis of previous conversations with John, on his public utterances and writings and with an ear for the style and cadences of his delivery.

In the speech he made many of the points that were to be a repeated theme with him – unity in diversity and respect for difference, the need for compromise, for government to be built on trust and for politics to prevail over violence, the architecture of the structures which would address the resolution of conflict in Northern Ireland in parallel with building all Ireland relationships (over which unionists would have a veto) which could lead to a unity of people rather than territory: 'the fourth green field (Northern Ireland) empty of people means nothing to me'. It was also the first time an Irish politician directly asked Irish-Americans not to send money to the IRA – 'Would you pull a trigger or throw a bomb for that is what your dollar will do?'

Meantime, as the new ministers got to grips with their tasks Faulkner was steadily losing his as backbench supporters were leached away by bullying, intimidation and peer pressure. The election, in February, to Westminster of eleven unionist MPs out of Northern Ireland's twelve pledged to oppose Sunningdale was a melodramatic quantification of opposition to Faulkner that was to signal trouble ahead. The new assembly was a bear garden, with ministers subject to verbal (and in one case physical) abuse as Faulkner's opponents within unionism sought to make the place unworkable.

Nevertheless the votes were there to endorse Sunningdale after a fractious debate. Few of those who heaved a sigh of relief at the outcome had noticed a newspaper advertisement calling for action by industrial workers, or a quiet little man standing in the lobby. This was Harry Murray, a shop-steward in the shipyard – the man who literally had his hands on the levers of power.

Next morning, 15 May, saw the start of what became commonly, if inaccurately, known as the Ulster Workers' Strike. There were sporadic pickets that made the route to work difficult, but not impossible. What was galling was to see the police fraternizing with those who blocked the highway, often in the most intimidatory fashion, and the army standing idly by as citizens were obstructed, abused and forced to turn back.

There is little point in trying to rewrite history, but few of those associated with the executive will believe that the protest action could not have been contained by firm and decisive (and not necessarily punitive) action during the first few days. After that it turned into a popular movement that became unstoppable. Few either will absolve the Labour government for failure to enforce the rule of law or to support the institutions (which, of course had been set up by their predecessors and of which they felt no sense of ownership). Secretary of State Merlyn Rees was particularly supine, maintaining that the roads were clear even as irate ministers brought him to the window of his office to point out the pickets blocking the entrance to the Stormont estate. The approach of the Northern Ireland Office was to invoke the aid of the trade unions, who were themselves split and impotent on the issue, and to rely on the leadership qualities of Len Murray, General Secretary of the Trade Union Congress, to lead the men back into work. So all action was deferred until the Monday morning when Mr Murray and a sad little retinue assembled at the entrance to Belfast's Harbour Estate to lead the workers back to their cranes and lathes and generators in the shipyard, in Shorts aircraft factory and in the West Power Station. Unfortunately, no one turned up, the pickets having simply transferred to the suburban housing estates, blocking the routes to work for most people in an even more intimately intimidatory fashion.

The screw was turned too in the increasing restriction of electricity supply, of deliveries of milk and bread, of farm feeding stuffs and oil and petrol. Since most of the bodies involved either in the generation or distribution of energy were either subsidiary to or clients of the Ministry of Commerce, John Hume as minister was in the eye of every storm. He displayed enormous energy in drawing up emergency plans, in trying to galvanize management in the industry to take control. He shared with other ministers the feeling of impotence at having no control over, or even influence on, the deployment of police or security forces, which might at least in the early stages have been used to keep the roads open and protect the right of ordinary citizens to go to work.

There were two dramas being enacted in parallel at Stormont. One, clearly a tragedy, was the unfolding progress of the strike and the feebleness of governmental response, the other, with all the appearance of a farce, was the insistence of SDLP backbenchers on the immediate confirmation of the powers and functions of the Council of Ireland, opposition to which was what had brought people out into the streets in the first place.

The approach to the energy problems was determined by plans that had been drafted earlier to deal with a totally different kind of strike, one that was industrial rather than politically motivated, and involved the use of troops to man the power stations and to ensure the distribution of oil. At first it all seemed possible. Both the army engineers and the Electricity Board people were optimistic. We were told there were troops standing by, ready to be flown in from Germany, Gibraltar, Hong Kong and Singapore, and on nuclear submarines all over the place, able and willing to work the generators, and the people who had sorted out the Ruhr after crossing the Rhine in the Second World War would easily cope with Ballylumford and the West Power stations and the local distribution network. The only lurking doubt was the need to involve middle management – and the larger, and unstated one, whether a Labour government would ever allow the army to intervene in an industrial dispute, however motivated, for fear of setting a precedent in the case of a future power strike in Britain.

As the man carrying the heaviest load, John Hume had not only the stress of his ministerial responsibilities as everyone looked to him for an answer, but the fact that he was leading an almost nomadic life – unable to go home most nights, in danger wherever he travelled as a visible and highly recognizable bogeyman in unionist eyes. He stayed one night with us in Strangford and I reflected on the irony of sitting in the dark with the Minister for Light, waiting for the indulgence of the strikers to provide us with a brief period of illumination to work on the details of the Oil Plan.

Going into Belfast next morning in a police car, there were long queues outside the strikers' headquarters in a leafy street near Stormont, as businessmen, shopkeepers and middle-class professionals sought permits to open their shops or acquire fuel. This was when it struck me that there had been a transfer of allegiance from the legitimate elected government to a group of activists acting through the muscle of shadowy underground forces, a transference of the heart of middle unionism once they saw where personal advantage (and real power) lay.

Ministers did not get much comfort, either, from the BBC which treated the strikers as the moral and democratic equivalent of the elected government, or from a spokesman for the Electricity Board with the most doom-laden voice imaginable, predicting dire disaster until the final threnody: 'We have reached the point of no return'. Nobody seemed to reflect that he was a junior official who could have been replaced as spokesman at the stroke of a ministerial pen.

On the domestic stage, the SDLP and Faulkner's people were battling it out over the terms of reference of the proposed Council of Ireland. The SDLP were still insisting on the strongest and most inclusive body, Faulkner's men seeking to dilute the role and delay the process so as not to further inflame the protestors on the streets. Oddly, some in the SDLP seemed to put the future form of the Council of Ireland above the immediate survival of the executive (despite the obvious paradox that if one element fell, so did the whole project). I remember discussing this with Eddie McGrady when he maintained that the SDLP had only agreed to power-sharing in order to get a Council of Ireland (a point confirmed by Gerry Murray, quoting Eddie some years later). This did seem to be putting the cart before the horse, but may account for the persistence with which John Hume had pushed the issue at Sunningdale.

A compromise proposal which was acceptable to SDLP ministers was rejected by the party's Assembly Group, to the dismay of Gerry Fitt, who called on Rees for help. Stan Orme, minister in the Northern Ireland Office and friend of many of the SDLP leaders, was dispatched to read the riot act, after which the SDLP reluctantly agreed a compromise which would see a slimmed-down council delayed until after the next elections to the assembly. By then, however, it was too late.

By then, too, the army had decided (or had been told) that they could not help, that they could not operate the generators or learn how to regulate the distribution system on any reasonable time scale (despite the fact that the system was being played like a fiddle by a group of men, none higher than a foreman). Middle management too had baled out, the Electricity Board was more difficult, and there were fears of sabotage that would take years to repair if the troops came in.

Ministry officials, too, had begun to corporately distance themselves from their minister and, subconsciously at least, to assert that the departmental priority was to preserve the system (rather than the executive). It is of the nature of bodies like this to fall in love with the great systems they have created and to see saving them as the prime objective of public policy and in the long-term public good. I always thought it the supreme irony when it was discovered in the post-strike post mortem that the Ministry of Agriculture had broken ranks and done business with the strikers in order to secure the power supply to the fridges in the pedigree semen bank. What a miserable epitaph for a collapsed polity.

The final straw was Prime Minister Wilson's infamous 'spongers' speech in which he so described those whom he accused of accepting subsidies and benefits from the UK government but refused to accept the lawfully elected government. This ensured that even the most moderate unionist lined up behind the protest – a sharp lesson to governments that if you are not prepared to take decisive action against agitators, at least don't go round insulting them.

I have never subscribed to the commonly held view that it was the Council of Ireland that brought down Sunningdale. This, I believe, was the presenting issue, used to cloak the very deep-seated aversion among unionists to sharing power with Catholics and nationalists. This view (which was shared by Lucy Faulkner) was confirmed when, at a seminar at Queen's University to mark the fortieth anniversary of the strike, Glenn Barr remarked that what they (Ulster Defence Association/Ulster Workers' Council) really objected to was power-sharing, which they opposed even before the Council of Ireland came on the agenda, but the latter proved to be the easier ground on which to rally support.

Soon it was all over. The troops did not come in, the milk was not delivered, the cows were not fed, power supplies diminished and people could not get to work. Faulkner, briefed by permanent secretaries on the social and economic impact of the strike and the danger to public health, decided to resign along with his unionist colleagues. The SDLP attempted to stay on – a futile gesture – and Rees pulled down the curtain on a noble experiment.

On the last evening, Faulkner, a life-long tee-totaller, was giving his immediate staff a farewell drink in an atmosphere of doom and gloom when John Hume came in to take his leave. 'Well', he said, joining in, 'There's always drink at a wake'.

The last act of this phase of John Hume's political career was played out in the Constitutional Convention in 1975–6. This was in many ways a re-run of the assembly, minus the executive, shorn of any legislative or representational role, and charged with finding a form of government acceptable to both communities. At best this was a cynical exercise designed to keep Northern Ireland off the boil and to transfer blame for failure to solve the problem to Northern Ireland politicians and away from the British government. Frank Cooper, Permanent Under Secretary in the NIO, was reported as saying that they kept making the questions progressively easier in successive elections, and local politicians kept on failing. At worst, the convention was designed to fail in order to give cover for a more radical shift in policy. There was suspicion at the time, confirmed in recently available papers and memoirs, that the government was negotiating with (or at least playing footsie with) the IRA on the assumption that the convention would fail.

Not that there was much chance of success. The unionists, flush with victory and triumphalist after the fall of the executive, came not to negotiate but to bulldoze the opposition into providing a route map for a return to majority rule as near as possible like the old Stormont, with no concession to minority sensitivities and no Irish dimension. The result was a dialogue of the deaf, and a majority report railroaded through which the government rejected as not meeting their basic requirement of cross-community acceptability.

John Hume made two important speeches at the convention. The first in the opening session (when there was still some vestigial hope that business might be done) was one of the great set-pieces of the convention, a really memorable speech delivered with passion and eloquence. In an irenic appeal for a spirit of compromise, he set out SDLP ideals and attitudes and their basic negotiating position. Many of the themes that were to form the staple of his discourse over the next three decades are here introduced. First (a lesson perhaps drawn from Sunningdale and the executive), he cautions all parties against misunderstanding or misrepresenting the position and motives of their opponents. Then there was the need for a fundamental re-examination of group values and traditions, to work together without flag-waving or the trappings of romantic nationalism, the value of richness in diversity, the right to the expression of a cultural identity, the need to build trust, to work together, to spill sweat, not blood – and a final recognition of the difficulty of finding compromise when there was confusion in the language of discourse: 'One day we will begin to understand what we actually mean by the words we use'.

The other speech, his final major contribution to the debate, was, symbolically, delivered to empty opposition benches, the unionists having chosen to attend a wedding on the day allocated to the SDLP. It returned to the themes of diversity and rights-based institutions, the need for parties to recognize the position of others without abandoning their own, that a united Ireland was not worth dying, or killing for, that he sought to unite people, not territory, admitting the principle of unionist consent, and that the speed of development in an imagined Ireland could be controlled by the majority in the North.

There was one spark of life in the process before the blinds finally came down. A sub-group of the United Ulster Unionist Council, an umbrella group for most unionist Convention members, led by Bill Craig and including representatives of the other parties, almost reached agreement with the SDLP on a proposal for a voluntary coalition. John Hume, fearful of being wrong-footed, was holding out for an arrangement which would last over two parliaments. They seemed, over a weekend, to be within touching distance of agreement when Ian Paisley (perhaps under pressure from his church elders) disowned the negotiations and ended Bill Craig's political career and set the process of finding a settlement back by a quarter of a century.

Incidentally, that John Hume was right to be suspicious is confirmed for me by a remark attributed to Glenn Barr reported in the John Burton papers in INCORE (International Conflict Research Institute), that 'Craig has reassured his Vanguard followers that the pressures of a strong security policy would force SDLP out of government and unionists would have the field to themselves'.

John Hume's brief period in ministerial office was a short interlude in a long and distinguished political career that led him to the European Parliament, an international reputation and the Nobel Peace Prize. It was important in the Northern Ireland story in that he and his colleagues in the SDLP, along with the Faulkner unionists, showed that Catholics and Protestants, unionists and nationalists in Northern Ireland could work together in government for a common purpose, and that in working together they learned to know and trust each other. It was the fleeting proof that it could be done which sustained those, like Hume, who were to spend the next twenty-five years pursuing the holy grail of shared responsibility and joint government in a stable and peaceful Northern Ireland, until 'Sunningdale for slow learners' was finally achieved in the Good Friday Agreement.

As to his performance in office – it is hard to say. It was a totally abnormal situation in which he kept his head when older and more experienced politicians were losing theirs. The normal tests of ministerial performance – the ability to develop policies to meet the needs of society and to carry them through to delivery, to command respect among peers and in the wider society, to foresee problems and to innovate, to network and to advocate – given the untimely end of the experiment, were not available to him. There is little doubt, by the evidence of his behaviour under pressure and his subsequent performance, that, like Hamlet, 'if he had been put on, he would have proved most royally'. He had all the attributes of a good minister, but also, given his sapiential authority in any group, his ability to take the long view, the ability to communicate complex propositions to a general audience, the command of language and the facility with which he could draft papers and statements, enfolding conflicting propositions in phrases of Delphic lucidity, the tendency to work behind the scenes, to keep his own counsel and to keep the cards close to his chest, all mark him out as a mandarin manqué. Yes Minister! Yes indeed.

John Hume and the Irish Government

SEÁN DONLON

In this contribution I propose to deal with John Hume's influence on Irish governments' approaches to Northern Ireland from 1969 to 1987, years that witnessed the outbreak of civil unrest, the first attempt to establish cross-community institutions in Northern Ireland, their collapse and the gradual movement towards a comprehensive agreement. During that period, as an official of the Department of Foreign Affairs I held the posts of Consul General in Boston (1969–71), Counsellor/Assistant Secretary General in the department in Dublin but travelling extensively in Northern Ireland (1971–78), Ambassador in Washington DC (1978–81) and Secretary General of the department (1981–87).

There are two background elements that are relevant to an understanding of Hume's achievement.

First, for decades after the foundation of the state there was little public or political debate in the Republic about Northern Ireland and little contact between politicians in Dublin and their counterparts in Belfast, even those on the nationalist side. There was a general acquiescence in Éamon de Valera's approach that the British had partitioned Ireland and that it was a matter for them to undo it. That was the basis for propaganda campaigns abroad in countries with a significant Irish diaspora. In reality, however, these campaigns were designed mainly to impress domestically. There was little discussion of Northern Ireland in the Anglo-Irish political/diplomatic channel which was, of course, at times busy with other political and economic issues. The sterility of Dublin's approach to Northern Ireland is best illustrated by the almost complete lack of contact between the administrations in Dublin and Belfast until the meetings between Taoiseach Seán Lemass and Prime Minister Terence O'Neill in 1965. Until then, necessary cross-border contacts on practical matters such as transport, power and waterways was conducted by officials who met under the radar, sometimes under the stands at Lansdowne Road on the occasion of international rugby matches.

Second, there was no specific government department or official tasked with the responsibility for Northern Ireland. Nobody monitored and assessed what was happening there and there was no strategy for achieving the frequently stated aim of Irish unity. Because Ireland's 1937 constitution declared Northern Ireland to be part of the national territory, it was deemed not to be a matter for the Department of Foreign Affairs. And until the early 1970s the Department of the Taoiseach was essentially a secretariat for the cabinet and was not in any sense a policy formulation or implementation unit dealing with Northern Ireland or other major policy issues.

It is ironic that the first move in removing the barriers between Dublin and Belfast came not from Dublin but from Belfast, from Prime Minister Terence O'Neill. On the Dublin side the arrangements were handled by the secretary general of the Department of Finance, T.K. Whitaker, who was to become an influential adviser on Northern Ireland to successive governments for almost half a century. The Lemass-O'Neill meetings did not, however, immediately lead to a major shift in Dublin's political policy. Partition was still the issue and London had to fix it. When organizations such as the Dungannon-based Campaign for Social Justice (CSJ) and the Westminster-based Campaign for Democracy in Ulster (CDU) began to document evidence of widespread discrimination in employment and housing, Irish embassies were discouraged from distributing the material. Minister Frank Aiken's view was that while highlighting discrimination might have the effect of comforting nationalists in Northern Ireland, it ran the risk of helping to cement partition if these 'peripheral' issues became the focus of policy and were satisfactorily dealt with.

The first public questioning of Dublin's sterile Northern Irish policy was by Donal Barrington in his 1957 Tuairim pamphlet *Uniting Ireland* and his article in *Studies*, 46, pp 379–402 in the same year. His central theme was that partition was not forced on Ireland by Britain but was necessitated by the conflicting demands of two groups of Irish people. The political reaction at the time was not overwhelming, but the seeds planted were later to bear fruit. The next influential contribution came from John Hume who in his two articles in the *Irish Times* on 18/19 May 1964 set out the agenda that was to dominate his own political life and was also to be influential in Dublin and ultimately in London, Washington and Brussels as well. The three principles underlying his agenda were: violence was rejected, there could be no Irish unity without the consent of the Northern Irish majority, and there had to be a recognition that nationalism was an acceptable political belief and that people in Northern Ireland and elsewhere were entitled to advocate it and work towards achieving its goals. Again, the immediate political reaction in Dublin was not overwhelming though Garret FitzGerald has acknowledged Hume's influence on his 1964 article, 'Seeking a National Purpose', published in *Studies*, 53, pp 337–51. The articles by Hume and FitzGerald may well have also had an influence on the historic Lemass/O'Neill meetings a year later.

The Department of Foreign Affairs became involved in the Northern Ireland Troubles by chance and by the personal initiative of a middle-level official, Eamon

Gallagher. The unrest that produced the Troubles had been building up since the latter part of 1968 though the initial public reaction in Dublin was muted. The explosive events of the summer of 1969 culminating in the Apprentice Boys' march of 12 August, which occasioned serious rioting in Derry and elsewhere in the North, caused Dublin, London and indeed other capitals to begin to focus on what was happening. The Irish government struggled to formulate a response and the situation was not made easy by the frequent and conflicting views brought by the many delegations and individuals coming from Northern Ireland to lobby government and other politicians. The situation was further complicated by a split in Fianna Fáil essentially on the issue of the use of violence. Meanwhile, the British government had established a discreet listening post in a house called Laneside in a residential, leafy suburb near Holywood in Co. Down. It was staffed by senior civil servants and security officials whose role was to monitor and assess the political and security situation, keep in contact with the key players and report to the relevant ministers in London.

It was against that background that Gallagher took a personal initiative, neither informing nor seeking the approval of senior colleagues. A native of Donegal, he was a regular weekend visitor to his sister in Letterkenny who was a friend of a Derry woman, Kathleen Desmond, who in turn was a friend of John and Pat Hume. Gallagher asked her to set up a meeting for him with Hume and it took place in Hume's then home in Derry towards the end of August. As the year went on, Gallagher began on his weekends off to travel to Northern Ireland to see Hume and others that Hume had introduced him to or recommended to him. Based on these meetings, he wrote analytic reports which he submitted to the secretary general of the Department of Foreign Affairs who in turn passed them to the minister, Dr Hillery and the Taoiseach, Jack Lynch. It was some months before Gallagher's Northern Ireland work was given official recognition but by early 1970 a specialist unit was created in the department and Gallagher was made its head. There was no attempt to define his role but initially it seems to have been confined to liaising with nationalist representatives, notably Hume but including the core group of Gerry Fitt, Paddy Devlin, Ivan Cooper, Paddy O'Hanlon and Austin Currie, all of whom were members of the Northern Ireland Parliament and who were to combine in 1970 to form the SDLP.

The role of the department as a policy adviser was clear in so far as it dealt with Dublin-London relations, the United Nations and other foreign policy matters. In relation to Northern Ireland, however, it remained undefined and the personal role of Whitaker was still central, especially to Lynch. He was, for example, the main drafter of Taoiseach Jack Lynch's landmark Tralee speech in October 1969, in which for the first time an Irish government committed itself to the principle of unity by consent as well as making it clear that the use of violence was rejected in all circumstances, principles which Hume had enunciated in 1964.

Hume's energies in 1969–70 were devoted to forming and consolidating the SDLP. Though it is clear that much of the groundwork was done by himself and Currie, the building of a team which would be broadly representative was key and the recruiting of Fitt and Devlin from Belfast was a priority. Think-in meetings, usually in relaxed and sociable surroundings in Bunbeg in Co. Donegal, were an important element in creating a cohesive and unified approach. Fitt, as the only Westminster MP and the longest-serving elected representative, became leader though this was frequently a formal rather than an actual position. Initially, he and Devlin wanted their labour affiliations to be prioritized and highlighted in the party's name but when the first sample page of notepaper spelled out LSD, the Labour and Social Democrat Party, Devlin recognized the distraction that association with drugs and money would create and it became the SDLP. In addition to his work in Northern Ireland, Hume began to spend significant time in Dublin seeking financial support for the party but also selling his agenda to politicians and the wider southern public. He became a regular fixture on RTÉ radio and television and cultivated key media people such as the editor of the *Irish Times*, Douglas Gageby, the radio and television host, Gay Byrne, and the editor of the *Irish Press*, Tim Pat Coogan. He also frequented Leinster House and indeed anywhere where he might meet politicians, journalists and other opinion formers. There is no doubt that his activities in those days of political turbulence North and South did much not only to steady the nationalist ship but to change people's concept of Irish unity and how it might be achieved.

By the summer of 1971 the situation on the ground in Northern Ireland had deteriorated and the inadequate and unbalanced response from the administrations in Belfast and London had brought the SDLP to the view that continued participation in the Northern Ireland Parliament was unlikely to achieve progress. Hume conceived the idea of an alternative 'Assembly of the Northern Irish People' as an opposition forum to the North Ireland Parliament. A few meetings were held in Dungannon and Dungiven but as the situation continued to deteriorate and violence escalated, it became clear that nationalists acting alone could not hope to achieve the necessary reforms. Hume now enrolled the Taoiseach and they agreed a common policy objective, namely to get rid of the Northern Parliament and replace it with a power-sharing administration. This seems to have been the first time an Irish government and representatives of Northern Ireland nationalists agreed to co-ordinate their activities. The Taoiseach's initial overtures to British Prime Minister Ted Heath were rebuffed but by the end of September 1971 Lynch and Heath were in a dialogue that was ultimately to assist in bringing about the prorogation of Northern Ireland's Parliament and the introduction of direct rule from London in March 1972.

In a statement welcoming direct rule, Hume appealed to the Provisional IRA and to the majority community. To the latter he said 'we do not regard our political achievements as a victory over you, rather we regard them as a step forward and an opportunity for all of us. We ask you to join us on the road to permanent peace ...' The response was not encouraging. Unionists hugely resented losing 'their' parliament and blamed the SDLP, the Provisional IRA and Dublin. The Provisional IRA for their part were equally unenthusiastic responding bluntly that 'the war goes on'. Nothing daunted, Hume embarked on intensive behind the scenes moves to achieve a ceasefire. He entered into talks with the IRA leadership and with British government representatives and prepared the ground for direct talks between the British government and the IRA. Those talks took place in a private house in London and the IRA delegation included the then 25-year-old Gerry Adams. A ceasefire was agreed and the stage seemed to be set for fruitful negotiations. It was, however, a short-lived ceasefire and it collapsed in July 1972. At the time Hume concluded that internal divisions and the political immaturity of the IRA leadership made them unreliable interlocutors. It was to be many years before he talked again to them.

In developing his contacts in Dublin, Hume was careful at all times to be even-handed with the three main political parties, Fianna Fáil, Fine Gael and the Labour Party. From the beginning, the SDLP had fraternal links with both the Irish Labour Party and the British Labour Party and the latter agreed that they would not run candidates in Northern Ireland for Westminster elections. Hume also reached an informal understanding with Jack Lynch that Fianna Fáil would not organize or run candidates in Northern Ireland, an important arrangement at a time when there was a minority element within the party anxious to establish an assertive Northern Ireland profile.

With the introduction of direct rule, intended to be a short-term arrangement, the focus for the SDLP and the Irish government became the creation of structures to replace the old Stormont. In close collaboration with the SDLP and the Irish government, the British government developed detailed proposals for a power-sharing government in Northern Ireland and a structure that would recognize the 'Irish Dimension' of the problem, that is, a Council of Ireland to deliberate on matters of mutual, island-wide concern. By the spring of 1973 an outline of a package had emerged which included significant political reform. Elections were held in Northern Ireland in June that year and the SDLP emerged as the overwhelming representative of the nationalist community with twenty-two per cent of the votes. Hume almost immediately began an informal dialogue with the leader of the main unionist party, Brian Faulkner, and this quickly led to formal inter-party talks in Belfast involving the Unionist Party, the SDLP and the Alliance Party. Both government and opposition in Dublin were kept informed and by October sufficient progress had been made on the formation of a power-sharing executive in Northern Ireland that Hume persuaded Faulkner to take the courageous next step and begin conversations with Dublin. Faulkner agreed and the secretary of the government,

Dermot Nally and I travelled to Faulkner's home outside Downpatrick in Co. Down to initiate discussions which would facilitate the creation of structures to represent the 'Irish Dimension' and deal with thorny issues such as security co-operation, extradition and the status of Northern Ireland.

Once the groundwork had been done and there were reasonable prospects of a tripartite Belfast/London/Dublin agreement, a conference was arranged for Sunningdale in England early in December 1973. There the Irish and British governments together with the three Northern Ireland parties reached agreement, *inter alia*, on government in Northern Ireland, North-South arrangements, the status of Northern Ireland, extradition and security matters. With effect from 1 January 1974 Fitt became Deputy Prime Minister to Faulkner, and Hume, declining the post of Minister of Finance, became Minister of Commerce. He felt that in that role he could make the most effective contribution to the creation of jobs. It was, however, clear from an early stage that major elements of the unionist community were opposed to the arrangements and were determined to bring them down. The British government, now led by Labour's Harold Wilson, were not prepared or able to enforce their sovereignty. The Provisional IRA upped their campaign of terror and by May 1974 the Sunningdale arrangements had collapsed.

A most uncertain period followed. Rumours began to emerge that Wilson contemplated a complete British withdrawal from Northern Ireland. State papers now released and the publication of two books, *Roy Jenkins: a well rounded life* by John Campbell (London, 2014) and *Downing Street diary: with Harold Wilson in No. 10* by Bernard Donoughue (London, 2004), confirm the accuracy of these rumours. Wilson contemplated a unilateral, precipitate withdrawal regardless of the implications for political and economic stability on the island of Ireland. The steadying influence of Fitt at Westminster, of the SDLP with the Labour Party and of the Irish government in contacts with the British government were important elements in ensuring that Wilson's idea did not become policy.

Wilson appointed Merlyn Rees as Secretary of State in Belfast and he proposed a constitutional convention at which Northern Ireland politicians would be asked 'to consider what would be likely to command widespread acceptance'. The SDLP saw little prospect of anything constructive coming from this. If the British government had not been prepared to confront unionism to protect the Sunningdale arrangements what prospect was there that they would do so now? Reflecting his scepticism about the convention and against the background of the rumours of British withdrawal, Hume asked in a speech in August 1974 'what sovereign government anywhere in the world would allow part of its territory to decide for itself how it was to be governed, unless it was preparing to let it go?'

Hume's thoughts now began to turn to the United States and the possibility of winning support there for the achievement of his agenda. He had some familiarity with the US which he had visited in his credit union capacity in the 1960s. He had also visited Boston briefly in November, 1969. That was my first personal contact with him. (We had overlapped briefly when we were both clerical students at the national seminary in Maynooth in the late fifties but I did not know him there.) He had been invited to speak at the Boston Donegal Association and Gallagher in the department had asked me to facilitate him. It was not a particularly successful visit. The copy of the RTÉ film *John Hume's Derry* which he brought with him was in a European format and could not be shown in the venue with a normal US projector. Nor had the association invited local politicians or the media, which Hume had expected. The only politician I was able at short notice to arrange to meet was the then Speaker of the US House of Representatives, John McCormack, who was a great friend of Ireland's and of de Valera in particular, but who was now approaching retirement and not well-versed on recent developments in Northern Ireland. McCormack did, however, advise Hume that his focus should be on the centre of US political power, Washington DC, rather than on Irish-America. This seems to have influenced Hume's subsequent approach in the US.

He met Senator Edward Kennedy, at the latter's request, in 1972. After the Bloody Sunday killings in Derry, hearings were held on Northern Ireland in the US Congress but Hume had been unable to attend because of the turbulent situation in Derry and elsewhere. Later that year when visiting Germany for a NATO conference, Kennedy asked to meet Hume and a meeting was arranged at the Bonn residence of the Irish ambassador, Seán Ronan. That was to be the beginning of a long and fruitful relationship between the two and Kennedy quickly became committed to the Hume agenda. It was at Kennedy's suggestion that Hume spent a term as a Fellow at Harvard University's Centre for International Relations in 1976. This gave him the opportunity to become familiar with the US political system and to begin relationships with prominent Irish-American politicians including the Governor of New York, Hugh Carey, the New York Senator and academic, Daniel Moynihan, and the person who was to become the most influential figure on US Irish policy, Speaker Tip O'Neill. Hume worked closely with the Irish embassy in Washington and especially with the political counsellor, Michael Lillis, who had established particularly close relationships with O'Neill, Kennedy, Moynihan and their staffers, Kirk O'Donnell, Carey Parker and Tim Russert. Lillis had seen the possibility of harnessing the good will of major US politicians and the close involvement of Hume, an authentic voice of Irish nationalism from Northern Ireland, was essential. Hume now became a regular visitor to the US, a speaker at important Irish-American and US foreign policy fora and a frequent voice in the US media.

The major breakthrough in US policy on Ireland came in August 1977 when President Jimmy Carter issued a statement that had been carefully crafted by many hands including those of Lillis and Hume, working closely with Bob Hunter from the US National Security Council. In the statement offering US

intervention in Ireland, a first for a US government, Carter called for the establishment in Northern Ireland of a government that would command widespread
acceptance and for a just solution which would involve the Irish government. In
addition – and this was specifically at Hume's request – Carter pledged that in the
event of a settlement, the US would join with others to encourage job-creating
investment. That was the seed that led to the creation of the International Fund
for Ireland (IFI) when the Anglo-Irish Agreement was signed in 1985. Mainly with
US and EU funds, the IFI has to date made a significant contribution to economic development in Northern Ireland and border areas. But of even greater
importance, the Carter statement created the precedent which encouraged the
very significant subsequent US involvement in Northern Ireland, notably by
President Clinton.

The political situation in Northern Ireland in the late seventies continued to
be bleak and violence dominated. Hume's attention turned to Europe and to the
institutions of the European Union (EU), then the European Economic
Community, which he often referred to as the organization that had done most to
reconcile the warring parties of the Second World War, especially France and
Germany. In 1978 he became an adviser in the office of Irish Commissioner Dick
Burke and, as he had done in his stint at Harvard in relation to the US political
system, he now devoted himself to learning on the ground the complex working
of the European institutions. This was a helpful apprenticeship for his own membership of the European Parliament to which he was elected in 1979. For those
elections, the first direct elections, the British government had proposed that the
first past the post system used in the rest of the UK should be applied in Northern
Ireland. This would have resulted in no nationalist seat. Intensive lobbying at
Westminster by Fitt and Hume with critical support from the Irish government,
especially Minister for Foreign Affairs Garret FitzGerald, ensured that a single,
transferable vote system was introduced exclusively for Northern Ireland thus
ensuring that one of the three seats would go to a nationalist. Hume won the seat
with just over twenty-five per cent of the votes cast, suggesting that he had managed to win some non-nationalist as well as nationalist support.

There were three important leadership changes in 1979. Margaret Thatcher
became UK Prime Minister, Hume succeeded Fitt as leader of the SDLP and
Charles Haughey succeeded Lynch as leader of Fianna Fáil and Taoiseach.
Opinions on Haughey were divided, within his own party, in the country as a
whole and within the SDLP. His involvement in the 'Arms Trial' in 1969 – he was
acquitted of the charge of conspiring illegally to import weapons – and his association with the green wing of Fianna Fáil led to suspicions about him by some in
the SDLP. Hume had skilfully managed his relationship with Haughey in the seventies when he had been restored to ministerial office by Lynch, but he always
appeared to have some doubts about Haughey's approach to the North not least

because of his continuing association with the Donegal TD Neil Blaney whose outspoken anti-Lynch views had led him eventually to break with Lynch and to set up an Independent Fianna Fáil party with an aggressive anti-British approach to Northern Irish policy.

Nevertheless, Hume welcomed the energetic and refreshing approach that Haughey brought to his new position and early on they shared views on the best way to make progress in relation to Northern Ireland. Hume advocated a two-pronged approach, namely, persuade the British to devise a balanced unionist/nationalist policy and exercise their sovereignty by implementing it and second, get all nationalist parties, North and South, to reassess their approach with a view to putting an agreed position to the unionists and to the British. He had for some time been promulgating the idea of a Council for a New Ireland in speeches and newspaper articles and he now put the idea to both Haughey and the leader of the opposition in Dublin, Garret FitzGerald.

On assuming office, Haughey embarked on a series of intensive meetings with officials and advisers with a view to formulating a position and preparing the ground for meeting Thatcher. As ambassador in Washington I was included in these meetings as was the ambassador in London. Haughey's marshalling of the arguments and the various options was impressive as was his apparent openness to a wide range of views. He had undoubtedly inherited much of de Valera's position that the British had created the Northern Ireland problem and therefore had the primary responsibility for resolving it. He liked Hume's emphasis on the British role but was less impressed by the idea of a Council for a New Ireland. He saw himself as the leader of Irish nationalism and did not want that position diluted, particularly by including FitzGerald whom he regarded as not being sound on the national question

His immediate focus was, however, on establishing a good relationship with Thatcher and at his first meeting with her in May 1980 – the 'silver teapot' summit, so called because he presented Thatcher with an antique silver teapot – he appeared to make progress. The idea of twice-yearly summits and the creation of intergovernmental structures were discussed and a second summit took place in Dublin in December that year. The communiqué issued after that meeting referred to the need jointly to study the development of the totality of Anglo-Irish relationships. Afterwards, Haughey implicitly and Minister for Foreign Affairs Brian Lenihan explicitly indicated that the constitutional position of Northern Ireland was now one of the matters for a joint Anglo-Irish study. Thatcher was furious and she made it clear to Haughey when they next met, at an EU summit, that any feeling of trust between them had been destroyed. Slim prospects of restoring a working relationship between the two were, of course, completely shattered by the pro-Argentinean position taken by Haughey during the ten-week Falklands War in 1982.

In June 1981 FitzGerald had been elected Taoiseach but held office only until March the following year. During that time, he and Thatcher did reach agreement on the creation of an Anglo-Irish Intergovernmental Council though their efforts to restore normality to Dublin-London relations were greatly impeded by the IRA hunger strikes in 1980/1. Thatcher's determination not to concede any of the IRA demands was opposed by Dublin, by some of the American friends and by Hume who was among many who tried without success to mediate. Eventually, but only after ten prisoners had died and huge sympathy had built up for the IRA, most of the demands were conceded. The political winner was the IRA which now stepped up its terrorist campaign again, while at the same time its political arm, Sinn Féin, intensified its campaign. When elections were held for a new Northern Ireland Assembly in 1982, the SDLP held its own by winning three times as many seats as Sinn Féin but the latter had now established a democratic legitimacy and gained a valuable foothold on the road to power. Neither party, incidentally, took seats in the assembly, deeming it to be toothless.

As often happened when politics in Northern Ireland were in a barren phase, Hume turned his attention elsewhere, this time to Dublin and to the achievement of his idea for a Council for a New Ireland at which nationalists, north and south, would review possible political structures to alleviate the Northern Ireland situation. At about the same time FitzGerald had launched a constitutional crusade that would include a review of the Republic's attitude to Northern Ireland. FitzGerald accepted Hume's proposal but on the basis that unionists would also be invited to join. Hume then approached Haughey, now the leader of the opposition, and he reluctantly agreed to participate mainly out of respect for Hume. In the event only the nationalist parties, Fianna Fáil, Fine Gael, Labour and the SDLP, participated. Hume had agreed with Fine Gael and Labour that the ideal candidate to chair the proceedings was T.K. Whitaker but this proposal was vetoed by Haughey and the President of University College Galway, Colm Ó hEocha, took the position. To avoid comparisons with earlier conventions, the title became The New Ireland Forum. It met from May 1983 to February 1984 taking evidence from a wide range of individuals and organizations, north and south. In its final report the forum outlined three possible structures for a new Ireland, namely, a unitary state, a federal/confederal state and a joint authority under which Ireland and Britain would have equal responsibility for the administration of Northern Ireland.

While the forum was at its work, Dublin and London were engaged in secret talks which were initiated by FitzGerald. The talks were led on the British side by Cabinet Secretary Robert Armstrong and on the Irish side by the Secretary of the Department of the Taoiseach, Dermot Nally. The broad objective of the talks was to recommend structures that would contribute to peace and stability in Northern Ireland but there were no detailed terms of reference and both sides worked in a non-confrontational, open manner and usually in informal settings. Hume was kept in the picture at all times by the Irish side and while it was assumed, particularly at the later stages, that the British side were keeping some elements of unionism informed, it transpired that this was not the case. There were hiccups along the way including the notorious 'out, out, out' remarks by Thatcher in relation to the three possible structures outlined in the Forum Report, but agreement was finally reached and signed by FitzGerald and Thatcher at Hillsborough in November 1985. The central point in it was that for the first time the Irish government had a role in relation to Northern Ireland. It could put forward views and proposals which the British government would be required to mediate and take into account. To facilitate the implementation of the agreement a joint Irish/British office was set up just outside Belfast and the Irish government was now physically represented in Northern Ireland for the first time. The agreement also had a built-in incentive for the North's parties to come to an arrangement for a devolved power-sharing administration: the role exercised jointly by both governments would be reduced in the event of an acceptable agreement between the parties.

Once the agreement was signed US President Reagan and Speaker Tip O'Neill announced the creation of the International Fund for Ireland to which the US and the EU committed significant funds. Hume's insistence on US financial backing, which he had secured from President Carter in 1977, now became a reality.

The 1985 agreement between Dublin and London and the support given to it by Washington and Brussels marked an important milestone in Hume's political career. It bore all the marks of the consistency of his approach. He, himself, frequently talked about stickability, setting an objective and sticking with it even when the odds on achieving it were slim. He was, of course, to go on and eventually see the full achievement of the agenda he had first set out in the *Irish Times* in 1964: the rejection of violence, the establishment in both parts of Ireland of the unity by consent principle and the recognition of the equal validity of unionism and nationalism.

Dealing with British Governments

DAVID McKITTRICK

British prime ministers don't often have direct physical encounters with other politicians, especially not inside Downing Street, but there was a moment when John Major and John Hume came into unusually close contact. It happened some days after Hume had urged Major to make a positive response to the latest moves in the peace process. The SDLP leader, under strain from relentless pressure and criticism, was anxious to rescue an initiative that seemed on the point of failure.

According to Hume: 'I remember meeting Major in Downing Street and as I was about to go out I caught him by the lapels. I just walked up to him, smiling, caught him by the lapels, and said, "Prime Minister, let me tell you something. Gladstone failed. Lloyd George failed. Churchill failed. There could be peace within a week – take the leap. The PM that brings peace to Ireland will go down in history more than a PM who puts vat on fuel". He laughed, and he said: "You are right". Privately I think that had a big impact on him'. The close encounter certainly lodged in John Major's memory, for years later he remembered it vividly: 'He took me by the lapels, very emotionally seeking a peace in Northern Ireland – for it passionately mattered to him – and said: "You can achieve it".'

Hume's encounter with prime ministerial tailoring might serve as a metaphor for his relations with London, since it encapsulated his relationship with successive British governments. He was forever urging Britain to make concentrated efforts, to launch far-reaching initiatives, to accept that an approach based primarily on security policy would not bring a solution, and to work to overcome unionism's deep-seated resistance to sharing power. He was one of the first to try to persuade Major and others that, after all the decades of bombs and bullets, republicans might be prepared to leave violence behind and enter political life. It took many years before London, or more specifically Tony Blair, became convinced that the IRA and Sinn Féin could be transformed from part of the problem to part of the solution. Similarly, it took years for Hume, and others who favoured a Sunningdale-type model of power-sharing and North-South structures, to convince Britain that unionists could be brought to share power.

In the 1960s it took a great deal to persuade British governments to pay any real attention to the state of things in Northern Ireland. It was pretty obvious to some in London that all was not well, yet Westminster's strongest collective instinct was to steer clear of involvement rather than think of how things might be improved. Next came a phase when the surge in street disturbances made it impossible to avoid sending in the army. This emergency measure did not work and within a few years Northern Ireland was ablaze, with almost 500 violent deaths in the year 1972.

With hindsight, the demands of John Hume and most of the civil rights movement had been modest enough, pitched as they were in terms of ending discrimination and seeking equality. Certainly Labour's Harold Wilson and James Callaghan found little to object to in the civil rights programme, which was very much in line with the zeitgeist of the day. It was a time of change in many parts of the world, and Northern Ireland turned out not to be immune to the general impulse for reform. Hume and other civil rights activists made a powerful and articulate case. Unionism was politically ill-equipped to oppose it, lacking committed supporters at Westminster, lacking articulacy and above all lacking effective anti-reform arguments.

In past years there had been sporadic criticisms of Westminster's attitude, with occasional articles in the British press such as 'John Bull's political slum'. When Gerry Fitt and a group of British Labour backbenchers raised complaints in the House of Commons, the attitude of both Tories and Labour was to erect a firewall, pointing to a convention that all criticisms of the unionist system were not to be heard at Westminster and should instead be referred to Stormont. There they were promptly dismissed. This ploy, for years successful at keeping Belfast at bay, was brushed aside as Northern Ireland descended into violence. The years that followed brought many crises for London, the SDLP and everyone else. British and Irish governments tried many approaches while simultaneously attempting to cope with republican and loyalist violence.

As for Hume, he applauded Edward Heath's efforts to put together the Sunningdale Agreement, and was sorely disappointed when its structures crumpled within months, brought down by a demonstration of unionist and loyalist street power. That event dramatically limited the room for manoeuvre, creating deep gloom in non-unionist circles. Although Hume never spelt it out publicly – from the start of his career he demonstrated a special talent for constructive ambiguity – it is quite clear that the Ulster Workers' Council strike convinced him that unionist politicians were highly unlikely to voluntarily share power with nationalists. SDLP figures say that from then on he listened carefully for signs of a unionist change of heart, attempting to follow up anything that sounded promising. But no one on the unionist side was up for a deal. Various unionists thought briefly about cul-de-sacs such as majority rule, integration and independence, but in the long years between the downfall of Brian Faulkner, the unionist leader who had accepted the Sunningdale Agreement, and the emergence of David Trimble in the 1990s, what prevailed was the immobilism of Molyneaux and the aggressive rhetoric of Paisley. Partnership was not on offer.

Hume continued to urge London to press unionists in the direction of sharing power but British governments, preoccupied with the IRA, saw no prospect of constructing a cross-community administration. In this near-vacuum he moved to bring in reinforcements in the shape of the United States, working with Irish governments to establish the United States as an important new player. In essence he saw little point in expending much energy to persuade unionism to make a fresh start.

The Hume-Dublin courting of Irish-America delivered considerable political benefits over the years, not least in helping to staunch the flow of money and weapons to the IRA. In the early 1970s some Irish-Americans sympathized with Sinn Féin and the IRA, a sentiment which led to large amounts of dollars being sent openly to republicans as well as a surreptitious flow of arms shipments. From the late 1970s on, Hume and Dublin made a severe dent in this by recruiting powerful Irish-Americans such as Edward Kennedy and Tip O'Neill for constitutional nationalism and in opposition to violent republicanism. Hume's impact was such that he was described as the most influential Irish figure in Washington, particularly within the Democratic Party. 'To see John Hume at a Democratic Convention is quite something', an envious British politician once remarked. 'He is feted on all sides and can hardly move for his retinue of senators and congressmen'. Historically, it had always been the ambition of Irish nationalism to harness the potentially huge political power of the US, both in terms of the administration and of the forty million people who described themselves on their census forms as Irish-American. British governments, on the other hand, were always extremely sensitive to the old Irish-American accusation that Britain was a colonial power exploiting Ireland. Some British ministers and diplomats displayed distinct resentment at what they regarded as the migrant Irish attempting to poison the wells of the special relationship between Britain and the US. According to one Irish observer: 'The British wanted to convince people that they were honest brokers, peacekeeping in Northern Ireland. But the basic assumption of many Irish-Americans was that they are effectively there as agents of occupation, active agents of injustice. That's what they were up against'.

Many of the millions of Irish-Americans were descendants of people who had left Ireland in painful and traumatic circumstances during and after the famine years, harbouring the sense that they had survived, and often thrived, while many left behind had died prematurely. For many Irish-Americans there was also a villain of the piece – the British, who in the simplified folklore of Boston and New York had deliberately neglected the Irish, refused to feed them during the famine and were still occupying part of Ireland. Hume and Dublin were disseminating no such message in the US, stressing instead that any idea of a British withdrawal was to be avoided at all costs. In fact, Foreign Affairs Minister Garret FitzGerald, worried that London might opt for a withdrawal, has told of lobbying Henry Kissinger, then US Secretary of State, telling him that Dublin might seek American assistance 'in persuading Britain not to embark on a course of action that could be so fraught with dangers'.

The view of many in London was that they would much prefer not to bring in the US to what was already a highly complex problem, although assistance in staunching the flow of Irish-American money and guns was of course welcome. But the British authorities regarded this as coming with a considerable price-tag in that Hume and Dublin were simultaneously harnessing US influence for their own political aims – which of course did not coincide with those of London.

It was an article of faith for Hume that a solution would only be found on a broader canvas than simply the UK, or even the UK together with the Irish Republic. In promoting this view he worked closely with Irish diplomats such as Washington ambassador Seán Donlon, Michael Lillis and others. This united front was highly successful in recruiting top-level US political muscle in his support, starting with Edward Kennedy and Tip O'Neill and eventually reaching presidential level. Jimmy Carter had briefly shown some interest but Ronald Reagan, though initially indifferent to matters Irish, became much more involved.

He knew little about his Irish ancestry before Dublin officials carried out detailed research and announced his family had been traced back to Ballyporeen. That, Reagan said, 'was when I finally learnt of the rich heritage my father had left me'. Intrigued, he was persuaded to pay a four-day visit to Ireland in 1984 and, in each of his eight years as US President, spent St Patrick's Day at the Irish embassy in Washington. This association gave the Irish invaluable political clout, with Reagan speaking publicly about Northern Ireland on at least fifteen occasions and frequently raising Anglo-Irish relations in conversations with Thatcher.

This was only a few years after the hunger strikes, when anti-British sentiment remained high, and when the Foreign Office was taking pains to stress the wider Irish dimension to the Northern Irish crisis in efforts to demonstrate to Americans that Britain was running Northern Ireland in a fair and balanced way. London was also keen to clamp down on republican fundraising, and to strengthen American willingness to extradite IRA suspects.

The net effect of all this was to establish the US as a significant new element in the efforts to bring the Troubles to an end, creating a precedent for the later remarkably close involvement of Bill Clinton. The impact of America on Britain was illustrated by John Major's reaction when Clinton allowed Adams into the US after denying him access for many years. 'I was frankly astonished', Major remembered. 'My first instinct was to pick up the phone and speak directly to the president and say, "What on earth's going on? Why has he suddenly got a visa?" We summoned the American ambassador and told him in very clear terms how upset we were. We passed on a message to Washington which I think was one of the strongest messages we ever sent out of Downing Street'. Major was clearly affronted by the very public illustration that, on this very important issue, Irish-American power trumped the influence of Britain.

Hume's longevity in frontline politics meant he had to deal with an ever-changing cast of characters in London. Totting them up, in fact, the Troubles involved six British prime ministers and no fewer than eighteen Northern Ireland secretaries of state. These encompassed some admirable figures but also some who were out of their depth, as well as a number more dedicated to promoting themselves rather than promoting peace. A brief review of British politicians illustrates the range of opinions of those responsible for Northern Ireland.

Prime Minister Harold Wilson, while strongly supporting civil rights, also toyed with schemes designed to lead to Irish unity. Ted Heath removed Northern Ireland's Parliament and government and replaced the latter with the short-lived power-sharing government under the Sunningdale Agreement, though opinion within his cabinet was initially divided.

Reginald Maudling was originally against abolition and bringing in direct rule. While Hailsham and Carrington spoke out against any move in the direction of Irish unity, Douglas-Home argued in favour of 'pushing the people of Northern Ireland towards a united Ireland'. After much serious thought, including studies of possible re-partition, the cabinet unanimously agreed that only direct rule could offer the necessary breathing-space for the construction of a cross-community settlement.

After Sunningdale fell Hume was to commend Brian Faulkner's 'courage and political agility' in leading the power-sharing executive. But he had no praise for Wilson and his hapless Northern Ireland Secretary Merlyn Rees, roundly condemning 'the pusillanimity of the Labour government in failing to resist the predictable destructiveness of the demagogues and paramilitaries on the extremes of unionism'. Giving way to the UWC strike was, he declared, 'one of the most squalid examples of government irresponsibility in our times'.

Hume also strongly disapproved of Rees' successor Roy Mason who took no political initiatives, largely froze out Dublin, and pursued a hard-line security approach which, he asserted, brought the IRA to the brink of defeat.

Margaret Thatcher also believed she was scoring a victory over republicans in her handling of the hunger strikes. When, at a private meeting, Hume urged her to make concessions she lectured him, according to the government minute of the meeting, that 'the people who had been killed by the IRA had no choice. The hunger strikers had a choice – any wavering on the issue of political status would be a licence to kill'.

There was clearly no meeting of minds on that point, and indeed during much of her premiership, and yet she was eventually to sign the Anglo-Irish Agreement, of which he was one of the principal architects. Of course he regarded it as a huge political step, giving Dublin an official role in Northern Ireland affairs, while Thatcher saw it primarily as a security instrument.

Secretary of State Jim Prior had particularly harsh words for Hume – perhaps understandably, given that the SDLP put the kibosh on his personal scheme for a limited form of devolution. Describing talking to Hume as 'rather like punching cotton wool', he was disparaging about his leadership qualities, writing in his memoirs: 'Neither the character of the man, his background nor the nature of his party enabled him to be a strong leader'. (It is worth mentioning that Prior was highly critical of many other Northern Ireland figures, for example, saying that 'Paisley's bigotry easily boils over into bombast'.)

Hume was doubtless relieved when, after Taoiseach Charles Haughey's brief and counter-productive flirtation with Thatcher, Garret FitzGerald and Irish diplomats such as Dermot Nally, Michael Lillis and Noel Dorr engaged with London in a much more serious, professional and less ego-driven way. Thatcher's Foreign Secretary Sir Geoffrey Howe was certainly impressed by both the British and Irish negotiating teams which produced the Anglo-Irish Agreement, giving major credit to them as 'a galaxy of skill'.

Howe later detailed the range of opinion in the Thatcher cabinet in the lead-up to the Anglo-Irish Agreement. He recalled Whitelaw being wary but in principle strongly supportive, while Prior was 'tenaciously and sensibly positive'. Lord Hailsham was the most guarded of those around the cabinet table, serving as 'a constant reminder of the unionist case'. Tom King too expressed serious concerns about the deal, regarding it as imbalanced, while Ian Gow, later assassinated by the IRA, could not accept it and resigned as a minister.

Douglas Hurd recalled the mood at a crucial cabinet meeting as cool and uneasy, describing his own feelings as ambivalent. Interestingly, he recorded a key unexpected intervention from Norman Tebbit, whose wife had been badly injured when an IRA bomb had exploded at the Tory Party's 1984 conference hotel in Brighton. 'The discussion was particularly influenced by Norman', Hurd wrote. 'There was special power in his voice and his support was crucial – any opposition from him might have scuppered the negotiations'.

Years later at the launch of the Downing Street Declaration Secretary of State Sir Patrick Mayhew made it clear he disapproved of Major's willingness to advance the peace process. A Dublin official wrote: 'Sir Patrick made no attempt to conceal his lack of enthusiasm. He remained separate from the milling politicians and officials, gloomily staring out windows for much of the time'.

In the end Major did not move far enough or fast enough for Hume. He did not collapse the process, but, with only a slim House of Commons majority and a number of troublesome right-wing backbenchers, he clearly felt his room for manoeuvre was limited. As for Hume, he had made few inroads into the Tory party at a personal level, since not many Conservative MPs took a great interest. A highly experienced denizen of Westminster wrote privately: 'British politicians have a low boredom threshold where Irish affairs are concerned. Serious, humourless, garrulous Hume – like FitzGerald – bored the Tories rigid'.

It was left to the next prime minister, Tony Blair, to bring the process to fruition, working with his adviser Jonathan Powell and Secretary of State Mo Mowlam, and with invaluable input from Irish diplomats such as Seán O'Huiginn and Dermot Gallagher. Hume's health had deteriorated so that he was no longer at the centre of things, though Blair in his memoirs lauded him as 'a great political figure and genuine man, who had vision and imagination and foresight when others were resolutely still in blinkers'.

In addition to the politicians there was important input over the decades from the army and police as well as various intelligence agencies. MI5 and MI6 were both active during the Troubles, in confrontation with the IRA and in charting political currents within it. While most of what went on in the secret intelligence world remains unknown, one glimpse of how things sometimes worked came in 1990 when MI5's John Deverell, head of intelligence in Northern Ireland, informed Northern Ireland Secretary Peter Brooke that a line of communication was open to the republican leadership. In those early days of the peace process, Deverell said he believed there was potential for progress and sought permission to explore further. Brooke gave the go-ahead, later saying: 'It was not negotiation. I was not sanctioning a whole series of things – it was the opportunity to carry on conversation'. Before Brooke approved the move he cleared his instruction to Deverell with Downing Street, with Thatcher's knowledge.

Probably the most fundamental fault-line within government separated the Northern Ireland Office and the Foreign Office. The Northern Ireland Office (NIO) saw itself as locked in a struggle against terrorism, particularly an IRA campaign aimed at defeating the state and removing Northern Ireland from the UK. The Foreign Office started from a different perspective, since part of its role was to pay close attention to opinion outside the UK, including the US and above all in the Irish Republic. The prevailing sentiment in the NIO was against the approach urged by Hume, Dublin and the generality of nationalists. Instead it favoured an internal settlement, concentrating on a centrist approach in the belief that constructing a coalition of moderate politicians would eventually lead the extreme elements to admit defeat and give up.

Hurd wrote of his Belfast officials: 'Most of the individuals who kept Northern Ireland going were in a vague way unionist by background and inclination'. Howe commented that Hurd was initially much influenced by 'his initial tutors who included the traditionalists in the NIO'. Certainly the higher reaches of the NIO showed no signs of approval for Hume, as revealed in comments made in various conversations, memoirs and documents which have emerged from the Public

Record Office. The following snippets, which were written at various times over the years, give a flavour of how the most senior mandarins viewed Hume.

According to one document: 'Hume has been recognized as a kind of lay saint throughout nationalist Ireland and the overseas Irish diaspora ... the reputation as the greatest living Irishman assiduously built up by John Hume over many years of persistent lobbying ... There are those who regard any degree of criticism of him as close to blasphemy ...

'He led his party in an autocratic and authoritarian style ... the constant repetition of a limited number of well-turned phrases created a sense of intolerable ennui amongst not a few of his listeners ...'

While some of this might perhaps be put down to good-natured joshing intended primarily to give other mandarins a bit of a chuckle, there was little sign anywhere of officials approving or endorsing Hume's ideas. Over the years various officials made it perfectly clear that there were few if any Hume fans within the NIO, where the SDLP leader's approach was generally regarded as quixotic, wrong-headed, and indeed an obstruction to efforts to build a centrist solution which would isolate the extremes.

The day-to-day running of Northern Ireland was often left for long stretches in the hands of the NIO, in conjunction with the army and police. But at a number of points other, more powerful, parts of the British establishment intervened and took over control. This tended to happen at times of crisis, when powerful figures in London became alarmed at the level of violence, as well as concluding that the NIO's approach of doggedly pursuing an internal settlement was highly unlikely to deliver.

The prime instances of this involved the Foreign Office, the Cabinet Office and, crucially, the personal involvement of British prime ministers. Each episode involved significant input from Hume and Dublin, and each produced important developments regarded by constitutional nationalists as significant advances. The four main examples were the 1973 Sunningdale Agreement, the 1985 Anglo-Irish Agreement, the close relationship that developed between Major and Albert Reynolds, and Blair's partnership with Bertie Ahern. (Blair's aide Jonathan Powell commended Major as 'the first prime minister since Lloyd George to take a real and sustained interest in Northern Ireland'.)

A vital insight into a fundamental departmental divergence came from Sir Kenneth Bloomfield, who for decades was one of the most important figures in the governance of Northern Ireland. He was the most senior Northern Ireland-born figure in the NIO and the head of the Northern Ireland Civil Service. A key adviser since the 1960s to unionist leaders such as Terence O'Neill and Brian Faulkner, Sir Kenneth has provided, in two volumes of memoirs, a fascinating insight into how the Anglo-Irish Agreement came into being. He was later to survive an attempt by the IRA to assassinate him: they placed a necklace of bombs around his home. Luckily he and his family escaped unscathed. He went on to become a dedicated campaigner on behalf of 'the disappeared', a number of people murdered and secretly buried by the IRA.

In his memoirs Sir Kenneth set out an insider's view of how Whitehall took over from Stormont in deciding the future course of policy. The agreement of course was based on a deal with Hume and Dublin, a deal that angered all shades of unionist opinion. In his books Sir Kenneth provided a detailed description of how this came about. His strong belief was that he, who had for years served faithfully as the senior Northern Ireland voice, was pointedly excluded from the process.

The key politicians on the British side were Thatcher and Geoffrey Howe, while the key officials were her cabinet secretary, Sir Robert Armstrong, and Sir David Goodall of the Foreign Office. The team did not include Sir Kenneth. He considered himself objective, but did not see either Armstrong or Goodall in that light. Armstrong, he wrote, had worked under Heath, who 'had treated Faulkner and his unionist colleagues with something approaching brutal contempt', and under Wilson who during the UWC strike 'had excoriated a whole suffering community as spongers'. Goodall, he wrote, was a likeable individual 'but with strong Irish connections and an Ampleforth education (a reference to the English Catholic school) was unlikely to have much affinity with the Northern Ireland majority'.

Sir Kenneth described the British line-up as imbalanced and deeply flawed, since the Irish government was careful to keep in step with John Hume who he noted, 'deployed a remarkable influence on the policies of successive British and Irish governments'. The UK government, he complained, did not have the same close relationship with unionist politicians or Northern Ireland civil servants.

He had always detected 'traces of patrician arrogance' in the Foreign Office, recalling that the diplomat who chaired one meeting 'showed no more interest in my views than if I had been an observer from Outer Mongolia'. Sir Kenneth was only allowed to see the agreement when it was virtually finalized, and when he did he was shocked and 'went through days and weeks of mental agony', contemplating resignation or a personal appeal to Thatcher. He ruefully concluded, however, that 'in terms of departmental weight the NIO was a frigate in competition with battleships'.

He detected in his exclusion 'an inference that one could not wholly be trusted to be objective, coupled, perhaps, with the fear that one might offer inconvenient advice if afforded the opportunity to give it'. The London perspective on all this was set out by Sir David Goodall years later, after his retirement. From the beginning, the Foreign Office man said, the NIO were 'very sceptical, deeply sceptical' about the whole exercise.

The NIO had various confrontations, he said, with one Irish negotiator whom they viewed as untrustworthy. He went on: 'I think they thought these bright characters, Armstrong and Goodall from the Foreign Office, are taking this ball and running with it – they really don't know anything about running the province, they have no idea of the consequences of all this, and it's all very well for them to have these bright ideas but actually they're very dangerous ideas'.

> From a British perspective there was a feeling that everything triable had been tried in Northern Ireland and nothing worked and that we'd simply run out of ideas, so that something had to be done. And the NIO, their problem was they didn't really have anything else to suggest, that was their problem. Their scepticism I had every sympathy for, but the fact was that nothing was happening.

And what of unionist politicians, who like Sir Kenneth were kept in the dark? According to Goodall: 'The attitude to the unionists from the beginning was that they had made it so abundantly clear that they wouldn't tolerate any form of Irish dimension. The judgment was made that if you were going to go into confidential negotiations with the Irish you simply could not take the unionists into your confidence'. And of course that was a great weakness in the eventual agreement, that it was conducted over the heads of the unionists. 'I honestly have often wondered about it but I don't see how anything else was possible, given the attitude of the unionists at that time'.

In other words, a conservative government headed by Thatcher, the most unionist of Tory leaders, had put much thought into how to handle Northern Ireland, weighing up the approaches recommended by the NIO and unionism and by Dublin and Hume on the other. And London concluded that the status quo was not an option, that a fortress mentality offered no way out of the Troubles, and that despite many difficulties a new direction was needed.

Britain might not have acted in this way had it not been alarmed by the advance of Sinn Féin after the hunger strikes but the route into the new era of Anglo-Irish cooperation which eventually brought the Troubles to a close was fashioned by constitutional nationalism.

And one of the key figures in pointing the way was a figure who – figuratively and on occasion literally – persisted in gripping British lapels.

Hume and Unionists

ARTHUR AUGHEY

The Danish polymath Piet Hein is popularly known for his gruks (or in English, grooks), which are derived from the first two letters of 'grin' (laugh) and the last two letters of 'suk' (sigh). These may be described as short aphoristic poems which, as the name implies, at one and the same time make you smile in appreciation and sigh in recognition. One of these gruks runs: 'As pastor X steps out of bed he slips a neat disguise on/ that halo round his priestly head is really his horizon'.[1] If one were searching for a maxim which captures succinctly unionist suspicion of John Hume that is as good as it gets. And it was not just unionist suspicion, for others were equally critical of the confusion of the personal vision and the radiant truth, most notably Conor Cruise O'Brien. The long-drawn sigh of unionists was acknowledgment enough that the world had been too easily misled by Hume's halo, if that alliteration may pass. As one former Free Presbyterian recalled, Ian Paisley used to bridle at the praise for Hume's moderation. 'I remember the way he used to snarl about "Saint Hume".'[2] This point does not merely express distaste for personal self-righteousness even though historically minded unionists might think of Hume as Henry Labouchere did of Gladstone: that they did not object to him always having a card up his sleeve, but they did object to his insinuating that the Almighty had placed it there. If this were just a case of complaining that Hume was a nationalist, the popular response would be: 'so what?' If it were also just a case of complaining that Hume had used high-flown language merely to out-manoeuvre unionists in political debate, the popular response would be: 'serves you right'.

However, the complaint incorporates a number of more serious but interrelated criticisms that link the personal and the political. These criticisms were put to Hume very directly by the former *Irish Times* political journalist (and former General Secretary of the Ulster Unionist Party) Frank Millar in an interview

1 P. Hein, *Grooks* (Cambridge MA, 1966), p. 14. 2 E. Moloney, *Paisley: from demagogue to democrat?* (Dublin, 2008), p. 192.

which, at the time, the SDLP leader thought would become 'seminal'. The first was that his understanding of unionists was narrow and hackneyed and which, despite its claim to imaginative freshness, was incapable of acknowledging their basic entitlements as citizens of the United Kingdom. If republicans believed that unionists were merely dupes of British imperialism then Hume's abiding thought was that they found themselves in the wrong 'relationship'. The second was that Hume's horizon, like the Danish pastor's, remained a limited one despite the apparent breadth of his vision and focused exclusively on 'facing down the union-ists' who were still believed to 'hold all power in their hands'. The implication of Millar's question was that Hume could see unionists only as having sinned against the destiny of the Irish people, a very nationalist and very traditional form of political self-righteousness. And the third was that the aim of his politics – albeit by conviction and principle non-violent – perceived unionism not as a political tradition to be reasoned with but as an obstacle to be removed. Or as Millar put it bluntly, in unionist eyes Hume and his party have 'lived off the backs of the IRA since the beginning of the Troubles', pushing the same agenda only by different means.[3] In sum, even as a sympathetic academic interpreter concluded, 'Hume's greatest failure was his inability to engage at an intellectual level with unionist arguments'.[4] The purpose of this chapter is to consider the validity of those criti-cisms and to re-assess that conclusion.

ON THE IDENTITY OF UNIONISTS

Any political tradition is a tricky thing to get to know and unionism is no excep-tion to that rule. Indeed, unionism is an ideological abstraction from diverse pur-poses and, given the range of attitudes embraced by the term, division within it is sometimes as bitter as rivalry between it and nationalism. Any definition needs to be sensitive to that diversity and perhaps the clearest expression of unionist iden-tity remains the Ulster Covenant of 1912. The covenant was concise – 189 words – and yet it conveyed the complex relationship which was – and, in a sentimental sense, remains – characteristic of unionist argument. Perhaps surprisingly, given its political prominence today, the word British was not used at all. It begins with a statement of what political scientists would call the instrumental value of the Union: its importance for the material well-being of all citizens. If this appears like a contract with a mobile phone company that is not all the covenant says. Instrumentalism is balanced, second, by a statement of non-instrumental belong-ing in the United Kingdom: defined as the 'cherished position of equal citizen-

3 The full interview can be found in F. Millar, *Northern Ireland: a triumph of politics* (Dublin, 2009), pp 3–19.   4 G. Murray, *John Hume and the SDLP* (Dublin, 1998), p. 187.

ship'. Both of these are set, third, in the context of political allegiance: loyalty to the Crown – the closest thing we get to an idea of the British state where material entitlement and political obligation meet.[5] This links, fourth, to an appeal to values held in common: civil and religious freedom. Finally, the covenant points to what economists call the equalisation of risk – expressed there as the unity of the Empire but proclaimed today as welfare solidarity across all parts of the state. Of course, the specific historical conditions of this covenanting idea are now dead but what is living in the text is very contemporary and very relevant. For example, there is no presumption that everyone and everywhere in the Union are the same. Suitably updated and rephrased for the new world of devolution, it may be said to propose that different nationalities elect to stay in constitutional relation with one another and that this relationship constitutes an affinity giving meaning to the term British. To put that in language familiar now in Northern Ireland but of relevance elsewhere in the United Kingdom: multi-national affinities are sustained on the basis of consent and people can only be convinced by constitutional arguments that they themselves are already prepared to accept. In this view, the Union comprises a principle and an ideal. The principle is free association (elective) and the ideal is multi-nationalism (affinity). This means that the shape of the United Kingdom at any time is always open to negotiation, exhibiting the dual aspect of contract – instrumental bargaining for resources between nations, regions and central government – and solidarity – mutual support and risk sharing. Indeed as Kidd has argued the Ulster version of unionism has shared its paradoxical character with the Scottish variety in which 'a kind of cultural nationalism' also 'co-existed happily with loyalty to the British state'.[6] This paradox of identity may be called (after Goethe and Weber) 'elective affinity'.

A paradox like elective affinity is unlikely to find favour with one's political opponents where the temptation is always to look for one-sidedness and contradiction. Had not unionists denied choice to nationalists during the Home Rule crisis and had they not closed off their expressed affinities with the rest of the island under the old Stormont regime? Indeed, even those who treat unionism sympathetically have found it difficult to hold together both elements of the paradox. Thus David Miller's influential history of unionism, *Queen's rebels* (1974), identified another paradox but resolved the paradox into an 'external relationship', emphasizing famously its conditional nature, conveying the impression that Protestant allegiance was entirely instrumental.[7] The two parts of the paradox fell apart, one might suggest, as it encountered the force-field of nationalist interpretation. According to Ian McBride this force-field has been difficult to escape such

---

5 R. Rose, *Understanding the United Kingdom: the territorial dimension in government* (London, 1982), p. 62.   6 C. Kidd, *Union and unionisms: political thought in Scotland, 1500–2000* (Cambridge, 2008), p. 176.
7 D. Miller, *Queen's rebels: Ulster loyalism in historical perspective* (Dublin, 1974).

that unionist identity 'is usually interpreted as a tactical alliance designed to maintain colonial privileges rather than a bona fide expression of emotional commitment to British culture and values'. This partial view, he thought, ignores the 'substance' of a subject far more complex than such a simple and one-sided reading allows.[8] McBride's criticism of that purely cynical relationship is reflected in the argument of Neil Southern who also challenges a one-dimensional interpretation. He was critical of much of contemporary political science which employs terms like 'strategic political alliance' and 'convenient means' to imply that unionist politics can be understood only as a negative manoeuvre designed to secure local cultural and political dominance, again a familiar trope of Irish nationalism.[9] In a variation of the paradox of elective affinity, Tom Hennessey, who had been one of David Trimble's assistants during the negotiation of the Good Friday Agreement, thought that the concept of 'affect' helped to explain the politics of unionism. 'Affect may be unformed and unstructured but nevertheless highly organized and effectively analysable, a term which denotes a more-or-less organized experience, with empowering or disempowering consequences'. As historical conditions change, the balance between Irish-ness, Ulster-ness, British-ness and Northern Irish-ness change as well.[10] Or, to put that otherwise, the affinity of political belonging and the elective calculations necessary to secure that political belonging adapt to the times. To argue that opposition to Home Rule then and to Irish unity now is all to do with a self-interested unionist 'surrogate for the appeal of nationality' and nothing at all to do with principle is both partial and self-deluding.[11] The evidence suggests that unionist identity 'is not the result of them choosing to be British – as if before deciding to be British they neutrally assessed the identities open to them and weighed up their options' but is the political expression of genuine historical affinities.[12] Given the tendency to read unionism in a one-dimensional fashion, perhaps Hume's failure to grasp the subtleties is excusable. As a party political leader his priority was not to understand unionism but to change it and, inevitably, the wished-for outcome was read back into his understanding.

As Peter McLoughlin's account of his intellectual history makes clear, Hume's view is that the division in Ireland is 'primarily psychological' and that the unionist desire to maintain that division has been the product mainly of fear.[13] Their fear is ultimately irrational and it has had pathological political consequences. In this

8 I. McBride, 'Ulster and the British problem' in R. English and G. Walker (eds), *Unionism in modern Ireland* (Dublin, 1966) , p. 1. 9 N. Southern, 'Britishness, "Ulsterness" and unionist identity in Northern Ireland', *Nationalism and Ethnic Politics*, 13:1 (2007), pp 78–9. 10 T. Hennessey, 'The evolution of Ulster Protestant identity in the twentieth century: nations and patriotism' in M. Busteed, F. Neal and J. Tonge (eds), *Irish Protestant identities* (Manchester, 2008), pp 257–8. 11 A. Jackson, *The Ulster Party: Irish unionists in the House of Commons, 1884–1911* (Oxford, 1989), p. 121. 12 Southern, 'Britishness, "Ulsterness" and unionist identity in Northern Ireland', p. 102. 13 P.J. McLoughlin, *John Hume and the revision of Irish nationalism* (Manchester, 2010), p. 29.

condition of unreason, unionists have been persuaded to maintain a relationship – membership of the United Kingdom – which denies their real affinity with the rest of the island and has sustained in them a false sense of supremacy and privilege. And because the British government chose to underwrite that relationship in Ireland in 1921, it is mainly responsible for unionist intransigence. One can see how this leads to a conclusion reminiscent of Rousseau. If the irrational will of unionism is committed to partition, its real will cannot but admit the truth. How they might be 'forced to be free', of course, was the key dividing line between the SDLP and the IRA. Most unionists, argued Hume in 1971, will concede 'the inevitability of a united country' and he thought there was 'little point in evading any further the inevitability on which all are agreed.'[14] Unfortunately, this inevitability was something which an unsound tradition was dedicated to frustrate. As such unionists were and remain a suitable case for treatment. The elements of that treatment are already implied in Hume's understanding. The British 'connection' is exactly that – an external guarantee. Unionists believe that it is necessary for their well-being but it denotes nothing other than their dependence. What is required is either for those unionists enlightened enough to free themselves or for the British government to persuade them to act according to their real will. This remained the consistent refrain of Hume's key speeches for four decades. In the first instance, Hume's call was for those in the Protestant community who have a proper vision of affinity with their fellow Irish and who cherish their Irishness 'to step forward now and present us with proposals for a new Ireland that is acceptable to Protestantism as opposed to unionism'.[15] There is an element of truth here because many unionists continue to demonstrate an affinity with things Irish, at least in their own way, but do so on terms that should not be confused with the requirements of nationalist ideology. In the second instance it is the duty of the British government to create the conditions in which unionists 'can perceive and pursue their true interests'.[16] Hitherto, successive Westminster administrations have simply allowed perverse unionist 'suspicions, self-doubts and prejudices' to stand in the way of doing what is inevitable.[17] The consistent message is this.

The 'true interests' of unionists have been lost by clinging to the British guarantee. They need to exercise self-confidence and self-reliance and 'believe in themselves as their own guarantors in a future shared with the other people of the island of Ireland'.[18] They are invited to dispense with the external British guarantee and to accept the only guarantee that is worth having, that of their fellow Irish people. This happens to be the only condition of their 'safety' and ultimately the only one of 'value'. In other words, Hume's invitation to unionists is to set aside Northern Ireland's constitutional position and to engage as equals in the common

14 McLoughlin, *John Hume and the revision of Irish nationalism*, p. 34.   15 J. Hume, *A new Ireland: politics, peace, and reconciliation* (Boulder, CO, 1997), p. 71.   16 Ibid., p. 79.   17 Ibid., p. 81.   18 Ibid., pp 79–80.

aspiration for a new Ireland, where 'agreement threatens no one'. The landscape here becomes the political equivalent of Field Day's cultural 'fifth province', a transcendent location supposedly distinct from the old nationalist vision of homogeneity, one now respecting 'diversity'. Yet it only proposes to resolve real problems within an imaginary but very traditional nationalist shell. While the desire for a non-sectarian republic is clear, there remains a cultural blind spot – precisely those who need to be convinced, those whose 'elective' sense of political and cultural being is elsewhere 'affined'. That same cultural blind spot is repeated in Hume's speeches. They too conjure up the same sort of transcendent location where the fact of the Union and democratic support for it no longer function and unionist false consciousness will be corrected at last. Hume's design is to liberate political debate from its entanglement in unfortunate empirical detail, to substitute aspiration for actuality and to play fast and loose with the principle of consent. Hence, the familiar response of former Ulster Unionist leader James Molyneaux – that the priority in Northern Ireland should be an acceptance of 'reality' – becomes understandable in context.[19]

As Millar concluded from his *Irish Times* interview with Hume in 1989, such grandiose plans would never survive for a moment actual engagement with Ulster Unionists. It was obvious that they would refuse to move within the horizon of Hume's halo because they were never enchanted by the disguise. Their suspicion has always been that the SDLP leader's speeches were never addressed to them in any case but at others, like the British, Irish and United States governments, which had the power to implement his vision by 'persuasion'. Though unionists might laugh at Hume's so-called 'single transferable speech' and sigh at his wilful misrecognition of their position, this was a unionist problem and not Hume's. His criticism was equally consistent – that unionists failed to engage with him and not vice versa. One could say that Hume became a convenient scapegoat for unionist incapacity and inarticulateness, rather as Macauley wrote of critics of Machiavelli who, finding delinquents too numerous to be punished, select one to 'bear the whole penalty of an offence in which they are not more deeply implicated than those who escape'.[20] In Hume's case, his offence was that he did it better than the others. However, if the failings of the unionist imagination during the Troubles are obvious, they are replicated in Hume's own thinking. McLoughlin's conclusion is judicious. Hume's underlying assumption was that unionists 'were a constituent part of the Irish people' and so, despite the effort of him and his party 'to accept the authenticity of unionists' British identity', the assumption undermined the intention.[21]

19 A. Purdy, *Molyneaux: the long view* (Belfast, 1989), p. 79. 20 T.B. Macaulay, *Machiavelli, in critical and historical essays* (London, 1967), pp 18–19. 21 McLoughlin, *John Hume and the revision of Irish nationalism*, p. 229.

HUME-SPEAK

Another sympathetic student of Hume's political career once observed how his supposedly flexible language conveyed to many commentators on Northern Ireland that he was an honest broker and not a partisan politician.[22] This misinterpretation, in other words, confused the medium (a brave and moderate voice) and the message (an accomplished propagandist for a nationalist solution). Nevertheless, to be able to work that sort of rhetorical effect speaks highly of Hume's political skill. And it was a skill that supposedly straight-talking unionists would denounce as the verbal fog of cunning Irish blether. However, why should a politician use language precisely when vagueness (or what his critics would call, the pious cant of Saint John) was more likely to bring dividends? How might Hume's undoubted achievement be specified?

The author Mario Vargas Llosa, who decided subsequently to pursue a career in politics, once described the key transition to be from one use of language to another. He did not claim that the difficulty he found in making that transition to lie in forsaking literary truth for the dishonesty of the political world. Rather, it lay in moving from one sort of linguistic effort in the cause of clarity to another sort of linguistic effort in the cause of calculated ambiguity. Vargas Llosa found that the art of politics involved its own discursive discipline just as taxing in its demands as the writing of a novel or a learned essay. To formulate ideas and proposals in such a manner as to be both persuasive and ambiguous was an experience that Vargas Llosa found challenging and profoundly disturbing. But he accepted that it was part and parcel of the political craft. Not to acknowledge its necessity and therefore to fail to become proficient in the lexicon of ambivalence was to lack seriousness as a politician. To eschew it altogether would represent a dereliction of professional duty. Vagueness, elusiveness and allusiveness are necessary not only to attain self-interested ends but also to avoid potentially destructive – or self-destructive – political dogmatism.[23] This is the art of what during the 'peace process' of the 1990s, in which Hume was intimately involved, became known popularly as 'constructive ambiguity'. However, it was not Hume's mastery of the elusive and the allusive alone that misled those commentators. There was another and possibly more significant factor in play. To put it simply, Hume was speaking within a narrative of Northern Ireland's history and politics which favoured his 'flexible language'. Though he certainly gave that narrative an imaginative expression, the flow of interpretative sympathy was in his favour. As Millar admitted, unionists had lost the propaganda battle very early on in the Troubles and they found themselves invariably cast – probably to those very commentators

22 G. Drower, *John Hume: peacemaker* (London, 1995), p. 17. 23 M. Vargas Llosa, 'Vargas Llosa for President: a novelist's personal account of his campaign for the presidency of Peru', *Granta*, 36 (June 1991).

who found Hume persuasive – as the 'guilty party'.[24] This gave rhetorical advantage to Hume from the outset, though it was an advantage he had to exploit, and his exploitation of it put unionists consistently on the back foot. Indeed, such was their discomfiture over the years that it prompted one of them to propose an elaborate philosophic distinction to explain Hume's success.

Peter McLachlan, who had been an adviser to Brian Faulkner in the early 1970s, submitted a paper to the Opsahl Commission that proposed a fundamental distinction between nationalist and unionist discourse. He identified what he called two very different political 'theologies', one of which derives from Aquinas and is deductive in form and another which derives from Calvin and Luther and is inductive in form. The logic of the first, argued McLachlan, is best revealed in the speeches of Hume as well as in the negotiating strategy of the SDLP. They both reveal broad, general frameworks from which principles of advancement are deduced and from which they never budge. The logic of the second is found in the speeches and negotiating strategy of unionists which deal in specifics and build into a framework of defence from which they never move either. He thought that 'the two just bypass each other and no wonder they do not agree'.[25] There is a certain superficial plausibility to that argument. For instance, it appears to capture the repetitiveness of the 'single transferable speech' or Hume-speak of which unionists (and not only unionists) always complained. Nevertheless, its weakness is more obvious than its strength for Hume's distinctive rhetorical advantage can be understood otherwise and its partisan character more mundanely specified.

In the terminology of the political philosopher Robert Berki, all political ideals involve two ways of 'seeing' an issue. The first he termed vision and the second, insight. Vision perceives a transcendent objective in a process of becoming. Insight identifies the means to achieve that objective as well as the obstacles in its way. The two are interdependent.[26] Hume's vision proposed an Ireland yet to be, a united people in which Protestants, Catholics and their respective traditions would contribute their common energies ('spilling their sweat together rather than their blood'). It is a vision of destiny. Insight perceives the obstacles to the achievement of this new Ireland. It sees in particular British bad faith, unionist intransigence and the denial of self-determination for the Irish people 'as a whole'. What eases the painful insight of present division is the belief that the vision is inevitable (to use Hume's own word). On the other hand, the unionist vision is fixed on the world as it is – rather, a Northern Ireland but only with unionists left alone and free from nationalist subversion. That vision is long-standing. In May 1912, at the height of the Irish Home Rule crisis, the *Ballymoney Free Press* proclaimed: 'The

24 F. Millar, *David Trimble: the price of peace* (Dublin, 2008), p. 199.   25 Cited in A. Pollak (ed.), *A citizen's inquiry: the Opsahl Report on Northern Ireland* (Dublin, 1993), pp 37–8.   26 R. Berki, *Insight and vision: the problem of communism in Marx's thought* (London, 1984).

statement of Unionist Ulster is that it merely wants to be let alone'. Unfortunately, it continued, 'since Satan entered the Garden of Eden good people will not be let alone'.[27] Unionist insight, consequently, sees the militancy of republicanism and Irish bad faith in a common determination to undo the state in Northern Ireland. Putting these two ways of seeing in the context of the recent Troubles, and to use mechanical terminology, 'commentators' tend to perceive nationalism as the active political force and unionism, the resistant political force. Given the pre-judgment Millar accepts, it becomes very easy to give 'active' and 'resistant' the moral loading of 'progressive' and 'reactionary', thus immediately skewing to Hume's advantage the perceived relationship between the communities within Northern Ireland and between the two parts of the island.

In another submission to the Opsahl Commission, the cultural critic, Edna Longley, captured brilliantly the consequences of this ideological encounter between ways of seeing. She was unconvinced by the novelty of Hume's language and did not detect a profound distinction, as unionists did not, between his desire for an 'agreed Ireland' and the old conception of a 'united Ireland'. In an implied rebuke to the McLachlan thesis, she proposed that the unionist position is 'not essentially due to a bad case, bad conscience or Calvinist prohibitions or talking outside the congregation, but to defending the *status quo*.'[28] This is a key perception, for Longley believed that the one matter on which Hume's argument remained stereotypical was on the topic of Ulster Protestants and about whom 'his ideas are utterly unreliable'. Indeed, his frequent comparisons of Protestants with the whites of South Africa or with the whites of Alabama were particularly crass and insulting and simply replayed the traditional Irish practice of defining one's political opponents according to its worst elements. This has consequences for how one understands the way in which an 'agreed Ireland' can be delivered, something which is considered in the next section of the chapter. At this point, it may be said that it denies the value of institutional arrangements expressed in the language of permanence and which are capable of providing an alternative to the vision of unity. There were, and remain, differences of emphasis and commitment within the SDLP on this matter. There are also differences of perspective between northern and southern nationalists and between both of these and supporters who do not live in Ireland at all. However, whatever coherence there is to Irish nationalism consists in a consensus about the injustice of partition and an obligation to work for its removal; however, that obligation may be qualified by insights of prudence. This gives a dynamic, imaginative character to the nationalist argument on the 'soaring dove' principle – it can afford to be imaginative and to soar above the mundane because its intention is to move beyond the confining limits of the present.

---

27 Cited in P. Bew, *Ideology and the Irish question* (Oxford, 1994), p. 47.   28 A summary of her submission can be found in E. Longley, 'Challenging complacency', *Fortnight*, 135 (Mar. 1993), pp 20–3.

In this case, one can see how McLachlan could be impressed by the soaring dove aloft in the blue sky of Hume's thinking. And for Hume, of course, veto was the negative, and exclusive, default position of those unionists whose eyes could not be raised to his heights of possibility. By contrast, he emphasized relentless positivity but only insofar as it involved movement in a nationalist direction. Take, for example, this response to the Downing Street Declaration of 1993. Hume noted that there had been talk yet again of vetoes but that 'is a negative way of looking at' the possibilities. 'Surely the time has come to be positive, and to seek and work for agreement, the challenge of which is to persuade one another that neither side wants victory, but each wants an agreement which respects our different heritages and identities, which is the only basis for stability in any society'.[29] It is clear from the context of the speech that by 'agreement' he means movement in a pre-determined direction. As such, it is a partial and dishonest claim for Hume's own veto is smuggled in under the rhetoric of progress. Every political reversal for unionists became something for the SDLP to be conservative about and to defend. For example, the Anglo-Irish Agreement of 1985 meant that Hume was opposed to any attempt to tamper with its provisions (veto) while he continued to talk about a further agreement which would transcend it in importance ('soaring dove'). In short, the agreement was incorporated into rhythms of the single transferable speech and whatever concessions it made to the narrative of destiny were banked for good. That 'effectively meant that unionist retrenchment could be avoided: future negotiations would have to be based on the starting position of Dublin having a consultative role in the north'.[30]

In this way, at least, for 'many commentators', the positive was accentuated and the negative was concealed. For most of the 1990s, it appeared that Hume's transcendent agreement implied that all existing arrangements were up for discussion, except Articles 2 and 3 of the Ireland's constitution (which Hume had defended at Sunningdale), in which the parties would engage without a veto, except that of the Irish people's right to self-determination; in which consent was essential, except when unionists needed persuading; and where coercion must be removed, except when it is called persuasion. The persistent calls for 'imagination', for a new 'atmosphere', for 'realizing' potential, for 'moving the process forward', represented attempts to put the call of destiny ahead of contingent details, one of which was unionist dissent from that destiny.

In an analysis of the political language of Hume in this period, one scholar concluded that despite claims to the contrary, especially his use of 'post-nationalism', he remained wedded to the fundamentals of nationalist discourse. Of course this is

29 Hume, *A new Ireland*, p. 121.   **30** C. McGrattan, 'Nationalism and the Anglo-Irish Agreement: equality, identity and ideology' in A. Aughey and C. Gormley-Heenan (eds), *The Anglo-Irish Agreement: re-thinking its legacy* (Manchester, 2011), p. 88.

not to suggest systematic deception or bad faith 'but rather that his reassurances and concessions to unionism are ultimately likely to prove inadequate because they are informed by a conception of the Northern Ireland "problem" and a reading of history which cannot be reconciled with unionism through the reworking of language'.[31] Hume's trademark re-definition of unionism as an Irish tradition which must sort out its relationship with the rest of the island gave primacy to the nationalist aspiration to unity, from which all else must be deduced. This did not appear to be very different from the traditional objective of anti-partitionists. In her criticism of the SDLP leader's 'linguistic tug of war', Longley concluded that Hume tries to yank unionist 'off their UK base, then to pull them across the border'.[32] Why, though, should Hume be held to a higher standard of political virtue than others? One answer – the one which unionists would make – is because he presented himself as an honest broker who claimed to know better than anyone else what was required. Certainly he was a frequently exasperated and irascible prophet, if only because others failed to act according to reason or in line with their real interests. Nevertheless, there is one important mitigating factor in that critique and it is this.

Unionists too played the game of reductionism, in this case reducing Hume's message to 'what he really means'. And what he 'really meant', they were convinced, was to trundle them into a united Ireland. Even if that were true, the failure to respond rhetorically, at least, to the challenge left the field open to Hume to establish the parameters of debate. In truth, there was a profound gulf between the brutalism of the republican vision, with its violent insights, and the discourse of Hume-speak. The SDLP was not Sinn Féin and their respective political cultures were, and remain, radically distinct. Indeed, one of the motivations of IRA terror was to make sure that common ground between unionists and nationalists could not be secured. To put that bluntly, as one Tyrone republican did, the killing of local security force personnel was intended to stop 'the unionists doing a deal with the SDLP'.[33] Perhaps nothing captures better the difference between constitutional nationalism and republicanism than such cynical and casual viciousness. That being the case, Hume's increasingly intimate association with Gerry Adams became one of the surprises of the Troubles. It is a development which requires explanation if unionist criticism (and, again, not only unionist criticism) is to be understood correctly.

THE PEACE PROCESS

A personal recollection can be introduced here. At a witness seminar on the Anglo-Irish Agreement of 1985 a few years ago which was held at University

31 M. Cunningham, 'The political language of John Hume', *Irish Political Studies*, 12:1 (1997), p. 20. 32 E. Longley, *From Cathleen to anorexia: the breakdown of Irelands* (Dublin, 1990), p. 15. 33 H. Patterson, *Ireland's violent frontier: the border and Anglo-Irish relations during the Troubles* (Basingstoke, 2013), p. 198.

College Dublin, one of the senior officials on the British side was asked if subsequent events had conformed to expectations. There was a slight hesitation: 'Well, the one thing none of us expected was that John Hume would shortly be talking to Gerry Adams'. This did appear counter-intuitive for two important reasons. The first was that Hume's moral stature rested on constitutional nationalism's tradition of non-violent pursuit of civil rights. Or as one rather sceptical journalist put it, 'the SDLP grew used to sitting back and telling journalists and voters alike: "You must like and support us because we are not Sinn Féin, we don't kill people, and our leader is a great guy".[34] Moreover, the widespread respect for Hume personally tended to insulate both him and his party from critical challenge. The second was that the British and Irish governments, at the behest of Hume, had devoted political resources to sustain the SDLP in Northern Ireland against insurgent republicanism. Indeed, that had been one of the primary objectives of the Anglo-Irish Agreement. 'Perhaps this was the most unintended consequence of the agreement: that something designed to shore up and defend constitutional nationalism from republican challenge would instead see a gradual osmosis between the two dominant currents of northern nationalism'.[35] Reflecting on the impact of that moment, especially on unionists, is like trying to remember a tune that many who lived through it now find difficult to recall or that, for a younger generation, was never known. One reason for this has been the historical displacement effect of the Good Friday Agreement of 1998 which for some is retrospective absolution for all political sins of the past. It is the halo effect now complemented by the Nobel Peace Prize effect. But the ideological character of what has become known as Hume-Adams is worth exploring.

Here Hume's understanding of unionism, and his judgment of what he believed was necessary for agreement, intersect. He shared with Adams a common perspective that unionists are an obstacle. The former's experience of the failure of the power-sharing executive in 1974 convinced him that unionists would act as a block on progress. In his own terms, of course, he had good reason to believe that this disposition was ingrained and the lesson he learnt was informed by a deep personal sense of victimhood and betrayal. Certainly unionist politicians showed little generosity to, or understanding of, the SDLP's position in the aftermath of the Ulster Workers' Council strike. Yet one has to be cautious about the easy attribution of blame for the fall of the executive and the subsequent political deadlock in Northern Ireland. At that time Hume was talking of the power-sharing institutions being nothing other than an 'interim solution' and warning the Irish government that it should never succumb to the 'false liberalism of placating' unionism.[36] If unionists suspected that the SDLP was committed to a 'united Ireland or nothing' then here

34 S. Breen, 'A puff of change', *Fortnight*, 362 (June 1997), p. 7. **35** H. Patterson, 'Republicanism and the peace process: the temptations of teleology' in A. Aughey and C. Gormley-Heenan (eds), *The Anglo-Irish Agreement: re-thinking its legacy* (Manchester, 2011), p. 101. **36** H. Patterson, *Ireland since 1939: the persist-*

was apparent confirmation. McLoughlin, whose book is studiously fair on the problems faced by Hume, thought that at Sunningdale he had lost sight of the SDLP's founding principles and 'appeared to assume that Irish unity could be achieved through unionists' acquiescence rather than their active assent.'[37] From that perspective, Hume was indeed a victim, but a victim of hubris as much as he was a victim of loyalist protest. Whatever one's judgment, there is no doubt that it confirmed a view that the unionist obstacle had to be dealt with. Now, you do not negotiate with an obstacle for it is an object of unreason. You either try to blast it out of the way or you try to circumvent your way around it. Republicans were engaged in the first activity, even if they defined it as a struggle against British imperialism in the interest of which unionism was merely a local and deluded agent. Under Hume's leadership the SDLP was engaged in the second activity. In an interview in 1979, he had dismissed unionists as 'one of the most right-wing forces in Europe; nobody else would stand for them anywhere'.[38] And the most dramatic example of the outworking of that policy and that dismissal was the Anglo-Irish Agreement that had excluded unionist engagement on principle. It is worth following through Hume's logic as the peace process unfolded.

In a speech delivered at the beginning of the Hume-Adams strategy, he provided bitter criticism of unionism which one senses is an honest statement of his thinking. Unionists he describes as 'a petty people'. They no longer harbour any trace of the civil and religious liberty of which the covenant had boasted. Their only principle has been 'exclusivism'. Their leaders were never committed to peace and stability and for seventy-five years, especially in the period of the recent Troubles, never produced a single new idea or proposal. 'Where else in the world', he asked, 'would a powerful and influential government, such as the British, have tied the whole basis of their policy to such a pathetic and leaderless bunch of politicians?' He concluded by asking: 'Did anyone need to look any further for the roots of violence?'[39] That short passage reveals intellectual arrogance as well as intellectual contempt and if there was one thing that invariably threw Hume into a bad temper it was the thought of unionists 'making the political weather'.[40] The implication of the argument is clear. Why would anyone think it either wise or necessary to negotiate with people like that? And if unionist politicians want to know why the IRA is murdering their constituents then they should look to themselves for the reason. If this is the sort of view which Hume was conveying to Adams in confidence then the emergence of a common position is not mysterious. Indeed, according to Ed Moloney, Adams had asked Hume as early as 1988 to put together a common nationalist position in order to dismantle the unionist veto, a more

ence of conflict (Dublin 2006), p. 239.   37 McLoughlin, John Hume and the revision of Irish nationalism, p. 218.   38 S. Deane and B. Fitzpatrick, 'Interview with John Hume', The Crane Bag: The Northern Issue, 4:2 (1980), p. 40.   39 Hume, A new Ireland, p. 107.   40 D. Godson, Himself alone: David Trimble and the ordeal of unionism (London, 2004), p. 119.

effective combination of blasting and circumvention.[41] Of course, neither Hume
nor his party could or would agree to that course and it took another decade for
the IRA to admit the failure of its terror campaign. However, in its talks with Sinn
Féin in 1988 the SDLP agreed that 'the real question is how do we end the British
presence in Northern Ireland'.[42] This helps to put into context Sinn Féin's electoral
overhaul of the SDLP in the course of the next two decades.

The Hume-Adams talks gave those who were disposed already to be hostile to
Hume's politics sufficient justification for claiming that the halo had slipped at
last and that his real character had been revealed. It was not only unionists who
pointed the finger at the same old 'united Ireland or nothing' nationalist but also
critics in the Republic of Ireland claimed their warnings were now proven. For
O'Brien (423), it merely disclosed the emptiness of all that Hume-speak about
agreement between the two traditions while confirming that the real objective was
again to circumvent unionists and coerce them by other means.[43] For Proinsias De
Rossa, then-leader of Democratic Left, the fashioning of a common strategy with
Adams meant that Hume was 'now exposed as another tribal leader whose main
asset is that he says tribal things very slowly and very quietly'.[44] His saintliness was
now openly questioned. However, the case for the defence can be put simply.
Winston Churchill famously claimed that Stanley Baldwin's policy of appease-
ment in the 1930s had put 'party before country'. Hume's supporters would say
that he did precisely the opposite and put country before party. The light of that
halo effect serves to banish all other dark thoughts about his political motivation.
And surely the end justifies the means? Is not Northern Ireland now at peace? Is
there not agreement now between the people of the island? Does this not signal
the triumph of not only constitutional nationalism but also that the banalities of
the 'single transferable speech' were nothing other than truisms? Was not Hume's
petulance and short-temper justified when his bona fides were challenged? Has he
not in the end been proved right and all his critics proved wrong? The evasive
answer to these questions, and one which happens actually to be the honest
response, is that nothing in politics is an unmixed blessing.

If that British official had not expected that after the Anglo-Irish Agreement
Hume would soon be talking to Adams, then it was not inevitable that the peace
process would deliver Sinn Féin dominance of nationalist politics in Northern
Ireland. For those unconcerned about partisanship it may not matter that the consequence of Hume's personal style of politics and his priestly horizon is that the
SDLP has now lost its position not only of political but also of moral leadership
within northern nationalism. The relationship of the personal and the political
was put concisely by Malachi O'Doherty to the late Eddie McGrady. Surely the

---

41 Ed Moloney, *Paisley*, p. 338. **42** H. Patterson, *The politics of illusion: a political history of the IRA*
(London 1997), p. 209. **43** C.C. O'Brien, *Memoir: my life and themes* (Dublin, 1998), p. 423. **44** Cited
in Murray, *John Hume and the SDLP* (1998), p. 197.

problem for the SDLP after Hume-Adams, he suggested, is that 'the SDLP wrote character references for Sinn Féin'. Did not Hume urge party members 'to accept that the IRA was not criminal'? And if he was prepared to 'play John the Baptist to Adams' Jesus' did not those voters who agreed simply take their votes to Sinn Féin?[45] Disraeli once accused his party leader, Sir Robert Peel, of catching the Whigs bathing and stealing their clothes. That is always happening in politics. One can argue that it was Sinn Féin that now stole the SDLP's political clothes but that this act of theft constitutes a decisive victory for Hume's policy. There is a more serious criticism of Hume, however, and it comes not only from without the SDLP but also from within and it is a variation on O'Doherty's point. It is that Sinn Féin did not have to steal the SDLP's moral clothes because they had been gifted already by Hume. In the long run (in which we are anyway all dead) is that important? Is it any more important than the electoral pre-eminence of the Democratic Unionist Party (DUP) among Protestants?

There is an argument that politics helps to transform party culture as well as programmes. In local conditions it means that the logic of the consociational framework of the Good Friday Agreement has now made both Sinn Féin and the DUP 'stakeholders' in the institutions and thus provides both of them with incentives to be participative rather than anti-system. That entails a choice 'between stealing their opponents' clothes and wearing them, or showing that they remain wolves in sheep's clothing'.[46] The positive judgment is that Sinn Féin and the DUP have made their choice. The outcome of that choice has imposed itself upon party politics, softening rather than hardening doctrinal positions, all misleading rhetoric to the contrary being discounted. That argument is not without its merit but there is also an 'and yet': and yet one cannot help observing that the undoubted benefits of a peaceful society notwithstanding, a certain brutalism of official political discourse has been legitimized as a consequence.

CONCLUSION

This chapter has been sceptical about McLachlan's view that Hume and the unionists talked past one another because their politics were determined by different logics. Whatever explanatory value that interpretation might have, it should not be confused with the assumption that neither party understood one another. The truth is that they understood one another all too well. As the historian A.T.Q. Stewart believed, underneath changing events 'the fundamentals of Irish history remain largely unchanged'. In a damning aside on the pieties of community rela-

45 M. O'Doherty, 'Last stoop standing?', *Fortnight*, 434 (Mar. 2005), p. 11.   46 See P. Mitchell, B. O'Leary and G. Evans, 'Northern Ireland: flanking extremists bite the moderates and emerge in their clothes', *Parliamentary Affairs*, 54:4 (2001), pp 725–42.

tions (and, perhaps, the clichés of Hume-speak), he claimed that there is no mis-understanding between nationalists and unionists in Northern Ireland. 'Nor do they need to get to know each other better. They know each other only too well, having lived alongside each other for four centuries'. In short, the contemporary political question 'is not just a clash of cultures; it is a culture in itself, a point overlooked by most observers'.[47] Knowledge, in this case, is not the kind of subtle understanding that would impress the historian, the cultural critic or the political scientist. It is not the kind of knowledge, in other words, which is an end in itself. It is instrumental knowledge concerned with means to an end. Unionists were certainly an obstacle to the achievement of Hume's political end and he knew enough about them to calculate the options of success. And those calculations were informed by his experience of the collapse of the power-sharing executive in 1974. Hume's intention was to win a political argument and not to conduct an academic seminar. He would be open to criticism for being limited and partisan in these nationalist objectives only if one really believes in his sainthood and in his possession of a horizon-less halo. If anyone should be critical of Hume it is those who share his political horizon, his former colleagues in the SDLP. That Hume put country before party is a proposition which requires serious re-examination. For it can be rephrased thus: Hume did put party before country only it wasn't the SDLP. It was Sinn Féin. Unintentional and ironic, perhaps, but it is a fact nonetheless. His relentless pursuit of personal conviction, and his conviction that his judgment was always correct, closed down options other than a peace process promoting the interests of Sinn Féin. Maybe his room for manoeuvre was limited but it is also possible that his vision was equally limited. The remarkable legacy has been a republican re-writing of history in which Hume's, and the SDLP's, contribution to peace is being systematically marginalized. Here is another irony. After years of political division, this republican revision of the past is a concern which unionists and constitutional nationalists both should share.

---

47 A.T.Q. Stewart, *The shape of Irish history* (Belfast, 2001), p. 185.

Shaping the Peace

MARK DURKAN

CHALLENGING MINDSETS

A key to understanding John Hume's sense of purpose in the Hume-Adams process, and all that went on alongside and beyond it, is to understand his own reading of history. In particular, it is important to recognize that the concentrated effort he brought to reconditioning the analyses and attitudes of the adherents of 'physical force republicanism' was not the singularly obsessive political project that some suggest betrayed a disregard for his career-long commitment to reconciliation with unionism. While he showed a resolute determination in his pursuit of a new wavelength of dialogue and understanding with those who justified the IRA violence he repudiated, he also persisted in his commitment to ensuring a broader bandwidth of partnership between divergent Irish political traditions, and between these islands.

There has been little acknowledgment by unionist politicians or commentators that large portions of his arguments in Hume-Adams – not least those shown in the 1988 SDLP papers given to Sinn Féin – proffered degrees of validity around unionist perspectives, and refused to ignore realities of history, geography and politics. The case that he was bringing was not just to challenge Sinn Féin's legitimization of IRA violence but also to confound their delegitimization of the unionist tradition.

Sinn Féin accounts of Hume-Adams also fail to reflect this dimension of the exchange, or his emphasis on the costs and consequences of the ongoing IRA campaign. Instead they represent Hume's role as one of recognizing the failure of their exclusion, as though that was a cause of the conflict, which if remedied would enable their contribution to peace.

Too many treatments of John Hume's pivotal role in the peace process portray his motive of achieving an end to violence as an end in itself. That is to overlook the concurrent mission to bring about new relationships in new agreed institutions. John's own dogged justification of Hume-Adams, in the face of heavy political challenge and intense personal criticism, has been layered into a misinterpretation that his then dismissal of unionist political objections reflected a dismissive disregard for unionism at large. His tough love message about the 1985 Anglo-Irish Agreement as a harbinger of 'unionist catharsis' and his reference then to the 'need to lance the unionist boil' had previously brought some resentment. This helped to feed the unfair misrepresentation that he was simultaneously 'legitimizing the men of violence' and 'delegitimizing' unionism.

The reality was that John Hume had seen the purposes and prospects of the Anglo-Irish Agreement as entailing important new challenges to the rationales of both political unionism, and what he called extreme nationalism's physical force tradition. This was rooted in his historical analysis that two 'solution frustrating' mindsets had been created or compounded by both the denial of Home Rule and the undermining of the Sunningdale Agreement.

Hume posited that defiance of Home Rule and Sunningdale had ingrained an attitude within political unionism, that maintaining sectarian solidarity, along with a concomitant threat of force, ensured a veto over any course that might be favoured by constitutional nationalism and agreed by Westminster. He held that Home Rule and Sunningdale, in their respective times, both reflected the will of the 'sovereign parliament' supposedly recognized by unionists, and the broad democratic will of the Irish people, yet intransigent unionism had confounded them both by its readiness to resort to force or the threat of it. Consequently, political unionism had taken this syndrome as the lesson for its default position.

In his interpretation, these same events also had a negative conditioning effect on some republican mindsets too. The lesson for them was that negotiation with the British, in pursuit of agreed change and institutional accommodation, was futile, as the British had shown that the threat or fact of unionist force trumped anything else. For him, this interpretation that 'even if you get the British to agree something, you won't get it', galvanized the mindset that repudiated nationalist constitutionalism and resorted to marshalling degrees of physical force to override prevalent British considerations and the inexorable unionist veto.

These assessments partly informed John Hume's instinctive drive for a new British-Irish framework that could confound those mindsets that militated against democratic agreement in the North and on the island. His seminal article in *Foreign Affairs* in spring 1979 reflected other historical perspectives about previous failure, where the framework for the solution had not matched the framework of the problem. He argued from there for the British and Irish governments to marshall their combined authority and legitimacy in an intergovernmental approach, which he wanted the US and Europe to encourage. This would in turn create a different context from the failed 'narrow ground' which had trapped politics in the North.

This belief that British-Irish relations could find a new plane was also based on his historical assessment that Britain's involvements and choices in Ireland had been largely conditioned by wider geo-political considerations – mainly contests with, or threats from, continental powers. Even before he became a MEP in 1979, Hume believed that common membership of the EEC could create a context for a changed relationship between Britain and Ireland. He went on to argue that the unfolding European experiences of pooling sovereignty, sharing interests in shared decisions, and relaxing borders, would also offer a new 'psychological framework' that could allow – or require – the two rival nationalisms, locked in the narrow ground of the North, to relate differently.

Such thinking infused more and more of his outlook and his output in what he eventually dubbed his 'single transferable speech'. In canvassing this new paradigm which could release us from inherited prejudices and assumptions, he was challenging both traditional unionist and nationalist outlooks to realize a new context.

It was his long-held interpretations of history that were also condensed into his constant premise that the problem was about three sets of relationships – within the North, between the different traditions and parts of the island, and between Ireland and Britain. He posited that any purported solutions to this historic problem had failed (or would fail) because they ignored one or more of these relationships and the realities attached. Again this was a double-barrelled critique, both of received unionist assertions, and nationalist assumptions (as well as an indictment of British government policy). While this was long dismissed, discounted and variably disputed by more traditionalist or defensive adherents to both outlooks, it remained his persistent theme, which was further shorthanded into the language of 'three strands'.

BIG PICTURE

As well as the long view of history, John Hume always maintained a sense of the 'big picture'. In the face of grave outrages, rights violations, provocative prejudice, frustrating failures, and so many occasions for rage or despair, he was close to obstinate about not indulging in mood politics or reacting to reaction. While abhorring violence in all its forms and from all forces, he eschewed 'the politics of the last atrocity' and 'what-aboutery'. He would always reflect that 'the underlying problem has not changed therefore the solution has not changed'. He never gave up on the essential ingredients in the SDLP's first policy document, *Towards a New Ireland* (1972), and in the Sunningdale Agreement, of power-sharing in the North and all-Ireland institutions, although he determined that the political route to these objectives required a new British-Irish axis to be established first.

The SDLP rejected Secretary of State Jim Prior's 'rolling devolution' plan in 1982. The objections were not just to its exclusion of an 'Irish dimension', or the

failure to stipulate power-sharing in the possible incremental devolution it envisaged. For Hume, the British government had totally abandoned the prospects
from the 'totality of relationships' dialogue that had begun between Haughey and
Thatcher. Having disastrously mishandled the prisons issues and the hunger
strikes, the British government were now resorting again to a fatally flawed pursuit of a 'purely internal settlement'. He shared the deep sense of party colleagues
that their constitutional nationalist engagement could not be reduced to seeking
concessionary consideration as a free-standing internal minority in the North.

While 'nationalist alienation' was understandably much talked about at that
time, it was a term whose growing currency seemed to rankle Hume who admon-
ished colleagues about the risk of a self-unwinding analysis. No part of him was
tempted into participating in the rolling devolution scenario, even to prove its
inherent futility. He and his SDLP colleagues saw the trap of dead end choices for
them in that assembly plan. To take part in the exercise, and hold out for power-
sharing, would inevitably lead to intransigence, recrimination and a sense of failure. Moreover, to subscribe cross-community support to a tranche of rolling
devolution which would then be exercised on a majority rule basis would lead
inexorably to failure and frustration.

He also worried that an apparently purely abstentionist stance could be
recruited by others to portray the dead end futility of constitutionalism per se, and
capitalize on such visible evidence of complete alienation as added justification for
physical force over democratic engagement. The Home Rule and Sunningdale
messages for physical force advocates could appear to be endorsed by the SDLP
succumbing to any of the three dead ends which the plan entailed.

Wary of the language around alienation, he fully felt the sense of it and recognized the risks. One of the risks to which he was personally alert was the danger of a
newly compounded sense of alienation between northern nationalists and the South.
He was mindful that the broadly cross-party consensus of the main southern parties,
attuned with the SDLP, would not fully extend to the decision to be made on the
'Prior Assembly', if that was portrayed as the only constitutional show in town.

While he probably underestimated the potential electoral momentum for Sinn
Féin following their 1981 entry on to the electoral field, alongside their support for
armed struggle, he did not see their challenge as confined to the SDLP or the
North. There certainly could not be a purely northern response to whatever challenges their electoralism, alongside support for violence, brought.

NEW IRELAND FORUM

These were all considerations in Hume's proposal to have a Council for a New
Ireland, for which the SDLP would seek its alternative mandate in the assembly

election of 1982. This was realized as the New Ireland Forum which comprised representatives of the SDLP, Fine Gael, Fianna Fáil and Irish Labour. Meeting in Dublin Castle the forum's sessions helped to assert the sense that those whom the SDLP represented were part of the larger Irish body politic, and not just a detached internal minority in the North. It was not that symbolism mattered to Hume; but he conceived a substantive opportunity to develop a modern coherent constitutional nationalist understanding, which could underpin repudiation of republican violence, and simultaneously underwrite a new challenge, or offer, to unionists and the British.

In his contributions to the forum, John Hume typically refracted history to bring out different interpretations from the given positions and perceptions. In all the attention that focused on the forum report's three options of unitary state, federal/confederal state or joint authority, some missed the importance of Hume's fourth option, of anything else that might be agreed by democratic negotiation with unionism and the British. The forum's authoritative appraisal of the costs of violence became a buttress for further cogency in Hume's arguments as to the real impact of armed struggle. The affirmation of the principle of consent did not win it an audience in either unionism or militant republicanism, but would eventually prove to have produced significant coinage for future currency.

Other treatments will address more fully and authoritatively the great journey of work through the forum to the Anglo-Irish Agreement. While he lamented the crassness of what Garret FitzGerald called Margaret Thatcher's 'gratuitously offensive' rejection of the forum report's substantive options, John Hume did not get seized by indignation, but took care not to feed that mood, and he supported the resilient perseverance by the Taoiseach and his officials in developing discussions with the British government. This reflected his own belief that his fourth option, that is, that parties should enter negotiations to seek agreement, was the pertinent prospect, and the fact that Thatcher had made a point of stopping to tell him that, outside of the three options, she was committed to getting agreement with Dublin.

ANGLO-IRISH AGREEMENT

While full of appreciation for FitzGerald's application to achieving the 1985 Anglo-Irish Agreement, John did not like any line of argument that suggested something was needed to help the SDLP. It was not just being party precious that he disliked inferences about a crutch for the SDLP. Rather it was because he really did believe that the agreement, if Thatcher adhered to it in the face of unionist opposition, would change the context, and move mindsets in intransigent unionism and physical force republicanism.

He would make the point that, unlike Home Rule and Sunningdale, we could be looking at the 'unionist veto' over other British-Irish choices being trumped. If that happened, he held that a catharsis within unionism would lead to a necessary adjustment to not having all power in its own hands. He gave equal significance to the agreement's potential to refute the residual rationale for armed struggle, given the agreement's international status, the import of the British government's undertaking to facilitate a united Ireland by consent, and the seismic significance if London faced down political unionism's attempts to mobilize their previous veto.

This was not just the rationale he shared with party colleagues and suggestively aired in more public debate. It was a strong part of his argument to the Friends of Ireland in the US whom he persuaded to support the principle, then the prospect, and then the fact of a new British-Irish framework. He sold it to them not as an end or settlement in itself, or as mainly or solely a development that could lead to future and better dialogue between unionists and nationalists. The strong conviction he shared with them was that it could also serve to recondition the fixed and repeated arguments for armed struggle that sustained dreadful violence in Ireland, and whose inflated currency in the Irish-American constituency they were very conscious of.

When he assigned me to work in Senator Edward Kennedy's office in the summer/autumn of 1985, John gave me a brief to lobby other congressional offices to be ready to support a new agreement between the two governments with a new fund. Speaker Tip O'Neill's office, with his own direct personal commitment, orchestrated that lobby. It was clear to me that Kennedy, O'Neill, Moynihan and others were less taken with the prospective economic contributions of the fund and more seized of the potential of a new agreement to transform the arguments around the use of physical force and the British role in Ireland.

This was politically tested when Taoiseach Charles Haughey opposed the Anglo-Irish Agreement and sent Brian Lenihan to Washington to lobby Irish-American politicians against supporting it. Kennedy, O'Neill et al. stuck with Hume's read of events when they were asked to decide between Garret's stance and Charlie's. The persuasive factor was not the transactional construct of new inter-governmental arrangements, or the transformative impact that the International Fund for Ireland could have on some areas. It was their belief in Hume's argument that this could unfold a transfiguration from conflict and stalemate, towards his oft-advocated essential scenario of dialogue – free from violence – which could lead to an agreement which should threaten no one, and shared institutions which would allow a longer healing process.

In the House of Commons debate on the agreement, Hume deployed his familiar structured reasoning, seasoned with historical perspective. In the charged atmosphere of the unionists' 'Ulster Says No' campaign, more attention was being paid to how he thought unionism needed to respond to the prospect of their veto

being faced down, than to the adjusted understanding he also called for in traditional nationalist thinking. He cited the sixth century Convention of Druim
Ceatt, and St Columba's judgment on the vexed issue of whether those in the Irish
portion of the kingdom of Dal Riada owed tribute to the High King of Ireland or
the King of Argyll – his answer was 'let them pay tribute to both'. Hume later
alluded to that same historical context (and others) in the 1988 exchanges between
the SDLP and Sinn Féin. In the 11 July 1988 *SDLP response to questions raised in
discussion and in previous Sinn Féin papers* he included the following paragraph:

> In addition it seems to us to reveal a deep misunderstanding of the Ulster
> Protestant tradition to suggest that it is largely the British influence and not
> their own choice and their own reasons that make them wish to live apart
> from the rest of the people of Ireland. Do we not accept whether we like it
> or not that they have deep seated and deeply felt reasons of their own based
> on many historical factors for their differences; differences which go back
> beyond partition, beyond even the Plantation, differences which were vis-
> ible as far back as the 6th century? To underestimate the task of really
> accommodating the diversity of the Irish people is to really intensify our
> central problem and to continue to push difference to the point of division.

HUME–ADAMS

Many of the arguments Hume posited publicly after the Anglo-Irish Agreement
proved to be trailers for much of his later Hume-Adams discourse. These also
drew on the work of the New Ireland Forum, not least with updated critiques of
the cost of violence, and the relative burden of victimization attributable to republican paramilitaries as compared with their own rhetorical narrative. Those of us
working with John were not sure what weight to attach to apparently incidental
Donegal soundings between Belfast solicitor Paddy McCrory and himself on the
possibility of him talking to Gerry Adams, but it was clear that John was starting
to wonder if seemingly new tones from Sinn Féin signalled a possible reappraisal
or a new example of Orwellian presentation.

It was in early 1987 that Fr Alec Reid approached John under the cloak of the
Clonard Peace Mission, which was led by Fr Reid and colleagues at the
Redemptorist monastery at Clonard. John seemed open to exploring a possible
engagement with the Sinn Féin leadership, seeing this as a logical extension of the
case he was making publicly about the primacy of dialogue, the futility of violence, and the changing context afforded by the Anglo-Irish Agreement and wider
European change. He was circumspect about some of the apparently laden language Fr Reid was deploying, and wondered if there was a reliable foundation for

useful discourse. With a Westminster election expected within months, and the ongoing chill from unionist politicians still in protest over the Anglo-Irish Agreement, he was wary that talks at that point might be exposed to revelation and compound misrepresentation. His response was to agree to personal inter-party dialogue after the general election, and to continue to liaise with Fr Reid on framing the dialogue in the meantime.

In that interim, he was not very taken by the clunky *Scenario for Peace* released by Sinn Féin, but he allowed himself some encouragement that the wrong look-ing direction might be part of a long, clumsy, multiple point turn. He also took some working confidence from the fact that the prospective dialogue, via the Redemptorist priests at Clonard, had neither been leaked nor pre-empted with stunt offers or calls from Sinn Féin. However, he was having some misgivings about the intensity and weight of expectations inherent in some exploratory papers from Fr Reid at that time, even while being continually impressed by his driven application. Even a consummate politician found it hard to argue carefully with someone invoking the Holy Spirit with both regularity and conviction.

Indeed, John's feedback from the first meetings with Gerry Adams suggested that he found Adams ready to engage at a more exploratory pace than Fr Reid had suggested to both of them for more public presentation. While not one hundred per cent sure of the Sinn Féin leadership's preparedness to move towards a purely political approach free from IRA force, Hume was clear that the Clonard Peace Mission was an opportunity to test for new thinking, and that he had a personal responsibility to take it as far as he could.

When he asked me to go to Clonard as part of a 'seconds' channel in August 1987, he cautioned me not to be put off by Fr Reid sounding like he was asking for the SDLP to submit to a dialogue which would be premised on Sinn Féin's outlook, but to focus on a willingness for dialogue where each party could bring their respective analyses. In a quasi-tutorial mode Fr Alec would stress the need to be sensitive to the experiences and perceptions of Sinn Féin's and the IRA's bases, while I had to contend that the valid views of other 'bases' also had to respected if dialogue was going to be meaningful and carry support from people.

Fr Reid was very seized of the importance and value of public engagement between the leaderships of Sinn Féin and the SDLP in allowing republicans to have a starting point other than their exclusion and the futility of conventional political courses. The sooner the SDLP and the Irish government could be shown to be subscribing to the principle of self-determination in the same terms as 'republicans', he contended strongly, the sooner people could be persuaded that there was an alternative to armed struggle. He was not overly impressed by cau-tion that the use of violence might then be portrayed as the inevitable conse-quence of previous political delinquency by constitutional nationalism. However, he did acknowledge the concern that a reluctance to conform to a future Sinn

Féin position could be represented as undermining the basis of a non-violent IRA/Sinn Féin strategy, thereby giving the latter an assumed whip over others based on the threat of some reverting to violence. (This was typical of what was to become a recurring default argument over the course of the process.)

John Hume's response was not just to be wary of a superficial 'pan-nationalist' presentation as an apparent precondition for Sinn Féin leaders commending an alternative to violence. While able to justify those reservations on a number of grounds, he tended instead to concentrate on the goal of such a persuasion which, to be sustainable, would require factors more durable than constitutional nationalism appearing to now adhere to Sinn Féin's terms. It seemed to me that he believed, from those early meetings with Adams and Fr Reid, that together they could frame a context where the Sinn Féin leadership could bring about a renunciation of violence by the IRA; this, he believed, could also be the context for the wider dialogue and agreement with unionists and the British, which he held to be essential for a solution. I sensed from Fr Reid that his impatience with the reluctance to declare a new nationalist/republican axis gave way to his stronger belief that John Hume was very committed to the potential and purpose of the dialogue, and that the Hume-Adams chemistry (with his help) was developing well. He still made the case for a public dimension to the dialogue, so that key constituencies could think and talk differently. Perhaps for differing reasons, John Hume and Gerry Adams agreed that their private dialogue should widen to inter-party talks between the SDLP and Sinn Féin, with a public profile. For Fr Reid, the shocking series of events – and dangerous emotions in response to – Gibraltar, Milltown and the killing of two British Army corporals, added a real weight of obligation and moment to the Sinn Féin-SDLP engagement.[1]

The wider 1988 SDLP-Sinn Féin talks saw both parties test each other's analyses, assumptions and arguments around:

- self-determination,
- the rationale for armed struggle,
- the viability or legitimacy of constitutional approaches,
- whether the character of Britain's historic role in Ireland was changed or changing in the modern context,
- the roles, rights and reasons of unionists.

The papers exchanged then, and published when those talks ended the following September, show that John Hume tried both to take some of Sinn Féin's own

---

1 In March 1988, three IRA members were killed by British undercover agents as they reconnoitred the location for a bomb attack on British military personnel stationed in Gibraltar. Their funerals at Belfast's Milltown cemetery were attacked by a loyalist gunman who killed three mourners. At the funeral of one the slain mourners in West Belfast two British Army personnel who had mistakenly driven into the cortege were dragged from their car and murdered. Fr Reid who was present ministered to them in their dying moments.

1 John Hume graduate

3 John Hume at Stormont rally calling for the new university to be sited in Derry, along with Mayor Albert Anderson and Eddie McAteer MP

2 John Hume with students meeting President de Valera at Áras an Uachtaráin

4 John Hume with crew filming *A City Solitary* in 1964
5 John Hume with Taoiseach Jack Lynch

6 John Hume, Gerry Fitt, Austin Currie and Paddy Devlin
at early SDLP press conference
7 John Hume assisted from civil rights demonstration

8 John Hume at sit-down protest against internment without trial
9 John Hume with SDLP colleagues Hugh Logue (left) and Ivan Cooper (right) under British Army arrest following anti-internment rally

10 John Hume and colleague ministers and officials
of the 1974 power-sharing executive
11 John Hume addressing SDLP annual conference

12 John Hume, Leader and Séamus Mallon, Deputy Leader of SDLP
13 John Hume with Taoiseach Garret FitzGerald, Chair Colm Ó hEocha,
Opposition Leader Charles Haughey, and Tánaiste Dick Spring
at opening of New Ireland Forum.

14 John Hume with President Reagan, Speaker Tip O'Neill
and Senator Edward Kennedy

15 John Hume and Ian Paisley
16 John Hume with Taoiseach Albert Reynolds and Gerry Adams
following IRA ceasefire

17 John Hume with President Clinton in Derry
18 John Hume and SDLP colleagues, Good Friday 1998

19 John Hume, Bono and David Trimble following Good Friday Agreement

20 John Hume displays Nobel Peace Prize medal and certificate

21 John Hume addresses audience following presentation of Nobel Peace Prize

22 President Clinton with John and Pat Hume

23 John Hume meets the Dali Lama

24 John Hume and President Nelson Mandela

25 The Hume family

given premises and carry them over a different course of experience and logic, and also to offer some new premises that allowed and required new approaches. While he made the moral argument against violence in the late twentieth century, he knew that it would be idle to rest on it. He sought to uproot the rationale that IRA violence was a legitimate response to an illegitimate British presence. He challenged their reliance on 'theological' or 'academic' arguments about the abrogation of self-determination, which ignored realities of difference among the people of Ireland, and excused the excesses and counter-productive effects of violence. While key arguments are repeated throughout the papers, they carry new nuances and reflect the flavour of some of the oral exchanges in the meetings between party delegations.

History was recruited in a number of his arguments. As well as the previously quoted example of St Columba's advice at Druim Ceatt, he invoked Wolfe Tone and Parnell to highlight divisions among the people that predated partition, and which needed to be conciliated if we were to have a united people. He further cited the leaders of the 1916 uprising in Dublin, Patrick Pearse and James Connolly, who had decided on surrender to avoid further suffering being inflicted on citizens of the city. In his recollections of these meetings John gave examples of arguments about the current nature of the British role in Ireland. John and colleagues could concur with Sinn Féin that strategic and economic interests had motivated much of Britain's historic behaviour in Ireland. However, they argued that such considerations had changed and were further diminishing in the modern context of European integration, with the North having had no strategic significance in the Cold War, which was itself already being replaced by new East-West relationships. Sinn Féin had apparently then argued that Britain was definitively serving her own economic interests by its occupation of the North. They reasoned that the financial subvention was to afford the British economy a market it could dominate not just in the North but on the whole island. John pointed out that under that thinking the single European market would mean Britain would be subsidizing this market for continental economies.

His strongest arguments were for the historic significance of the Anglo-Irish Agreement, and the SDLP continually emphasized its import. This is reflected in the SDLP 5 September statement on the end of the talks:

> The SDLP has asserted that in Article 1 of the Anglo-Irish Agreement, an internationally binding agreement, the British government have removed the traditional republican justification for the use of violence. In that article … the British government have made clear that if the people of the unionist and nationalist traditions in Ireland reach agreement on the unity and independence of Ireland, then the British government will legislate for it, facilitate it, and leave the people of Ireland, North and South, to govern

themselves. In short, they are stating that Irish unity and independence are entirely a matter for those Irish people who want it persuading those Irish people who don't. It is clear from Article 1 and the Preamble to the Agreement that the British government have no other interest at stake in the exercise of Irish self-determination except that violence or the threat of violence shall not succeed. In this context the 'armed struggle' can only be a negative factor. The SDLP has not convinced Sinn Féin that this is the British position, but we would pose a question to every member of the Provisional Republican Movement … If the SDLP is correct, that this is the British position, do you agree that it removes the stated justification for the 'armed struggle' of the Provisional IRA?

For John Hume, getting acceptance of this case was then a compelling requirement. In meetings with governments or others, he would refer to the flow and weight of these arguments in the SDLP-Sinn Féin talks. In particular, he subsequently encouraged Peter Brooke, who was showing himself to be a secretary of state of some purpose, empathy and insight, to give authoritative British voice to the case made in the SDLP's 11 July 1988 paper:

> The second relates to our stated belief that Britain has no interest of her own in remaining in Ireland, that she has no strategic, military or economic interests and that if the Irish people reached agreement among themselves on, for example, Irish Unity that Britain would facilitate it, legislate for it and leave the Irish to govern themselves.

Peter Brooke articulated such words in what was seen as a surprising keynote speech in London in November 1990. The same words were incorporated in the later Hume-Adams document, which was really a draft declaration to be made by the Prime Minister and Taoiseach jointly. They then, of course, featured prominently in the actual Downing Street Declaration of December 1993, which strongly reflected the Hume-Adams draft, along with additional paragraphs addressing loyalist and unionist sensibilities, which drew on discussions between Archbishop Eames and others with loyalist and unionist representatives.

John Hume later recorded, in his lecture at Leeds Metropolitan University, that his effort had been to get the British to make explicit what Sinn Féin were dismissing as merely implicit according to the SDLP. It should be noted that he encouraged that message from Peter Brooke at the same time as supporting the Secretary of State's efforts to frame a talks process in which unionist parties would engage, moving beyond their 'Ulster Says No' boycott mode.

It also needs to be remembered that John Hume's dialogue with Gerry Adams and Fr Reid had not stopped with the end of the SDLP-Sinn Féin talks. Few had recognized the signal in the 5 September 1988 statement: 'The SDLP hopes and expects that the debate on these crucial issues which has begun will continue in the public and private arena ...' The Hume-Adams dialogue which continued with Fr Reid's committed cultivation, also involved the Irish government. Taoiseach Charles Haughey engaged directly with both Hume and Fr Reid, with Haughey's adviser Martin Mansergh helping to develop and refine the wording of the Hume-Adams document.

TOWARDS COMPREHENSIVE DIALOGUE

Crafting a possible joint declaration by British and Irish premiers which could be used as a definitive basis for a definitive ceasefire had become the key focus of the Hume-Adams effort. Fr Reid's travels and travails with each adjusted draft, as individual words or tenses were modified and fine-tuned, showed his belief not just that Sinn Féin leaders could be enabled to secure a ceasefire, but that John Hume might also be right about the possibilities of a wider, more inclusive process. While the burden of Fr Reid's efforts had originally been on achieving joint declarations, fronts or working axes spanning nationalism-republicanism, the key now was a more comprehensive and ambitious scenario. Both he and Sinn Féin, separately and differently, would still continue to press and test for measures or gestures of pan-nationalism, no longer as essential preconditions, but rather as additional political collateral to reinforce the appeal of an unarmed alternative strategy.

This graduation had not just come from the content of the Hume-Adams dialogue, but in the context of other unfolding processes which were well shepherded by Peter Brooke, and well-served by the Irish government too. Brooke's work to achieve a format where the unionist parties would be in talks with the SDLP, Alliance and the Irish government as well as the British was concurrent with his signals to Sinn Féin-IRA that they and the British government might find new ways of regarding each other. He clearly shared a belief with John Hume (albeit one that they might express differently) that the givens of the post-Anglo-Irish Agreement environment could now induce unionists to consider a talks agenda they had previously eschewed, and also persuade violent republicanism to turn a corner. The Irish government was equally aware of the nature of the continuing Hume-Adams engagement, and was also keen to achieve inter-party talks where the unionist parties would negotiate with both governments and all other parties.

Some have suggested that Hume must have believed that Hume-Adams was the only game in town in the early nineties, and that he was somehow averse to prospects in the Brooke, and subsequently Mayhew, talks. However, even more deeply than either government, Hume was seized by the possibilities that could stem from both processes of dialogue – not least because the format for the Brooke talks fitted squarely on his 'three sets of relationships/three strands' analysis, but also because both governments, as he had long advocated, were to be essential players and partners. When the very agenda was such an achievement for his long-held approach, why would he be cold to such talks? Having deflected urges for pan-nationalism, and having emphasized to Sinn Féin the essential requirement for respecting, engaging and reconciling with unionists, and having continually contended that unionists' abhorrence of the Anglo-Irish Agreement would adjust to grounds for new negotiations, John Hume saw what became the Brooke/Mayhew talks as a key opportunity for new understanding.

He felt that all these factors should obviate any likely anxieties from Sinn Féin that such talks would lead to the SDLP succumbing to an 'internal settlement' approach, which had been a stated fear of theirs after the Anglo-Irish Agreement. His efforts during the Brooke talks to achieve an 'international' chair and a non-Stormont venue (Armagh) for the Strand 2 negotiations, and to ensure that both London and Dublin would host some Strand 3 talks, were partly to assist in countering any such misperceptions.

I was one of the few who were privy to the fact that Hume-Adams was in train at the same time as the Brooke/Mayhew process. It was clear to me that John saw them both as necessary, compatible and potentially complementary. It seemed to be about building layers of understanding in both dialogue channels so that a convergence could be achieved. There was obviously potential tension in trying to ensure that the SDLP did not adopt language or propositions in either channel that could confound or be seen to contradict understandings in the other. Without breaching the supposed confidentiality of the Brooke/Mayhew talks, a large portion of my conversations with Fr Reid at this time were about reinforcing assurance on that account. He usually seemed content, but was still concerned that diligence might be overtaken by political optics. (It was only with later media revelations that John Hume (and I) came to know that the British government had moved to provide Sinn Féin with some tracking briefs on the Stormont talks.)

BROOKE/MAYHEW TALKS

John Hume had been wont in the exchanges with Sinn Féin to refer to a cited reality 'whether we like it or not'. Similarly, when inter-party dialogue started in the Brooke/Mayhew process he stressed the importance of all of us recognizing each others' realities 'whether we like them or not'. Indeed he pushed for parties to try to agree 'realities' about our situation, and then to try to agree 'requirements' for a solution based on those realities. Because *Realities and Requirements* was deemed to be Hume-speak, the paper that the parties eventually agreed was headed *Themes and Principles.* It was not only compatible with everything the SDLP had argued or agreed with Sinn Féin, but it would be in line with the terms of the Hume-Adams proposals for a joint declaration by the British and Irish premiers.

It is also significant that the same Hume proposition that a negotiated agreement should be put to referendum, North and South on the same day, was tabled in both the SDLP-Sinn Féin talks in 1988 and in Brooke/Mayhew. He said in 1988 that the argument with Sinn Féin, who resiled from the idea, had run around self-determination, democratic validation, partitionism and the unionist veto. Nevertheless he remained convinced of the power and potential of the concept of such articulated self-determination by this generation of the Irish people validating agreed institutions and invalidating violence in any cause. Unionist parties then also resiled from agreeing the idea in Brooke/Mayhew, mainly citing concerns about a perceived southern veto on self-determination by the people of Northern Ireland. However, they acknowledged the motive and rationale behind the proposition and indicated that in a context of a possible agreement they could look at its potential merits and their concerns again.

When it came to proposed institutions in Brooke/Mayhew, Hume was conscious of not prejudicing the terms of the understandings in Hume-Adams, but also of the particular danger, from the SDLP's perspective, of the talks becoming embedded in Strand 1, with Strand 2 being deferred or dimmed. John was clear that Mayhew was no Brooke: Mayhew made it equally clear that he did not share Brooke's regard for Hume's outlook.

On an evening in Inishowen, John told me that the SDLP's proposals for Strand 1 would include 'a commission' of three people directly elected across one constituency who would form and oversee the executive administration alongside, and accountable to, an elected legislative assembly. The difference from the Sunningdale coalition model seemed to carry a number of considerations. An executive formed by assembly coalition numbers could prove vulnerable to volatility in other elections, as happened to the power-sharing executive after the February 1974 general election. A voluntary coalition model would be seen as casting some parties only in an opposition role, with consequences of diminished buy-in in a referendum and subsequent outright opposition. He confirmed that he had Sinn Féin in mind in this thinking but, at least as pertinently, also the DUP. Indeed when British ministers subsequently voiced doubts about any possible unionist interest in the model, John Hume countered that Ian Paisley might not rule it out. He pointed out that Paisley would fancy his prospects of topping the poll, as in European Parliament elections. He then observed that Ian Paisley would always oppose anything where he was not on top, but would be different where he might be number one!

It is important to register that the idea of directly electing three people to form the administration was the first proposal for elective inclusion by mandate in executive office. The SDLP's later proposals in the 1996–8 talks, for an executive appointed by d'Hondt, carried the same essential elective inclusion principle to a more open, less stilted level. So contrary to various accounts, the thinking for a model other than a negotiated 'voluntary' coalition did not start with Sinn Féin's entry to talks, or the Blair or Ahern governments.

Of course, unionists scoffed at the overall 'commissioners' proposal, deploring the impression of an 'international' rather than 'internal' solution. However, a delegated sub-committee from the four parties in the 1992 talks produced and proofed an outline paper (without prejudice and full of 'coulds') to be tabled for 'plenary' negotiation that clearly posited the option of a directly elected 'panel' of three alongside an assembly. This paper was not actually subjected to plenary negotiation by party principals, some of whom had differing reasons for not wanting to be drawn into such detailed Strand 1 modelling at that point.

This episode was subsequently cited by unionist politicians, after the Hume-Adams dialogue came to public notice again in the spring of 1993, as John Hume having vetoed a possible four-party agreement or scuppered those talks. Their further insinuation, also carried in some academic writing, was that he had abandoned those four party prospects in favour of the Hume-Adams process. None of the later versions of this narrative highlight that the draft 'there could be' paper was exactly transposed as the Strand 1 paper in the *Framework Documents* from the two governments in February 1995.

It was true that John Hume had not expected a draft paper to be 'pre-negotiated' in the talks sub-committee, which shadowed his own original proposal for electing three executive principals outside of, but accountable to, a legislative assembly. His reservations about the plenary negotiations to follow had as much to do with his concern to have the Strand 2 (and 3) talks started. He was worried that, in the time-limited period[2] set aside for the talks, there was a risk of all the concentration by other parties and the British government falling on building a putative Strand 1 model. In the context of the concurrent Hume-Adams dialogue he was self-conscious about ending up appearing to be talks-locked into the realms of purely internal settlement. While he expressed tactical misgivings quite graphically to party colleagues, however, he did not exercise a veto on the negotiations or upend the talks.

As it happened, Jim Molyneaux was particularly lukewarm about negotiating more substantively on devolved powers and structures at that time. The subgroup's paper was banked without designation and without formal plenary debate. Hume and Molyneaux then personally brokered an understanding on moving the talks into Strands 2 and 3, including sessions in both Dublin and London.

---

2 Unionists had only agreed to the talks provided they took place in the intervals between meetings of the Inter-governmental Council. Protracted discussion on procedural matters had exhausted much of the time available for substantive dialogue.

TOWARDS CEASEFIRE

John Hume was not aware during this time that the NIO were providing some level of insight to Sinn Féin on these talks. I subsequently reflected on Fr Reid's communications at that time, and his ongoing cautions against an internal settlement, or producing an outcome without Sinn Féin being engaged in all-party talks. He would also point out that all-party talks should include an all-Ireland level, to be consistent with lines suggested in earlier SDLP-Sinn Féin exchanges, and options being canvassed in the dialogue channels that he was tending. My assumption was that he was maintaining this contact as part of his 'constant gardener' approach, and showing some general insight from Irish government sources.

As someone directly involved in those Stormont sub-group talks, I was fully aware of the ongoing Hume-Adams discussion, sometimes with shared journeys to or from our respective encounters. I understood that Hume believed that both exercises were about building the basis for future shared negotiations and the class of agreed outcome which he believed could only be achieved from such fuller dialogue. The challenge was to ensure that there could be convergence achieved, not just within the respective political channels but between them. For him it was about building layers of understanding and creating the context of dialogue in the absence of violence, where parties and governments would agree new institutions on that firm new ground. This would summarize the personal briefing I gave Dick Spring, as new Tánaiste and Minister for Foreign Affairs, in early 1993, when he sounded me on disparate talks processes on which he had been officially briefed, and on John's strategy and wider prospects.

The inter-party exchanges in Brooke/Mayhew included unionists upcasting the earlier Hume-Adams and SDLP-Sinn Féin talks, with John and colleagues defending the rationale. He and we contended that inclusive dialogue with violence ended could work to produce a workable agreement across the three strands. A strong burden of the unionist challenge to this line centred on questioning the quality or reliability of a ceasefire, even if one was achieved, and the sense of threat that could attach to such negotiations. John's repeated stipulation of 'no guns on the table, under the table or outside the door!' did not convince them.

So John Hume did not abort the Brooke/Mayhew process because of the Hume-Adams agenda. Nor did he regard those talks as a failure, which then propelled him anew into the Hume-Adams scenario. Hume was careful, in the ongoing tuning of the Hume-Adams text for joint declaration by the Taoiseach and the Prime Minister, to ensure that nothing contradicted any of the understandings expressed during the Brooke/Mayhew talks.

The media revelation in April 1993 of meetings between Gerry Adams and John Hume brought adverse commentary, unionist complaint and also a lot of nationalist questioning, North and South. The reaction was toned in shock, anger or bewilderment. Loyalists and unionists ratcheted up allegations around a pan-nationalist front, with loyalist paramilitaries in renewed targeting against and physically threatening SDLP figures. As in the earlier Hume-Adams phase, there was particular anguish in some victims' voices. For some, the revelation that such talks were not a new initiative but ongoing was more troubling than reassuring, given the continuing IRA violence. All the obvious real and rhetorical questions were hurled at John and the SDLP. Over the course of that year, Hume was sub-jected to constant vilification by columnists in the *Sunday Independent*; other com-mentators in the North and Britain also joined the impugnment. But the messages of support for John, trust in his motives and the integrity of his non-violent prin-ciples also came through.

Some party colleagues had been previously briefed on the bones of the then-drafts from Hume-Adams. But even they were taken aback by the reaction and mischaracterization following the re-surfacing of the dialogue. This included obvi-ous misgivings about Sinn Féin's soundings on it all. Hume's response to col-leagues' acknowledged concerns was to recap on the issues in the original SDLP-Sinn Féin talks, to re-assure them that the efforts on a joint declaration were consistent with positions offered in the other inter-party talks, and to read out from the most recent draft version of it.

Colleagues were encouraged that the text they heard corroborated John's case. Their misgivings centred on trying to understand how Adams could be sincerely working on the logic of such an approach while justifying the violence of the IRA, including arguably new lows, such as Warrington only weeks earlier,[3] and sustain-ing other Sinn Féin rhetoric. The questions were not about John's motives but the purposes and capacity of others. There were also questions about how an outcome to Hume-Adams might be expressed, and various impressions of possible British and unionist responses. Séamus Mallon, while critically cautioning on key points of presentation and of substance, spoke of the need to be prepared to take this right down to the wire in difficult conditions. John also repeated, by way of reas-surance, that if this initiative failed or proved folly, he would personally take the consequences, and not the party. (This became the form, with varying emphases, for subsequent SDLP leadership meetings.)

The heated political response to the talks' revelation from 10 April, and the variable public reception, made a case for a joint statement to confirm the nature of the dialogue and affirm its purpose for peace. Hume's concern was to offer assurances on the intent and content of the talks to those who had genuine mis-givings, and to rebut the more partisan critics. Fr Reid, who liked the idea of joint lines from the two leaders and their potential resonance, was very keen for a declaratory message that would get across the sense of what was being seriously

3 An IRA bomb in Warrington, England, on 20 March killed two young children and injured many more.

worked on. His response to sensitivity that the terms of such a statement should avoid misrepresentation about a pan-nationalist front was 'and what would be so wrong with that?'

When John phoned me from one of his discussions with Gerry Adams and Fr Reid to read a draft statement, I knew by the way he asked me to listen to and transcribe parts of it that he wanted a second opinion because he had some anxiety. He readily accepted the observation that, while the draft had obvious lines from the SDLP book, the weight of its particular words on self-determination could be read as him now subscribing to a Sinn Féin view on which we had shown clearly qualified differences in the 1988 papers. I was also concerned that the draft seemed to be advertising the significance of their own agreement, and little recognizing the requirements for wider agreements. When he rang for the amendments I drafted, he suggested further nuancing in a way that indicated he was glad to have employed a sounding option. He called later to confirm that they had agreed on the changes but 'new dispensation' (which was borrowing from the South African process) would appear instead as 'new peaceful and democratic accord'.

The 24 April Hume-Adams statement should have had the effect of allaying some genuine concerns and rebutting more fevered insinuations. While the language may have been more qualified than he would have ventured, Fr Reid seemed content that it would serve not just to rally some belief in the point and prospect of negotiation. For him, too, the fact and measure of such a joint statement could help the Holy Spirit move the governments towards the sort of declaration that would be required from them. John tried to use the statement's terms to reassure and rebut as required in the face of ongoing public, political and personal questioning, but this did not stem the sharply personalized invective. With the IRA's bombing at London's Bishopsgate happening at the same time it was not easy to get a hearing for the real import of their dialogue.

> ... we accept that an internal settlement is not a solution because it obviously does not deal with all the relationships at the heart of the problem. We accept that the Irish people as a whole have a right to national self-determination. This is a view shared by a majority of the people of this island though not by all its people. The exercise of self-determination is a matter for agreement between the people of Ireland. It is the search for that agreement and the means of achieving it on which we will be concentrating. We are mindful that not all the people of Ireland share that view or agree on how to give meaningful expression to it. Indeed we do not disguise the different views held by our own parties. As leaders of our respective parties we have told each other that we see the task of reaching agreement on a peaceful and democratic accord for all on this island as our primary challenge. We both recognize that such a new agreement is only

achievable and viable if it can earn and enjoy the allegiance of the different traditions on this island, by accommodating diversity and providing for national reconciliation.

While the concept of possible Hume-Adams proposals was now in common political parlance, none of this revealed that they were really drafting an intended joint declaration, not for themselves but for the British Prime Minister and the Taoiseach. Both governments were fully aware of this but for their own reasons did little to reflect this or relieve any of the excoriating criticism that was being heaped on Hume. The mixture of challenge, expectation and confusion in the public mood might have tempted John to let the public know what he had shared with party colleagues. But this would have shop-soiled the key elements of the plan for a joint declaration.

Their draft terms for that declaration, aka the Hume-Adams paper, were agreed by late spring/early summer. By agreement, John Hume had given this to Downing Street by June. Similarly, the Irish government had the final agreed Hume-Adams text into which they already had input via Martin Mansergh. The purpose now was that the two governments should concentrate on working together to bring the project of a joint declaration forward (to herald a ceasefire and subsequent inclusive negotiations). So over the summer months, in the face of mounting criticism, continuing IRA activity, and loyalist violence claiming it was targeted at a pan-nationalist front, John Hume was defending his talks with Adams as though they still had not reached a working conclusion, while the governments were conveying detachment. John was getting impatient at the lack of clear feedback from the governments. He was reflecting uncertainty he was hearing from Gerry Adams and Fr Reid respectively, that the reputed strong personal relationship between Albert Reynolds and John Major might not be enough to produce what was needed.

He told me at my wedding reception on 10 September that the three of them, Hume, Adams and Reid, had agreed that it should be made public that their talks had agreed a paper that was now with the governments. I thought this was right and only advised that it be done when John was in the country to field the reaction, and not when he was due to be in America. That was not quite how it worked out, resulting not just in the manner of John's announcement on the way to the United States being questioned, but some government sources suggesting no paper had been given.

The predictable mixed reaction ensued. The correspondence of support to John was growing even while the political and media criticism increased. The personal and emotional pressure on John and Pat Hume was palpable. This took on a bigger and deeper order following the IRA's murderous Shankill bomb massacre, the reactions to Gerry Adams carrying the bomber's coffin, and then the Greysteel massacre by loyalists.[4] John could feel all the pain and anger from these outrages, much of which was being directed at him. He could not easily hide his own emotions as he received thoughtful messages of encouragement alongside the understandable outrage.

His personal working aphorism that the problem had not changed, so the solution had not changed, was once again applied in testing circumstances. There seemed to be strains in the normally tight channels between John and the Irish government when Albert Reynolds replied in an interview that there was no way that the two governments could accept Hume-Adams. This and other impressions of detachment from the Hume proposition at this juncture evoked popular reaction, including among Fianna Fáil grass roots whose positive feelings towards Hume were manifest at their annual conference in November. John's office was contacted with the message that the Taoiseach had omitted the word 'simply' before 'accept', which had been in his prepared line to take. We established that similar reassurance was offered to Fr Reid. In subsequent comments and interviews Albert sought to assure that the two governments could, in Séamus Mallon's words, 'take the ball and run with it'. Along with some other stray phrases, he rightly stressed that John's position was that it was for the two governments to take initiatives and that Hume-Adams was pointing the finger at useful principles, but he also indicated that other soundings would also inform what he and John Major could do. The latter point reflected the efforts to include paragraphs more customized to unionist and loyalist perceptions alongside the worthy terms in the Hume-Adams draft declaration.

When the Downing Street Declaration came in December, John could not say so publicly but could show colleagues just how substantively the Hume-Adams draft had been transposed into the two premiers' joint statement. The more unionist-facing paragraphs did not detract from this. Indeed the balance and roundedness of the Major-Reynolds paper allowed party colleagues to reaffirm confidence that the process ahead could not only entail inclusive talks under a ceasefire, but could recruit relevant understandings already developed in the Brooke/Mayhew talks. This sense then made Sinn Féin's move to 'clarification' mode somewhat confusing and increasingly frustrating as it dragged out while IRA violence continued with new victims.

John's frustration in early November had led him to rashly state there could be 'peace in a week' if the two governments moved with the Hume-Adams scenario. As Sinn Féin appeared to string things out with requests for clarification and no sign of urgency towards an IRA ceasefire, pressure came back on John. While he thought that a decisive response should have been made to the declaration, he felt he had to

4 IRA bombers planted a bomb in fish shop on the Shankill Road, Belfast, that killed ten, including one of the bombers. A week later loyalist paramilitaries killed seven people in a public house in Greysteel, Co. Derry, in revenge.

show some patience for the SF leadership conversation with their base, conversations that he was being told were necessary and in hand. This was a period when the Sinn Féin leadership wanted to be seen proofing the two government's real meaning, and proving their own standing as potential negotiators in a new approach.

Some were diffident about the Gerry Adams US visa request that arose at this point, or suggested that conditional leverage might be applied, but Hume felt strongly that a positive gesture without obvious haggling or negative pressure from the British was the optimum response. Even though he could acknowledge (and even share) the concerns about predictable showboating, he argued strongly that allowing Adams to be seen to relate directly to the movement's Irish-American base would be the right call. He used all his lobbying clout in Washington to that end. He told all his congressional, White House and diplomatic contacts that a visa could move things forward, or at least remove an excuse.

While he was again having his currency castigated at home for Sinn Féin's failure to move as IRA violence went on, Hume was spending his political capital in the US to trump strong British lobbying against the visa. In some of the serial telephone exchanges, I had to caution Nancy Soderberg, President Clinton's adviser on Northern Ireland, not to pitch the National Security Council's advice against the State Department's line on any suggested prospect of Adams announcing a ceasefire in America or on return. While those who supported the visa decision did not expect that it would occasion a ceasefire declaration, they did succumb to disappointment that Adams showed no hurry to reward the risky political investment by the Clinton administration. This showed in the pointed scepticism that marked the later approaches around a visa for IRA activist Joe Cahill, as people in Washington as well as in Ireland were voicing frustration about the sense of being strung along. This mood was certainly building within the SDLP as people felt cynicism: about the 'PR circus' of the Adams' visa trip; the speculation that seemed to be played about developments around Easter; stories of soundings of key elements; other expectations allowed to grow then pass; ongoing IRA activity; and the recurring unionist contention that this was all a misadventure at the expense of dialogue and progress between the constitutional parties.

As before, Hume sensed all this as it touched on intermittent doubts of his own. But through it all he sustained his own confidence that a ceasefire had to come. This seemed to stem not just from his own intuition, but from his continuing contacts with Fr Reid and, not as constantly, with Adams. By the summer it was not only in public media that John Hume was being questioned about what had happened to his stated belief that the Downing Street Declaration would be the prelude to a definitive ceasefire. This was in turn supposed to provide the context for new, inclusive political dialogue. When these questions were reflected at difficult SDLP meetings that summer, colleagues did not doubt John's motives or judgment, but those of others. The talk was of 'lines to be drawn', 'calls to be made', 'how much more positioning, clarification or gratification does it take?' This reflected not just understandable political frustration but deep disgust that the IRA campaign was still being 'justified', after all the stilted efforts and taxing political strain to present the context for a well overdue ceasefire announcement.

At this time John could not divulge the basis for his then confidence about the ceasefire to come or a prospective time line. Party representatives were voicing doubts that were circulating widely. There were clear signals of impatience from the Irish government and weary misgivings in America. One of John's less intemperate ways of meeting colleagues' concerns into the summer of 1994 was to point to the need to prepare for future negotiations which would build on the agenda and other foundations from the 1991/2 talks and the Downing Street Declaration.

Fr Alec was aware that patience was wearing thin outside the provisional movement. John apparently told him that he could not brief his colleagues to reassurance by passing on his match reports on how well the Holy Spirit's game was going. To those who reflected the strains and doubts abounding, Fr Alec counselled that people should be told to see such a test of patience as a test of their political commitment or instinct. As well as invoking the Holy Spirit to aid their forbearance, he suggested that they might compare this with the allowances that could be made for unionism and the British in the conduct of politics, because republicans would make that comparison.

In this context, he expressed his own profound esteem for John Hume and his 'stickability' (John's word) in spite of all the pressure and any provocation. He said to John (and about him) that his consistency, determination and straightness of purpose were helping people to think differently about the course of politics and move for change. There was a mutual regard for each other's diligence and application over years of challenging effort. This was not flattery to deceive, as John fully appreciated Fr Alec's belief that Gerry Adams was uniquely placed to lead republicans out of armed struggle.

John did have a flicker of reservation, when, in the spring Fr Reid produced papers from another dimension of the Clonard Peace Mission's work with others who were engaging with loyalist paramilitaries. He was slightly apprehensive that worthy and welcome as this was, it might entail new delays or twists in the pursuit of the IRA ceasefire. I think he pointedly left it to me to receive and go through these papers with Fr Reid.

Fr Alec was firm in his belief that these prospects of a possible loyalist ceasefire would not turn into a precondition for a decisive IRA move. This was convincing to me and reinforced by other soundings which assured John. Then there was the converse anxiety about possible IRA sensibilities, that a loyalist cessation following an IRA ceasefire might be used to reinforce the pretence that loyalist violence had only been in response to the IRA's. Fr Reid was firm that this should not be an impediment to the IRA's 'own declaration'.

Even when he was sharing proposed timelines and elements of illustrative terminology for the IRA ceasefire, Fr Reid stressed the importance that the timing and terms had to be seen as the IRA's own. It would be presented as their initiative putting it up to others. Knowing when the ceasefire was to be announced, there was still apprehension for John given the doubts understandably circulating, the fear that some turn of events might be an excuse to hold it back and a degree of worry about what might be done in the IRA's name just ahead of the announcement. So John and Pat Hume displayed more a sense of relief than achievement when it did come. A degree of cynicism about the news-management and spin around it did not eclipse the real and personally emotional significance of the news and what John believed it would herald.

Peace Comes Dropping Slow

SEÁN O'HUIGINN

Reporting from a conference on Northern Ireland held in Virginia, US, in 1985, Sir Kenneth Bloomfield, the Head of the Northern Ireland Civil Service, penned a vivid image of John Hume, a fellow participant, as a man who had lost a fortune by continually backing the same number at the roulette table, until he was finally left, forlorn and bankrupt, staring at the numbers with no stake left to play.

Happily the fears Sir Kenneth may have harboured about Hume's political bankruptcy were to prove unfounded, but he was right on one point: Hume did back the same numbers at every table. They were, however, anything but the superstitious pick of a gambler. At the outset of his political career Hume had reflected very deeply on the nature of the Northern Ireland problem and formed his own ideas about how a fairer and more realistic and therefore more stable compromise between the conflicting interests could be put in place. Once he had decided these positions he backed them unswervingly throughout his career.

In the famous contrast between the fox who knows many things and the hedgehog who knows one big thing Hume belongs towards the hedgehog end of the spectrum. This is not to suggest any narrowness of character on his part. His ability to relate to widely different contexts was always one of his significant political assets. But the 'one big thing' that Hume knew was that the rough-hewn compromise of the 1920s, in reality more stand-off than compromise, was not fit for purpose, and certainly not for the purpose of allowing a fair and stable society to flourish in Northern Ireland. He saw the problem as the wider failure of Britain and Ireland to resolve their differences in the 1920s, a failure that they had pushed into a corner called Northern Ireland, whose problems derived essentially from unfinished business between the two islands.

The 1920s arrangements involved selective denials by all who operated them. Each government rejected the constitutional doctrine of the other on the issue. Unionists could not accept that their monopoly of power over a minority growing ever closer in demographic terms was either unfair or unsustainable. Hume found his own nationalist community divided between 'flight or fight' – a pathetically ineffective abstentionism, or a campaign of violence equally doomed to failure since, apart from the moral issue, it comprehensively ignored the realities and rights of the unionist community. The British presented their own role as the harassed adult dealing with the two sets of sectarian delinquents, artfully evading any notion that since they were by far the dominant influence in creating and sustaining the situation they had a correspondingly preponderant responsibility to correct its flaws.

Hume's entire political career can be understood as a struggle to replace all these patterns of denial with a more realistic and truthful acceptance of the complexities bequeathed by history. Since people cling to denial as a comfort zone, taking people out of their comfort zones will usually involve phases of anger and confrontation. If the Good Friday Agreement embodies and vindicates Hume's vision it is no coincidence that the approach to it included some of the most fraught and confrontational periods of his career.

The Anglo-Irish Agreement was a very important staging-post in Hume's project to 'retro-fit' the 1920s arrangements to provide a more sustainable compromise between unionism and nationalism. It marked the abandonment by the British of some of their own particular ramparts of denial. More importantly, from Hume's perspective, it circumvented the major obstacle of what was termed the unionist veto. Unionists were, subjectively or objectively, the incumbents of privilege. Since any change would involve some loss of that status it was logical rather than perverse on their part to resist change, a logic embodied with stentorian consistency by Dr Paisley and adroit immobility by Mr Molyneux during their long reigns as leaders of unionism. The agreement embedded the Irish dimension in intergovernmental arrangements, beyond the immediate reach of unionism. The perception, widely shared by unionists and nationalists alike, that unionists had a veto on change was comprehensively discredited. The unionists were quite right to see the agreement as a watershed moment. Their protests did lead the British to go slow on many aspects of implementation, but Mrs Thatcher's famed obduracy, which nationalists had found so baleful during the hunger strikes, now stood in edifying contrast to her Labour predecessors in the wake of Sunningdale.

The framework of the agreement was resolutely preserved in the years following its signature, allaying one of Hume's main concerns at the time. Mr Haughey's threat to repudiate the agreement if elected to government challenged both Hume's view that it was a potential catalyst and his iron rule of avoiding partisan alignment in the South. His influence with key Irish-American politicians and in the European Parliament easily saw off some ill-advised Fianna Fáil attempts to oppose the agreement in those quarters. The stresses engendered within the SDLP's own ranks were ultimately confined to a few resignations, none of far-reaching import.

The elections in the aftermath of the agreement were more reassuring for Hume than otherwise. That of 1986, after all unionist MPs had resigned in protest, saw the election of Séamus Mallon, both weakening the message unionists hoped the elections would send and adding a second formidable talent to the SDLP team in Westminster. In 1987 Eddie McGrady won a further Westminster seat, affording Enoch Powell, who lost the seat, a personal confirmation of his famous dictum that all political careers end in failure.

The incentives in the agreement for Northern Ireland politicians to negotiate power-sharing devolution foundered in the short term on unionist rage. Partly due to Hume's skillful prompting, the agreement was to prove fruitful in another unexpected direction, leading to the transformational change of the peace process.

The republican movement had for some time been operating an approach memorably summarized by Danny Morrison as combining the armalite and the ballot box, although few outside the movement would bother to draw distinctions between a full-time or merely part-time resort to violence. The movement's impractical millenarian goals and ruthless actions placed it outside the normal democratic framework. They were like the proverbial man with only a hammer insisting that every problem must be a nail, in short a force to be reckoned with, but not negotiated with, since their principles and methods could permit no constructive cooperation.

In reality the armalite and the ballot box were mutually limiting rather than complementary. The more thoughtful leaders understood that and also the limits of what the armed struggle could achieve, even with massive arsenals from Libya. Strategic choices had to be made.

As early as 1985 Sinn Féin leaders, working in conjunction with the Redemptorist Fr Alec Reid at the Clonard monastery in Belfast, and other clergy and lay people, had been making attempts to establish a political dialogue with church and political leaders. Most, predictably, came to nothing because of the ongoing campaign of violence. However, Fr Reid engaged with Mr Haughey, then in opposition, and subsequently wrote to John Hume in May 1986, who agreed to meet Gerry Adams.

Hume set out his familiar argument that the agreement meant the British were now open to Irish unity, subject only to the prior agreement of both parts of the island, thus making the campaign of violence counter-productive as well as wrong. Adams agreed that it would be helpful if the British were to state this position clearly and explicitly. He could not say what the IRA response would be but considered the only way to end the violent struggle was to develop a peaceful alternative. The two leaders formed a bond of personal trust, recognizing in each other a deep seriousness about the responsibilities of their respective leadership roles. Agreement was reached to hold formal dialogue between delegations from Sinn Féin and the SDLP in March 1988.

These talks did not bridge the differences between the two parties but they crystallized them. The papers exchanged are among the foundation documents of

what came to be termed the peace process. They put on record many of the formulations that Hume and ultimately the two governments were to develop in
future negotiations, in particular Hume's ingenious definition of the unionist
sense of British identity as a sub-set of Irish self-determination. This apparently
abstruse point had the very practical effect of making the manifest reality of the
unionist community compatible with the core republican doctrine of Irish self-
determination, enabling it to be treated as an Irish presence rather than an alien
implant. Hume insisted, with a deft invocation of Wolfe Tone, that agreement in
Ireland was a necessary precondition for ending the British connection.

The Sinn Féin documents were sceptical or interrogatory rather than polemi-
cal. They showed the party concerned to debate their positions rather than assert-
ing them as so many promulgations of blind republican faith. Although the talks
ended without agreement, republicans were convinced that the search for an alternative to their armed struggle could best be achieved by working with Hume. The
relationship between Hume and Adams was reinforced rather than otherwise and
their personal dialogue continued after the talks.

For the next few years the search for progress on Northern Ireland operated on
two levels, one in public view, one not. Unionist anger at the Anglo-Irish
Agreement was gradually yielding to a more sober assessment that the politics of
full-spectrum domination no longer offered a viable strategy to deal with the
nationalist community. If some accommodation was inevitable it might as well be
used to undermine the hated 'diktat', as they described the agreement.

Secretary of State for Northern Ireland Peter Brooke (1989–92), a subtle politician adept in the art of concealing art, launched a process with the constitutional
parties aimed at the ambitious goal of replacing the Anglo-Irish Agreement with
'a new and more broadly-based agreement'. After protracted wrangles on venues,
chairmanship and other procedural aspects the negotiations proper began in June
1991 in the now generally accepted SDLP three-stranded format to address relationships within the North, between North and South and between Ireland and
Britain. A former Australian Governor-General, Sir Ninian Stephen, was chosen
as independent chairman of Strand 2 where discussions on North-South relations
would take place. (That the British anticipated no great awkwardness from Sir
Ninian's independence may be inferred from their back-channel assurance to the
republicans that they proposed to ghostwrite his report.)

Suspended because of a meeting of the Anglo-Irish Conference in July, and
then because of the British general election, talks resumed with new personnel
from both governments and continued until drawn quietly to a close in November
1992.

The talks failed to bridge any major gap between the participants. Unionists
found the SDLP's opening bid on Strand 1 unacceptable, tantamount on some
readings to joint authority with a European dimension. They were frustrated that

the Irish government would not make a firm pledge in Strand 2 to drop Articles 2 and 3 of the Irish Constitution, which claimed jurisdiction over Northern Ireland – a keystone issue that Irish ministers felt should not be casually devalued in the foothills of the negotiations. Nevertheless the talks, the most significant such attempt since Sunningdale, were valuable both as educational dialogue and in breaking some ritualistic taboos to the benefit of subsequent negotiations.

Oliver Napier, leader of the Alliance Party, proferred a two-syllable explanation why these talks failed – 'John Hume'. Some felt the Irish government too saw the process as an interlude of necessary humbug, the implication being that they allowed a viable alternative to the peace process to wither on the vine. These accusations presumed a nearly absolute dichotomy between talks confined to constitutional parties and talks including Sinn Féin. In contrast, both Hume and the Irish government saw the Brooke/Mayhew talks and the peace process as potentially complementary rather than mutually exclusive. The Irish government never lost sight of the risk that the fraught process of bringing the republican movement into peaceful politics might end disastrously, either because the republicans might be in bad faith, or might themselves fail in all good faith. If the peace process succeeded, any gains from these talks could be carried forward. If it failed they were the only viable option left, two good reasons to take them seriously.

The point is worth emphasizing because there are people of goodwill who even now cannot reconcile themselves to the radical new approach that created the peace process. The policy of mobilizing the moderates on both sides to isolate the extremes seemed intuitively right, but it had never worked, in spite of having been tried in many variants. The reason was simple. The 'moderates' (a fluid concept at the best of times) feared their own extremes more than they trusted their fellow-moderates on the other side. Invited to swing a political trapeze across the sectarian divide, they had no confidence they would be gripped by supportive arms on the far side, and some suspicion their ropes might be cut through behind them. The hints that the republican movement might move to peaceful rational politics that the rest of the body politic could engage with gave hope of a transformation so valuable as to justify the manifest risks of pursuing it.

This second level of negotiations with the republican movement was pursued away from the public eye by both Hume and the Irish government, but also included intermittent backchannel conduits between the British and the republican movement. Haughey had declined to meet Gerry Adams but maintained indirect contact through both Hume and Martin Mansergh, the latter in his capacity as a Fianna Fáil operative. (It was only after the ceasefire that members of the civil service were permitted contacts with Sinn Féin.)

In autumn 1992 Hume sent Adams the first draft of *A strategy for peace and justice in Ireland*, the urtext of what became, after countless additions and subtractions from many hands, the kernel of the Downing Street Declaration. Haughey had flagged the initiative to Major as a possibility rather than a probability, but with Albert Reynolds' appointment as Taoiseach in 1992 it moved to centre stage. An enemy of vacillation, and always focussed on results rather than mere process, Reynolds felt, as Hume did, that if negotiations had failed to bring peace, then peace, an inestimable prize in all respects, would also transform the climate for negotiations.

The refinements of text in successive approximations of the Downing Street Declaration would require an exegesis as complicated as that of the origins of the Gospels (and indeed crumpled amendments Hume would occasionally proffer on some point of detail often bore more than a passing resemblance to scraps of papyrus).

Much of the redrafting at official level was an attempt to preserve Hume's valuable composite definition of Irish self-determination in terms that satisfied the governments' criterion that majority consent for a change of constitutional status in Northern Ireland was not diluted or compromised. Other redrafts sought greater clarity, or to weed out unintended corollaries, as with a version that implied a British commitment to legislate for an independent Northern Ireland. There was, however, one substantive point of difference between the Hume-Adams drafts and the final outcome. The British were willing to assume the role of encouraging agreement in Ireland but not the role of persuader for Irish unity. No-one in the Irish government was surprised at this outcome, although we felt it right to test fairly the acceptability of the drafts given to us. We looked at the out-come in the light of Hume's own argument that the fact of agreement had a value of its own, independent of the content.

The process of negotiations was conducted in a kind of variable geometry, led on the Irish side by Albert Reynolds and Foreign Affairs Minister Dick Spring, with the involvement on justice issues of Minister Máire Geoghegan Quinn. Official participation, including for this purpose Martin Mansergh and adviser to Dick Spring, Fergus Finlay, as highly active and creative participants, was concen-trated on five or six people. There were comparably limited numbers on the British side. Although given regular directions from meetings at prime minister or ministerial level, the process of negotiations was both fluid and drawn out. Hume repeatedly voiced impatience at their length and suspicions he was being left out of the loop. These latter concerns were largely unfounded in my experience, since no one doubted his gift for strategic thinking or his importance as a political leader whose support would be crucial for the success of any outcome. Moreover, the unchanging consistency of his ideas, while starving the media of novelty, made it easy for officials to 'channel' him on points of detail.

In these circumstances, it may have been a relief to him rather than otherwise when his on-going dialogue with Adams became public knowledge in April 1993. He issued a joint statement with Adams shortly afterwards. The hostility this evoked was all the greater since the IRA's Warrington bombing in March, with its two poignant child victims, was still fresh in everyone's memory.

Up to that point Hume had embodied, and arguably largely created, a moderate nationalist perspective on Northern Ireland, which enjoyed near consensual support in the South. His now public dialogue with Gerry Adams changed that. Even his admirers had misgivings, fearing that the vital distinction between democratic politics and political violence risked being blurred. Those, and there were many, who optimistically believed that if the South ignored the North, the North would obligingly vanish from the agenda, were aghast that Hume was now intruding the problem on them in the most problematic form imaginable . That view was stridently epitomized by the *Sunday Independent*, whose journalists, with a few honourable exceptions, hunted the designated quarry persistently and unashamedly as a pack. Hume attracted support also of course, much of it, encouragingly for him, coming from people outside the immediate realm of public life. The support of family and friends and of party colleagues meant it was never Hume 'contra mundum', but the storm of often venomous criticism must have taken its toll.

1993 had some claim to being among 'the best of times and the worst of times' of the peace process. That year added Warrington, Castlerock, Bishopsgate, Shankhill and Greysteel as headline atrocities to the steady drip of more routine incidents, and suggested a frightening potential for even greater escalation. October 1993 had the highest death-toll of any month since 1976. The Shankhill bomb and Greysteel massacre in particular seemed terrible omens of worse to come. The subsequent funerals showed one protagonist of the Hume-Adams dialogue shouldering the bomber's coffin, the other weeping publicly from the depths of despair, contrasting pictures but both equally bleak and comfortless to those who hoped for an end to the nightmare.

At the same time the year saw sustained efforts at political and diplomatic level aimed at finding a path to peace. Albert Reynolds (with the solid and committed support of Dick Spring, contrary to subsequent legend) was in sustained engagement with Hume and other channels, and with the British government, to create a platform from which all interests could pursue their conflicting goals through exclusively peaceful means.

Reynolds was always acutely conscious of the difficult context in which British Prime Minister Major operated, both because of parliamentary arithmetic and the mindset of the Tory party generally. He did his best to insulate him from accusations that he was negotiating with terrorism, a prospect Major famously declared would turn his stomach. Reynolds therefore highlighted the intergovernmental element in the hybrid ancestry of the proposal, and sought to remove Adams' fingerprints, a process that necessarily meant removing Hume's also. These efforts to protect Major's political flank aroused great misgivings, very clearly manifested in that year's

Fianna Fáil árd-fheis. Reynolds was later not amused to discover that Major's stomach had in fact withstood without convulsions the ordeal of protracted British contact with the republicans, carefully concealed from the Irish government.

This aspect of the process led to significant tension between Hume and the Irish government. Reynolds and Spring were exasperated when, at the end of September 1993, Hume and Adams issued a joint statement saying they had ended their discussion and had given the result to the Irish government. Hume then left on a visit to the United States, leaving an embarrassed government as the presumed custodian of a talismanic Hume-Adams document. This, as everyone involved in the peace process knew, but could not say, was a cluster of ideas and overlapping texts rather than tablets of stone. On Hume's return he held a well-publicized meeting with Reynolds and Spring, who engaged in another well-intentioned blurring exercise as to the nature and prospects of the Hume-Adams document.

In fact, those prospects seemed to grow dimmer with every passing week. London gave ever-clearer signals to both Hume and Dublin of misgivings and doubts about the entire process. These culminated in the British launching a new draft in the run up to the Dublin summit meeting of 3 December. This upended the finely tuned formulations the two governments had jointly elaborated over many months. Whatever its purpose, it offered nothing to advance an IRA ceasefire and indeed represented a rebuff that would probably have generated its own chain reaction. It was unclear whether the British were responding to the undoubted constraints on Major or indulging in a habit of their statecraft, to test very close to destruction whether the goals they pursued might not, after all, be secured for a cheaper price. The summit opened with an acrimonious exchange on British underhand dealings with the republicans before proceeding to the even more fraught operational issue of the proposed declaration. The discussions, including a tête-a-tête between Taoiseach and Prime Minister, increasingy replaced diplomatic euphemisms with expletives, and set a record for angry confrontation, which will hopefully remain unrivalled in the future.The outcome was a close-run thing, but to the credit of both sides ended with agreement to continue negotiations on the basis of the work already done, leading to the Downing Street Declaration a few weeks later.

Since Irish independence, the British-Irish relationship had been one of generally close practical cooperation with agreement to differ on the constitutional gaps that separated them. These latter were rarely allowed to undermine the necessary practical cooperation, but represented a potentially limiting fault line under it. The Downing Street Declaration was the most sustained attempt up to that point to agree how these gaps could be better bridged. It sought to reconcile the principles of Irish self-determination and unionist consent – non-negotiable for one or other poles of the negotiation – in language which, at some sacrifice of elegance, encompassed both. These densely grained drafts, which survived into the Good Friday Agreement, meant that doctrinal issues, which had given us the Irish

civil war, were successfully defused, leaving subsequent negotiations free to concentrate on the practical agenda.

Reynolds had availed of the goodwill of Lord Eames, Church of Ireland archbishop of Armagh, and the Revd Roy Magee, a Presbyterian minister, as interme-
diaries, and also incorporated libertarian principles advocated by the loyalist
paramilitaries, adding value to the declaration both in substance and in symbolic
openness to unionist concerns.

The eight months between the declaration and the IRA ceasefire tested the forbearance of those who had taken risks to reach out to the republican movement.
They understood fully that Adams' goal of bringing his entire movement into the
peace process was of the utmost importance but as a drawn-out process of clarification and other delays succeeded each other, their fingers itched for a fast-forward
button. Adams' visit to the US, which drove Major into meltdown, produced only
hints that backers of the peace process would not be disappointed. Meanwhile the
steady pattern of atrocities by the paramilitaries on both sides continued.

Hume appealed publicly and privately to the republican movement to recognize that the declaration removed their rationale for armed struggle and urged the
governments to provide whatever clarifications were needed to dispose of that particular obstacle. He was also facing a growing restiveness within his own party,
many of whom felt the republican response to his efforts for peace was merely one
of cynical gamesmanship.

A Sinn Féin conference in Letterkenny disappointed the hopes invested in it.
The incipient backlash, even among those supportive of the initiative, was fore-
stalled when the IRA declared a complete cessation of violence at the end of
August 1994, a transformational moment in the history of Northern Ireland.

The aftermath of the ceasefire showed a clear divergence between Dublin and
London on how to react to it. Dublin followed broadly Ronald Reagan's maxim
of 'trust but verify' while London's policy reversed that order. The British
launched a debate about the *permanence* of the ceasefire, a question that only history could reliably answer. Decommissioning was a much more formidable brake.
It was a goal generally acknowledged as both essential and attainable as one of the
practical corollaries of a political agreement. It was never time-critical so long as
the weapons were not being used. Taken out of sequence and loaded with unnecessary symbolic import, it was guaranteed to be an obstacle, and so it proved.
Political resources were diverted from more useful purposes to undo the effects of
the essentially tactical use that had been made of a particularly delicate and strategic goal to cover for Major's inability to move, delaying the achievement of both
decommissioning and progress towards agreement generally.

The interval between the ceasefire and the Good Friday Agreement began for
Hume with a lap of honour for his work in making a ceasefire possible. He derived
understandable satisfaction from events such as a standing ovation in the European

Parliament and the sense of vindication he enjoyed at that year's SDLP conference. He expressed this tactfully in a well-deserved tribute to the support his party colleagues had given him. He busied himself also with promoting economic support for the peace in the US and Europe.

As had been the practice of successive Irish governments when engaging in significant initiatives on Northern Ireland, he was consulted on the Framework Document we were drafting with the British government. This was the most detailed joint blueprint advanced by the two governments up to then. Unsurprisingly he was supportive, since the document, launched in 1995, incorporated many proposals derived from ideas put forward by Hume himself or the SDLP.

Gradually however these positive developments gave way to anger and foreboding on Hume's part as the political stalemate due to the decommissioning precondition lasted throughout 1995. It was the prospect of a visit by President Clinton to Northern Ireland at the end of 1995 that finally broke the stalemate, leading to a last-minute agreement to entrust the by now intractable issue to an international body chaired by US Senator George Mitchell.

The President's visit displayed a surefootedness that confounded his critics. The Mitchell Report in January 1996 showed a comparable level of skill. The report set out six principles as a public test for the democratic commitment of talks participants. While recognizing that decommissioning was a voluntary act that paramilitaries would not do before talks, it recommended they should do so during the process. In deference to David Trimble's demand for prior elections, the report cautiously listed the idea as a confidence-building measure, if properly mandated, generally accepted and within the three-stranded structure. This latter qualification addressed Hume's worry that elections might recast the negotiations on an essentially internal basis, but not his concern that they could lead to maximalist election platforms and waste time that should be devoted to negotiations proper. The British government accepted the report but highlighted the election dimension.

All calculations had to be reset when the IRA exploded a bomb on London's Canary Wharf in February 1996. In the absence of a ceasefire, Sinn Féin's exclusion from talks was axiomatic, but at a summit meeting at the end of that month the two governments agreed to convene interparty talks the following June. They also agreed on prior elections, under a novel system designed to ensure, among other things, that loyalist paramilitaries could get elected.

In February Hume and Adams met with the IRA. The ensuing IRA statement acknowledged the two men's shared desire to restore the ceasefire, but blamed its collapse on the British failure to launch inclusive negotiations, adding loftily that the IRA would only exercise its responsibilities if others did likewise. It was noticeable at this point that Hume began to give heightened emphasis to his joint referendum proposal, an instrument that could also democratically validate arrangements from negotiations without Sinn Féin, if the republican movement persisted with their armed struggle.

1996 was busy politically with the elections (where Sinn Féin came within five per cent of the SDLP vote), various proximity talks and the launch in June 1996 of formal inter-party negotiations (excluding of course Sinn Féin). However the increasingly looming shadow of the British general election diminished further Major's already small stock of political authority. There was a distinctly 'phoney war' tone to the negotiations in their initial phase. Hume was a participant, but left much of the work to his able lieutenants, led by Séamus Mallon, delegation he should have arguably practised more widely in his leadership generally.

On the streets, however, the war was not phoney. The streets also played out the now recurrent confrontation over the Orange Order march in Drumcree, a local conflict that had acquired a capacity out of all proportion to its real importance to polarize the political climate. (Unionists were beginning to react to the prospect of political change by brandishing more insistently the now very hollow symbols of their old supremacy, a process the outside world found baffling and alienating.)

The British and Irish general elections in 1997 brought onstage two new prime ministers enjoying firmer authority and, arguably, sharper skill-sets in regard to Northern Ireland than their two immediate predecessors. Tony Blair and Bertie Ahern reestablished, in their own very different idiom, the purposeful working relationship that had existed between Major and Reynolds, greatly enhancing the climate for negotiations.

Hume's private and public appeals for a new ceasefire had fallen on deaf ears but he believed that however brutal the collapse of the ceasefire and its aftermath, the republican movement wanted to come to the negotiating table and that both governments wanted them there. In July, Hume and Adams issued an optimistic statement, and a new ceasefire was announced two days later. Delicate manoeuvres were needed to bring Sinn Féin into the negotiations without precipitating a unionist withdrawal over the lack of decommissioning, but, with the help of some constructive if necessarily oblique choices by David Trimble, fully inclusive negotiations were genuinely engaged by the beginning of 1998. They culminated in the equally inclusive Good Friday Agreement, the most decisive gear-shift in the politics of Northern Ireland since its creation.

Hume's role in the detailed negotiation that finalized the agreement was fairly low-key. He satisfied himself they were within the parameters he had painstakingly designed and long advocated, bestirring himself mainly when these seemed threatened, for example, when Sinn Féin appeared at one stage to question the need for an assembly in Northern Ireland. Details within that strategic framework were of less concern to him. He probably felt he could rely on the dynamics of an inclusive engagement between unionism and nationalism to produce an acceptable outcome on this level also.

The Good Friday Agreement reflected credit on the art of politics generally, and on those directly involved in its preparation and conclusion in particular.

There were very few instances during its long gestation of anyone exploiting the process for partisan or personal advantage. The list of those who made crucial and very often selfless contributions to advance it will, one hopes, be recognized and honoured in history.

John Hume is assured of a prominent place among the names at the very top of that roll of honour. He and the party he led made peaceful reform their political mission. The unwavering rejection of violence at the core of their politics helped prevent Northern Ireland being overwhelmed by the violence that beset it in the way we have seen in other blackspots which lacked such a political bulwark. The second part of the programme, a long and patient campaign for reform, transformed Northern Ireland from an unfair society into one that respected all its citizens, nationalist no less than unionist, and could be accepted honourably by them.

Hume's personal contribution to this transformation was felt on many levels. His gift for conceptual thinking enabled him to redefine many of the traditional tenets of nationalism as vehicles for cooperation rather than confrontation. By refusing to let abstractions dominate his politics, he promoted a very necessary separation between sovereignty and issues of citizen's rights, so that no flag over Northern Ireland could ever again come to mean that winner took all.

He opposed a purely internal framework as he knew that Northern Ireland needed to escape the zero-sum game of its traditional politics and that this could best be done by linking it to wider contexts he cultivated. These also provided support for his reform plans, including the American dimension, which eventually contributed so much to the search for peace.

Hume could see from his native Derry that the paramilitaries were not exotics from outer space but were a product of the complexities of Irish history and might be persuaded to a better path by invoking that history.

It took his political acumen and sense of history to see the opportunity in the approach he received from Gerry Adams. It took his political courage to respond as promptly and positively as he did. It is easy to forget the depth of scepticism that greeted the initiative, born of long experience of unremitting IRA violence. The respect he had earned as a visceral opponent of violence and for the integrity of his political record made him an informal guarantor of the potential of the new approach, which otherwise might have collapsed under the weight of doubt.

Hume's Nobel Prize was for a lifetime's work. His career shows such consistency and continuity that it must indeed be treated as a whole but if one had to pick the period where his contribution was at its most decisive, and made at greatest cost to himself, it was probably in the decade between 1988 and 1998, when the Good Friday Agreement finally placed the coping stone on his work for peace.

Hume in Europe

BRIGID LAFFAN

John Hume was elected to the first directly elected European Parliament (EP) in 1979 and remained a member of that parliament until the 2004 elections, thereby serving five terms. He represented Northern Ireland together with Ian Paisley of the DUP and in turn John Taylor and Jim Nicholson of the UUP during this period. Because Northern Ireland lacked direct ministerial representation in Brussels as a region within a member state, its MEPs played a more central representational role than in other parts of Europe; the three MEPs were the major conduit between Northern Ireland and the European Union. In a parliament characterized by significant turnover at each election, John Hume's longevity as an MEP is remarkable. He was the predominant face and voice of constitutional Irish nationalism in the European Parliament. In his final speech to the parliament just before the 2004 EP elections, Hume ended with the following words: 'I express my deepest gratitude to you all for the great support that you give to peace on my own streets. Thank you very much indeed and I regret very much that I am leaving this great Parliament'.[1] This chapter explores the role Europe played in John Hume's political worldview, political strategies and activities during his lengthy and full political career. His success in 1979 in harvesting 140,622 votes (25.5 per cent) highlighted his popularity. His candidacy and electoral success had a major impact on the SDLP as it copper-fastened Hume's role as the most popular leader among nationalists. Paddy Devlin, his former SDLP colleague, ran against him in the election but did badly. Tellingly, the SDLP failed to hold the seat following John Hume's retirement in 2004 and the leadership of nationalist opinion in Northern Ireland passed to Sinn Féin.

'Europe' as inspiration, vision, model and arena of politics mattered to John Hume. It was core to his political ideology and principles. He developed a certain

---

1 John Hume, European Parliament Plenary, http://www.europarl.europa.eu/meps/en/highlight.html?query=John+Hume&url=http%3a%2f%2fwww.europarl.europa.eu%2fmeps%2fen%2f1408%2fJOHN_HUME_home.html.

idea of Europe and the role Europe could and should play in the search for peace and reconciliation in Northern Ireland, within the island of Ireland and between the two neighbouring islands. His work on and in Europe was also the playing out of his core political beliefs, principles, values and ways of being in the world. John Hume's principles started with a core belief in the importance of the individual in his/her family, his/her local community, and the region in which he/she lived. His early commitment to this philosophy can be seen in his immersion in the building of the credit union movement right across Ireland, as a means of empowering individuals and small communities to marshall their resources and build their family and community infrastructures. His involvement in the University for Derry campaign reflected his commitment to the building of his home city, and the development of its resources. Beginning with the local, John Hume later brought these beliefs and strategies into all of the theatres of politics that he was engaged with, the North, Dublin, London, Brussels/Strasbourg and Washington. John Hume's political achievements in Europe were a perfect fit with his entire political approach, a coherent part of the whole fabric of his political life

For John Hume, Europe meant its political and institutional expression in the European Community, now European Union (EU). Hume, through his use of narrative and direct political action, ensured that the SDLP was 'an active player in the Europeanization of the Northern Ireland problem'.[2] It fact it was the prime mover in exploring and exploiting the European context of the problem. John Hume came into the parliament with a burgeoning European and international reputation, which made him one of the best-known members of the then largest group in the parliament – the Socialist Group. When the group was choosing its officers in that first term following direct elections, Hume was unanimously elected treasurer – and therefore responsible for deployment of the formidable resources of the Socialist Group throughout the member parties in the various member states – an unusual honour for the single representative of the smallest party in the group. This role gave him extensive contact with all the member parties, and his resulting prestige and popularity were such that he was able to mobilize the Socialist Group in support of any initiative that he took in relation to Northern Ireland.

This chapter begins by looking at Europe as part of Hume's political narrative and the role Europe played as a model for conflict management and conflict resolution in Northern Ireland. Hume developed a consistent and coherent discourse concerning Europe that he deployed throughout his political career.[3] The discussion of Europe as narrative and model is followed by an exploration of Europe as

2 Peter McLoughlin, 'The SDLP and the Europeanization of the Northern Ireland problem', *Irish Political Studies*, 24:4 (2009), pp 603–19.   3 Michael Cunningham, 'The political language of John Hume', *Irish Political Studies*, 12:1 (1997), pp 13–22.

a political arena where John Hume plied his political craft and its role as a source of support for peace in Northern Ireland. John Hume, unlike Ian Paisley, was comfortable and at home in the institutions of the EU and supported the project of European integration in a deep sense. Hume came to the parliament with an already developed commitment to the EU and had a major impact on the pro-EU position of the SDLP from its foundation. There was a high degree of congruence between John Hume's core political beliefs and objectives and the process of European integration. His idea and ideal of Europe was closely related to his core political objectives and strategies in relation to Northern Ireland, the island of Ireland, and Great Britain and Ireland. Already in 1971 and 1972, Hume and the SDLP articulated a strong sense of what Europe represented and its potential role in conflict resolution in Northern Ireland.[4]

NARRATIVE AND MODEL

A core element of John Hume's interpretation of the conflict in Northern Ireland and his strategy to address it was to locate Northern Ireland in a wider European and global context and to use all available political channels and opportunities to Europeanize and internationalize the search for a resolution. In the influential US journal *Foreign Affairs* in 1979, a bleak time in Northern Ireland, Hume wrote that 'One of the few developments that has cheered those who believe that reason and moderation must prevail in Northern Ireland has been the growing interest in the problem on the part of responsible political leaders outside Ireland and Britain. This is particularly true of the United States, and to a significant extent, the European Community'.[5] Hume resisted the idea that the conflict in Northern Ireland was in any sense exceptional. Time and time again, John Hume asserted that Northern Ireland was the last remaining zone of conflict in Western Europe, an outlier that needed to be addressed, and that the conflict was not just a conflict between Britain and Ireland but a conflict that was linked to the Reformation and thus European in origin. For Hume, the conflict could not be reduced to religious differences but was a conflict about competing identities and sovereignties locked in different states.

The Hume narrative on Europe was multidimensional, nuanced and layered. First and most intensely was the idea of the EU as a peace project, a living example of the political reconciliation of erstwhile political foes. Hume often, including in his Nobel Prize acceptance speech, recalled the walk he took on the bridge between Strasbourg, one of the seats of the parliament, and Kehl in Germany in

4 I would like to thank Denis Haughey for his very rich and insightful comments on an earlier draft. 5 John Hume, 'The Irish question: a British problem', *Foreign Affairs* (1979), pp 300–13.

1979 when he went to his first session of the EP as an elected member. For him, standing on the bridge between these two countries offered a moment of reflection on the profound change that had transformed relations between France and Germany in a short time period after the war. The evidence of reconciliation between these two countries, the manner in which it was achieved, and the kind of political order that the EU represented was, for Hume, inspirational. Hume experienced in a deep sense European integration as an exemplar of successful conflict resolution. For him, 'The European Union is the best example in the history of the world of conflict resolution. For that reason, the principles at the heart of it should be sent to every area of conflict'.[6] Those principles are further teased out below in the exploration of Europe as a model.

Hume's European narrative went beyond the idea of Europe as peace project to embrace other ideas related to the kind of political order that the EU was, notably concepts of multiple and post-nationalist identities. This was part of his re-assessment and revision of Irish nationalism within a European context.[7] Hume's restatement of the Irish case in non-violent terms, and in terms appropriate for late twentieth- and early twenty-first century Europe was a beacon in the midst of the re-assertion of the physical force tradition of Irish nationalism. Hume subscribed to the view that the congruence between territory and identity, a hallmark of the traditional nation state, was separating out and losing purchase in the contemporary world. For him the traditional nation state was being re-configured in all kinds of ways by the process of European integration. The process of economic integration, particularly the single market, was reducing the salience of borders by turning borders into bridges. A Europe without internal barriers melded with his view that the traditional nation state was being transformed and exclusive national identities were losing their purchase. For Hume, post-nationalism, or re-configured nationalism, afforded the possibility of overcoming the dichotomy between unionist versus nationalist, and Britain versus Ireland. Rather, the forging of post-nationalist identities would allow for multiple identities to emerge within an integrating Europe thereby taking the sting out of the 'integrity of the quarrel' and the hardness of borders. Post-nationalism did not imply the transcendence of national identities; rather what mattered was their transformation within a new political setting. For Hume, identity was inclusive rather than exclusive, multiple rather than singular, mixed and entangled like a marble cake.

John Hume identified three core principles at the heart of the EU, namely respect for difference, layered institutional representation and integration as a healing process. These three principles had a major impact on his approach to conflict resolution and his proposals for new governance structures in Northern Ireland

6 Hume, European Parliament Plenary (see note 1).   **7** Peter McLoughlin, *John Hume and revision of Irish nationalism* (Manchester, 2012).

and between Britain and Ireland. He saw the identification and institutionaliza-
tion of these three principles as central to the Anglo-Irish Agreement and the later
Good Friday Agreement. Respect for difference captured in the phrase 'unity in
diversity' was constitutive of how the EU developed and was one of its core values.
Reading from the European script, acknowledgment of, and respect for, difference
was necessary to resolve the conflict in Northern Ireland. From Hume's perspective, the acceptance of diversity by both communities in Northern Ireland and
within the island of Ireland was a necessary step in the search for peace and conflict resolution. Difference in and of itself was not the problem as captured in the
following quote:

> Difference is not our problem. It is that we have pushed difference to the
> point of division. From that division springs the many symptoms that are
> a consistent cause of complaint and that waste so much time and energy
> that ought to be devoted to the central problem.[8]

Thus the acceptance of diversity and the insertion of that acceptance into agreements and governance arrangements addressing the conflict were central to his
ideology and strategy. Ireland had to create 'institutions that respect our diversity
but also allow us to work on our substantial economic ground together'.[9] The
second principle, layered institutional representation to capture the different
member states that made up the EU, resonated later in the institutional model
that evolved in the Anglo-Irish Agreement and the Good Friday Agreement.
Writing on the Anglo-Irish Agreement in 1996, Hume claimed that 'The structures established by the Anglo-Irish Agreement reflected those of the European
Union. This was no accident'.[10] According to Hume, the agreement's intergovernmental conference was modelled on the European Council of Ministers and its
secretariat analogous to the European Commission (EC). The European institutional model was even more apparent in the later Good Friday Agreement. The
d'Hondt system used for the allocation of political offices according to the share
of seats in the parliament was used for the allocation of ministerial office to the
parties in the Northern Ireland Assembly. The North-South Ministerial Council,
which meets in plenary and in different sectoral formations, was not unlike the
Council of Ministers, and meetings of the British and Irish heads of government
resembled the European Council.[11] According to one assessment, the Good Friday
Agreement institutions 'bear testimony to the effects of Europeanization on the
realization of post-conflict, post-sovereign state institutional arrangements for the

8 Hume, 'A new Ireland: the acceptance of diversity', *Studies: An Irish Quarterly Review* (1986), pp 378–83.
9 J. Hume, *Personal views: politics, peace and reconciliation in Ireland* (Dublin, 1996). 10 Ibid., p. 47. 11
Brigid Laffan, 'Ireland, Britain, Northern Ireland and the European dimension', *Working Papers in British-
Irish Studies* 27, IBIS, 10 (2003).

island of Ireland' and according to another scholar, 'the Good Friday Agreement of 1998 is by far the closest agreement to the model suggested by Haagerup', which is discussed below.[12] One of Hume's and the SDLP's innovative proposals for the governance of Northern Ireland in the early 1990s was the suggestion that a representative of the European Commission would sit on a regional executive involving the two governments and three elected politicians from Northern Ireland. The proposal did not fly because of unionist opposition but it is highly unlikely that the Commission would have ever consented to being directly involved in the governance of one part of a member state. President Delors made his opposition to the proposal known.

The third principle – healing – resonated with the manner in which European integration evolved through piecemeal cooperation, the spilling of sweat not blood according to Hume.[13] It reflected a particular kind of politics, a politics of compromise and partial agreement rather than zero-sum and winner takes all politics. In the European Union agreement was and always is slowly built from shared problems and common ground in an incremental process of shared and divisible sovereignty. No member states or political actors gets all that they want in any negotiations. Getting to 'yes' involved an in-built commitment to compromise and to understanding the views and needs of the other side. For Hume, the EU style and its underlying political culture had lessons for those who would pursue issues of sovereignty and territory in absolutist terms. It offered a psychological framework within which there could be 'growing appreciation that interdependence can be achieved without sacrificing independence'.[14]

During the 1980s and 1990s the concept of a 'Europe of the Regions' gained considerable discursive power in the politics of the EU. Powerful regions in Europe used the opportunity of EU treaty change to seek the further representation of regions at EU level. In addition, there were processes of decentralization and regionalization in many member states. The expansion of European structural funds and the Commission's preference for partnerships with regions within the member states all strengthened the concept of a 'Europe of the Regions'. Given Northern Ireland's position as a region within a larger member state, Hume's preference for multiple identities and his interest in and commitment to European regional policy, a 'Europe of the Regions' melded with his convictions about the importance of the local, the community and the region. In the European theatre, he quickly became a proponent of the concept of a Europe of the Regions, and not just because it might provide Northern Ireland an escape route from the suffocating dominance of Britain, whose interests in Europe were often the diametric opposite of the Irish

12 K. Hayward, 'Reiterating national identities: the European Union conception of conflict resolution in Northern Ireland', *Cooperation and Conflict*, 41:3 (2006), pp 261–84.   13 Hume, European Parliament Plenary.   14 Hume, *Personal views*, p. 113.

approach. In his first term in the parliament, John Hume put down a motion calling for measures to protect and promote regional languages and cultures in Europe.
This motion led to the Arfe Report, which prompted the establishment of the
European Bureau of Lesser Used Languages, set up in Dublin in 1984.[15] This was
part of his belief that small communities and small regions should be enabled to
protect themselves, protect their identities and cultures, and develop the resources
to promote their welfare and their prosperity. Later, he supported the institutional-
ization of the Committee of the Regions and promoted the growing density of relations across Europe's regions. In 1987, as a member of the Regional Policy
Committee, he was appointed as rapporteur of a report on regional problems in
Ireland. This report came at a time when the EU was moving towards a strengthening of regional policy both in terms of governance and resources. Hume's report
was very critical of the lack of regional structures in Ireland and the concentration
of power in Dublin. The report was widely debated but led only to a symbolic commitment to regionalism in Ireland. Regionalism never gained traction in Ireland
because of the importance of the county as a mark of identification, largely because
of the GAA, and the power of the centre. Notwithstanding his commitment to a
'Europe of the Regions', Hume also understood that governments and states, in this
case Britain and Ireland, had a powerful role to play in conflict management and
resolution in Northern Ireland.

ARENA FOR POLITICAL ACTION

The European Union was an important political arena, one of two relations
beyond Britain and Ireland that played a central role in Hume's search for a resolution to the communal conflict in Northern Ireland. As a long-standing MEP,
John Hume was a political actor in an institution that would gain in power and
influence from 1979 onwards, arising from direct elections and the Union's need
to respond to what was identified as a 'democratic deficit'. Within the EP and the
wider context of European politics, John Hume and the SDLP never positioned
themselves as a regional or nationalist party. Rather, from its foundation, the
SDLP was a member of the Confederation of Socialist Parties, one of Europe's
main traditional families and following Hume's election to the EP, he joined the
powerful Socialist Group, then the largest group in the parliament. He was a
member of the group's central bureau for most of his time at the parliament. This
afforded him an invaluable network and an ease of contact within the group and
in the parliament more widely as the bureaus were the main conduit for inter-

---

15 Arfe Report and resolution on Measures in favour of minority languages and cultures (11 Feb. 1983),
Official Journal C 68, 14.3.1983, 103.

group relations. His earlier appointment in 1977 as a political adviser to Dick Burke, Ireland's European Commissioner for Transport, Trade and Administration, gave Hume an insider's knowledge of how the Commission as an institution worked, an experience that Hume acknowledged as being very valuable.[16] John Hume arrived in the EP in 1979 not as a novice but as someone who knew and understood the complex political and policy making environment he was working in. His Commission experience together with his standing in the EP allowed him garner support for a number of initiatives that are outlined below.

Committees are the lifeblood of the EP in the tradition of continental European parliamentary democracy. John Hume's choice of committee during his tenure as an MEP reflected his interests and prevailing narrative on Northern Ireland and the EU. He was a long-standing member of the Regional Policy Committee of the EP, a committee that altered its title to include transport and tourism from 1999 onwards. He acted as a substitute on the Agricultural and Fisheries Committee from 1979 onwards which reflected the importance of these sectors, particularly agriculture, to Northern Ireland. He served briefly on the influential Institutional Affairs Committee (1987/88) and spent a full legislature on the Joint ACP (African, Caribbean and Pacific) Assembly and on the Delegation on Relations with the US. The ACP Assembly reflected his internationalist outlook and by the time he served on the US delegation, he was already a Washington insider with close contacts in the US Senate and House of Representatives.

John Hume was not interested in pursuing office goals for himself within the parliament other than ensuring that he served on the group bureau, nor was he active on a wide range of issues because for much of his time in the EP, he had a triple mandate and his priority was Northern Ireland. The record suggests that during his last five years in the parliament, he made fourteen speeches, asked five questions, made one motion for a parliamentary resolution and was associated with one written declaration. Hume's approach to the parliament was strategic and focused. He was interested in and committed to using the parliament as an arena to highlight the situation in Northern Ireland, to improve its economic situation and to bolster the role Europe could play in addressing the conflict.

Hume's first priority as an MEP was to put the situation in Northern Ireland on the EP and EU agenda. In one initiative after another, John Hume garnered attention to Northern Ireland and its needs through exploiting the economic and political opportunities offered by the EU. There was a remarkable consistency in his strategy, which can be summarized as getting an issue on to the agenda, ensuring that one of the EP's committees drafted a report, influencing the Commission to ensure eligibility and then moving on to a new issue having secured his objectives. In many instances this was done despite opposition from the British gov-

---

16 George Drower, *John Hume: man of peace* (London, 1995), p. 84.

ernment. He began, within six months of his arrival at the parliament when he sought and gained the support of a sufficient number of colleagues, to table a resolution calling for an examination of how the then European Community could assist the economy of Northern Ireland. The resolution was successful and the Committee of Regional Policy and Planning, of which Hume was a member, appointed Simone Martin as rapporteur to produce a report on the subject. She visited Northern Ireland at the end of September and early October 1980 to engage with relevant stakeholders and to develop an overview of the potential of the role of the EC. The Martin Report was the beginning of a continuous role for the EU's structural funds in Northern Ireland that would culminate in the peace funds.[17] Following the Martin Report, a regulation was passed providing for special assistance for Belfast, namely, the allocation of £63 million for housing development in the deprived inner city parts of the city because of its deteriorating economic and social situation. However, almost as important as the extra resources for housing in Belfast was the fact that this initiative established Northern Ireland as an area for special assistance in the European budget. That created a precedent which led to many special measures for Northern Ireland in the future (including the peace programmes), and especially the designation of Northern Ireland as an Objective One Region in the framework of the new and enlarged structural funds – even though Northern Ireland did not meet the economic criteria. Moreover, although the focus of the report was social and economic, it made reference to the civil unrest within Northern Ireland and its particular circumstances.[18]

John Hume worked also to extend special assistance to the rural parts of Northern Ireland. He was successful in his campaign to embarrass the British government to apply for a special programme for the less favoured areas in Northern Ireland, which massively enhanced the inflow of European resources into deprived rural communities across the region, thereby stimulating their development. Equally, his successful campaign to extend the borders of the Less Favoured Areas brought into the stream of assistance for deprived rural communities huge areas of Northern Ireland deliberately excluded by the old Stormont regime, because they were mainly nationalist. The extension was achieved following a resolution by Hume and a report by Irish MEP T.J. Maher. By virtue of this extension about seventy per cent of Northern Ireland's land area came to be designated as 'less favoured'. It laid down a blueprint for rural development programmes in the future, and which informed the utilization of the International Fund for Ireland monies at a later stage.

17 S. Martin (1981), Report drawn up on behalf of the Committee on Regional Policy and Regional Planning on Community regional policy and Northern Ireland. Working Documents 1981–1982, Document 1–177/81, 4 May 1981. **18** J. Mitchell and M. Cavanagh, 'Context and contingency: constitutional nationalists in Europe' in M. Keating and J. McGarry (eds), *Minority nationalism and the changing international order* (Oxford, 2001), pp 246–63.

Having started with the economic dimension of the crisis, Hume turned his attention to the actual conflict itself and sought to promote an EP led investigation with the tacit support of the Irish government. This would serve to draw attention to Northern Ireland within the then EC and take the conflict out of the UK domestic container. John Hume was widely credited with the instigation of the report[19] and being able to exploit the EP to acquire a wider legitimacy for the nationalist position.[20] The ambition to have the EP examine the conflict in Northern Ireland was a much more ambitious objective than studying the economy. In a series of resolutions, mostly tabled by Irish MEPs, the Political Affairs Committee agreed to undertake an investigation into the situation in Northern Ireland and appointed Neils Haagerup, a Danish MEP, as rapporteur. The decision to proceed with the report in February 1983 was remarkable given the trenchant opposition of the UK government and unionist politicians and the fact that Northern Ireland was part of a member state. The EU did not at this stage see itself as an institution that addressed conflicts in the member states.

The Haagerup Report began from the premise that the situation in Northern Ireland was one of the 'gravest political and social problems existing in the community'[21] but also acknowledged that the EC had 'no competence' to make proposals for changes in the constitution of Northern Ireland, a fact which gave some comfort to the UK government of the time although Jim Prior, the then Secretary of State for Northern Ireland announced that he would not cooperate with the report.[22] The sensitivity of the report for the UK government was highlighted in a note prepared by Baroness Elles, a Conservative MEP, for Margaret Thatcher four days before Haagerup presented his report to a special meeting of the parliament's Political Affairs Committee on the 12 December 1983. Baroness Elles was at pains to stress that the report was prepared entirely by Mr Haagerup himself, that no fact-finding mission to Northern Ireland by the Political Affairs Committee had taken place and that the EP accepted that it could not make proposals on changes to the constitutional position of Northern Ireland. However, even if Haagerup could not recommend any changes to the constitutional position of Northern Ireland, the report could exert influence by offering an interpretation of the conflict and possible solutions and by bringing a European and EU dimension to the problem.

The rationale behind the report was to explain to a non-Irish and non-British audience the complexities of the situation in Northern Ireland and to see how the

19 Hayward, 'Reiterating national identities', p. 268.   20 Paul Bew and Elizabeth Meehan, 'Regions and borders: controversies in Northern Ireland about the European Union', *Journal of European Public Policy*, 1:1 (1994), pp 95–113.   21 N.J. Haagerup, Report drawn up on behalf of the Political Affairs Committee on the situation in Northern Ireland, 19 March 1984, European Parliament Working Documents 1983–1984, Document 1–1526/83, p. 5.   22 Hayward, 'Reiterating national identities', p. 269.

EU and its institutions might contribute to improving the situation. The inter-pretation of the conflict arrived at in the Haagerup Report was relatively close to the SDLP's analysis and its suggestions for a way forward were broadly in line with SDLP preferences. The Haagerup Report strongly advocated a joint approach from London and Dublin in the following terms:

> calls upon the British and Irish governments to re-examine their individ-ual and collective responsibility for expanding and enlarging their mutual co-operation not only in matters related to security north and south of the border but also to use their influence with the two communities in Northern Ireland to bring about a political system with an equitable shar-ing of government responsibilities, which would accommodate the identi-ties of the two traditions, so upholding the ideals and the concept of tolerance vis-a-vis minorities practised in the two countries and in other EC Member States.[23]

In addition to the British-Irish dimension, the report advocated a power-sharing agreement within Northern Ireland. Observers suggest that the Haagerup Report and the EU more generally may well have nudged the Thatcher government towards the Anglo-Irish Agreement (AIA) which was signed a year later.[24] That agreement in turn was a precursor to the Good Friday Agreement, the agreement that transformed the governance of Northern Ireland. Thus, although the report was cautious and not very radical, an important marker was put down by the European Parliament that the Northern Ireland conflict was a legitimate area of European and international concern.

SOURCE OF SUPPORT

Although Northern Ireland's three MEPs disagreed fundamentally on many things and European Parliament elections underlined the depth of political polarization in the province, they worked together to ensure that Northern Ireland would ben-efit from the European Union budget and programmes. The two most significant EU policies were agriculture and regional policy. The latter became particularly salient following the major reform of European regional policy in 1988.[25] Certain aspects of European regional policy were challenging to implement in the context

---

23 Haagerup Report (1984), p. 9. **24** Dennis Kennedy, 'North-South relations in the European context' in Mary Browne and Dennis Kennedy (eds), *Northern Ireland and the European Union* (Belfast, 2006), pp 60–2. D. Phinnemore, L. McGowan, C. McCall and P. McLoughlin, 'Northern Ireland: 40 years of EU membership', *Journal of Contemporary European Research*, 8:4 (2012), pp 563–70. **25** Bew and Meehan, 'Regions and borders'.

of the island of Ireland. As a complement to the single market project, the Commission was an advocate of cross-border co-operation and included in its model of EU funding provision for programmes known as Inter-Reg, that were designed to facilitate joint cross-border projects. These programmes were initially met with suspicion and resistance from unionist politicians in Northern Ireland but gradually the carrot of budgetary support and the actual experience of working with counterparts from the other side of the Irish border was accepted as part of the landscape of public policy. The experience of working with Inter-Reg facilitated the establishment of a cross-border body for EU programmes, Special EU Programmes Body (SEUPB), as part of the Good Friday Agreement. It was one of the areas where there was both experience and tangible benefits of co-operation across the contested Irish border.

Hume stressed from the beginning that incremental economic co-operation that improved the social and economic situation in Northern Ireland had a significant role in the search for a new political order. Moreover, EU programmes provided a framework for cross border co-operation that was one level removed from the Dublin government. The EU went beyond its normal financial toolkit in the 1990s to both recognize and encourage reconciliation in Northern Ireland. Together with the unionist MEPs, John Hume lobbied for the establishment of the EU Special Programme for Peace and Reconciliation (Peace I, II and III). The title of the programme, Peace Programme, was enormously symbolic and signalled EU and member states support for developments within Northern Ireland. The Peace Programme was directed at the communities on the ground and because of the rules, access to financial support was contingent on designing intercommunity projects and processes. Moreover, the inclusion of the stipulation – largely at John Hume's instigation – that actions undertaken under Peace I and Peace II would have to be demonstrably additional was an important milestone in the struggle over the vexed issue of additionality, that is, of ensuring that EU money was not seen as a substitute for finance from the UK treasury by the UK authorities.

CONCLUSION

The core objective of John Hume's political career was to foster peace and reconciliation in Northern Ireland by creating the conditions for and fashioning a set of durable political arrangements that would capture the complexities of politics in Northern Ireland, the island of Ireland and between Britain and Ireland. Hume's attitudes towards Europe and the role Europe played in his political narrative, strategy and action must be understood in the context of this core objective. Hume was culturally and linguistically at home in continental Europe and experienced the EU as a peace project, not as a set of technocratic policy processes.

In the long struggle for peace from the end of the 1960s and the even longer search for a more inclusive set of political arrangements, John Hume drew inspiration from the European Union, from the manner in which it went about its business, from the kinds of institutional arrangements it created, from its politics of compromise and piecemeal cooperation, and from its emphasis on working towards a common interest. For these reasons, an emphasis on Europe as a model was central to his political philosophy and how he described the world. John Hume was a consummate political actor and understood that the EU was not just a model but an opportunity, an opportunity to internationalize the conflict, an opportunity to educate and remind others of the seriousness of the situation within Northern Ireland and an opportunity to garner material support for Northern Ireland through EU funding programmes. It was also an opportunity and arena to put forward SDLP preferences about the kind of political arrangements that should emerge. Hume also understood Britain and Ireland's joint membership of the EU had a profound impact on relations between the two islands and hence on their joint ability to address the conflict. His idea of Europe in the 1980s and early 1990s, a Europe of the Regions, a Europe of post-nationalist identities, a borderless Europe, did not prevail. The member states and national governments continue to be the most powerful political actors in Europe. But enough of that Europe did emerge to transform Europe's state system if not to transcend it. John Hume was an Irish European, a liberal nationalist who was himself capable of transcending and re-imagining the dysfunctional political system he was born into in Derry in 1937. Throughout his long political career in many different theatres, John Hume deployed his core political values and beliefs in a very consistent manner and managed to persuade other politicians and institutions of the need for profound change. John Hume was that rare thing in politics – a statesman – with ideas, convictions and consummate skill.

In America

NANCY SODERBERG

Simply put, John Hume drove US foreign policy on Northern Ireland for nearly three decades. Shirt always rumpled, glasses always smudged, Hume made lasting and real friendships with Irish-American leaders. His easy laugh, passion and love of a good story made him beloved of US policymakers. And they relied on his brilliant wisdom in shaping the US response to Northern Ireland's Troubles.

In the early 1970s, Irish-Americans were divided between those who supported the IRA and Sinn Féin and those who rejected violence and took their cues from John Hume and the Irish government. Some of the former supported the IRA and Sinn Féin not only with funds, but also sent weapons to the IRA to fight the British. Hume, however, aimed to direct Irish-America on a different path. He made inroads with political leaders in the United States by arguing for a non-violent path forward in Northern Ireland. One of the first people he befriended was Senator Edward (Ted) Kennedy, who was naturally drawn to Hume's non-violent method, as well as his emerging image as the Martin Luther King of Northern Ireland. They also bonded personally, with a shared love of good jokes, fun stories, and good food and good wine.

As British policy became increasingly security focussed, Kennedy strongly supported Hume and the goals of the Northern Ireland Civil Rights Association. Kennedy took an early interest in events in Northern Ireland. In his 1970 US bicentennial address at Trinity College in Dublin, Kennedy condemned Britain's approach, calling Northern Ireland 'Britain's Vietnam', and argued for reform. A close and intimate connection with Northern Ireland developed when Kennedy first met Hume in Bonn in November 1972 where he was attending a NATO Assembly meeting. They met at the Irish ambassador's residence on the eve of the ninth anniversary of the slaying of President John F. Kennedy. Together, the two agreed to work for a non-violent, pro-human and civil rights course for US policy towards Northern Ireland.

As the British security approach further intensified, Hume teamed up with Senator Kennedy, Senator Daniel Moynihan, Speaker of the House Tip O'Neill, and New York Governor Hugh Carey in issuing a statement on St Patrick's Day in 1977 urging Irish-Americans to support a non-violent approach, a cross-community dialogue and an end to the violence. That message initiated an annual statement that highlighted the differences between the two Irish-American camps. In 1981, Kennedy, Moynihan and O'Neill also founded the Friends of Ireland in Congress, lending further support to Hume's efforts to promote peace and reconciliation in Northern Ireland. The St Patrick's Day statement also became a way for Irish-American leaders in Congress to annually urge action on Irish issues.

Hume relentlessly built up a network of support for his message, first in Congress and then at the White House, working through the Friends of Ireland. President Jimmy Carter was the first US president to echo Hume's message, calling in 1977 on all sides, including Irish-Americans, not to support violence. His statement also promised additional US investment in Northern Ireland to support a political solution. Kennedy, who had pushed for the statement, called it the 'most important and constructive initiative ever taken by an American President on the Irish issue'.

Throughout the administrations of Ronald Reagan and George H.W. Bush, John Hume continued to push his message of non-violence, peaceful negotiations, and investment in Northern Ireland throughout the United States, always working through the Friends of Ireland. I became Ted Kennedy's foreign policy aide in 1985 and assumed the Irish portfolio. Every year, I would draft the annual St Patrick's Day statement, conferring with staffs of Senator Moynihan and Tip O'Neill, and, of course, John Hume. During my first month there, Hume sent over his top aide, Mark Durkan, to familiarize himself with the personnel and workings of the US Congress. We learned together.

Hume's pressure for US investment in Northern Ireland bore fruit when, in the wake of the 1985 Anglo-Irish Agreement, Congress created the International Fund for Ireland, which appropriated $20 million annually for creating jobs in Northern Ireland and the border counties of the Republic. Supported by President Reagan, the fund made good on President Carter's pledge. The fund is administered by an independent agency with contributions from not just the US but also other nations with large Irish populations, Canada, Australia and New Zealand, as well as the European Union. Incredibly in this age of partisan politics and budget cuts, the fund continues to thrive. In its three decades of work, it has invested nearly $1 billion in over 5,800 projects and stands as a living testament to John Hume's vision for peace, reconciliation and jobs.

While Hume had powerful allies in Congress he also had to face some vigorous opposition led by Congressman Mario Biaggi, a Democrat from New York. In 1977, Biaggi teamed up with Father Seán McManus, the President of the Irish National Caucus, to form the pro-Sinn Féin Congressional Ad Hoc Committee on Irish Affairs. The group advocated for the unification of Ireland, for a favourable immigration policy to the US for the Irish, and for the McBride

Principles, modelled after the Sullivan Principles in South Africa, which demanded investors in Northern Ireland adhere to non-discriminatory policies.

Hume argued strongly against the position adopted by the Irish National Caucus on the McBride Principles. While he approved of most of the principles, he believed some amounted effectively to a call to prohibit US investment in Northern Ireland. Hume's focus was on bringing investment and jobs. He believed both communities would gain from investment, not least his own constituents, many of whom suffered long-term unemployment. So, while a strong advocate of civil rights in the workplace, Hume did not believe in calling for a prohibition on US investment. Instead he favoured strong legislation in Northern Ireland outlawing workplace discrimination.

DEEPENING INVOLVEMENT

While Hume helped deliver US investment in Northern Ireland, peace still eluded him. Two to three hundred people a year were still dying from the violence. Following approaches from Fr Alec Reid, Hume entered a dialogue with Gerry Adams beginning in 1987, exploring ways to bridge the gap between his non-violent approach and Adams' belief that the British would listen only if the violence was maintained. Hume kept Senator Kennedy – and thus me – briefed on this dialogue. Although this initial contact with Adams did not succeed in ending the violence, the two men maintained contact, directly and indirectly, over the next two years.

By 1990, there was renewed hope with the new British Prime Minister, John Major. He took a more moderate approach to Northern Ireland than his predecessor, Margaret Thatcher, who had proclaimed that she would never negotiate with the IRA, a stand most determinedly demonstrated when she had allowed ten hunger strikers to die in 1981.

Major recognized the possibility of negotiations and found in his Irish counterpart, Albert Reynolds, a partner with whom he could work toward a solution to the conflict. On 15 December 1993, Major and Reynolds published a joint declaration, called the Downing Street Declaration, in which the British government committed itself to abide by the wishes of the majority of the citizens of the North, and the Irish government renounced its claim to the North until a majority of the people there agreed to change its status. This declaration opened the door for the first meaningful negotiations in a generation and would result in the Good Friday Agreement, a long four-and-a-half years later.

While Hume was cautiously supportive, he believed that the US government could play a key role in encouraging Adams and the republican movement to become fully engaged. Adams understood that the declaration offered a better chance for progress than he had seen in decades. But he also knew that he needed more in order to convince the IRA's inner circle to abandon its terrorist campaign and accept a negotiated solution. The declaration spurred him and others in Sinn Féin to intensify their pressure on the US to get involved to secure further concessions from the UK and instil confidence in the process. The form that pressure took was a request for an American visa for Adams.

During his 1992 campaign for the presidency, Bill Clinton had endorsed the more pro-Sinn Féin policy positions of the Irish-American lobby, partly because he wanted to win the New York primary, but also because he had long thought the US should play a more proactive and positive role in the search for peace. He had studied at Oxford as the Troubles emerged and had followed the situation since. Thus, in April 1992, former Congressman Bruce Morrison and others convinced him to call for a special envoy to Northern Ireland and to grant a US entry visa to Gerry Adams. Once I joined the presidential campaign in June of 1992, I had inherited this as Clinton's position, although I did not agree. When I went into the Clinton White House the following January as an official on the National Security Council, I took no action to implement the policy. And when Adams applied for a visa in 1993, the administration still flatly rejected it with no debate, leaving the issue to the State Department.

The Downing Street Declaration, however, changed the dynamics. At the time, we viewed the declaration as an impressive effort to move the peace process forward and gave credit to the two prime ministers for offering new positions that clearly tried to address both sides' more neuralgic phobias. We thought that it just might be the opening Sinn Féin needed to begin meaningful negotiations on an end to the violence. We expected to sit back and wait for their response. We recommended that the White House issue a presidential statement welcoming the Downing Street Declaration and pressing the IRA to take the next step by ending its campaign of violence. In biblical language President Clinton stated: 'I call on those who would still seek to embrace or justify violence to heed the words of Paul and cast off the works of darkness and put on the armour of light'. None of us had any intention of engaging Adams directly.

By December 1993, however, I had begun to pick up signs that real change was, in fact, afoot within the IRA. Key figures in the Irish-American community, especially Bruce Morrison, kept telling me Adams was slowly moving the IRA toward a peaceful strategy. They pointed to the week-long ceasefire, unannounced but effective 6 September 1993, as evidence of that shift, an event I had dismissed as not particularly significant in any longer term way. The move had been pushed by Irish-America to demonstrate the IRA's willingness to engage and had been timed to coincide with the visit of an Irish-American delegation to Belfast; we failed to grasp the importance of the gesture at the time. However, up until then the voice I had listened to most on the issue, John Hume, had been counselling me not to change our position on the envoy or visa issues. But by December, he had changed his mind.

ADAMS' VISA

I had kept in touch regularly with Hume and, in October 1993, I invited him to lunch in the White House mess, despite the ban on foreigners being invited into the mess, which I only later discovered existed! Over lunch in the windowless room covered in dark wood panelling, uniformed navy officers took our orders of soup and sandwiches. As we ate, Hume told me he had been discussing the issue of the expected request by Gerry Adams for a visa with Jean Kennedy Smith, Edward Kennedy's sister and the new ambassador to Ireland. While he was not yet ready to endorse the visa proposal, he said he thought things within the IRA were moving towards peace and advised me to watch events closely. That message surprised me because for the last decade, Hume had advised against engaging Adams. We spoke again in mid-December and, by then, Hume had changed his position. After careful consideration, and in light of the new atmosphere created by the joint declaration, he believed that giving Adams the visa would help the peace process and that the President should do it.

Hume had the best antennae for political change on the Irish scene. I knew then that if Hume was advocating that the President give Adams the visa, leading Irish-American members of Congress would give it serious consideration. I knew also then the White House would have to get more involved.

While the political side of the White House, and Irish-American politicians were in favour of sending a special envoy, issuing the visa, and of as much engagement as possible, no National Security Council or State Department official favoured these steps, with the sole exception of Jean Kennedy Smith. Ambassador Smith was beginning to make positive noises about the visa. She had long listened to John Hume and saw, long before I did, that the test of US engagement would come down to whether or not the US would reach out to Adams and give him the visa. Refusal to issue the visa would, at this stage, be a personal humiliation for the key figure trying to move the IRA away from the path of violence.

Irish-America politicians, including Congressman Bruce Morrison, New York Congressman Peter King and other members of the Congressional Ad Hoc Committee on Irish Affairs, pressed the President to fulfil his campaign promise of a visa. They were all calling the White House, including the Vice-President's Chief of Staff, Jack Quinn, one of the congressional liaison officials, Susan Brophy, and the head of Cabinet Affairs, Kitty Higgins, pushing hard for the President to respond to his friends in the Irish-American community. The respected William Flynn, CEO of the insurance company Mutual of America, ran a full-page ad in the *New York Times* calling on the US to engage. Signed by over 200 leading figures, the ad indicated the issue was moving out of the pubs and into the board rooms.

The political benefits to the President moving forward were clear. But the President's foreign policy team was concerned about the message granting a visa to Adams would send regarding the fight against terrorism. In 1994, terrorism was on the rise worldwide. The first attack on the World Trade Centre had occurred in February 1993, and movements around the world were targeting Americans. Congress was concerned. Politically, engaging the IRA held real risks.

In 1993, the IRA was one of the world's deadliest terrorist organizations, responsible for a conflict that had cost over 3,000 lives over the course of a generation. Despite his denials, Adams was part of the IRA's central structure. While there was no concern that Adams would explode a bomb during a visit to the US, there was real concern in law enforcement circles that he would use the visit to raise funds in the United States, and thus expand the lethal capacity of the IRA. Earlier, IRA supporters had recently purchased 2000 detonators in Phoenix, Arizona; these had been shipped to Northern Ireland and by late 1993 had already begun showing up in bombings. There was also a concern that some of the funds might be used to purchase stinger missiles which could be used to shoot down aircraft. The threat of terrorism had become a major focus of the US government. Letting in a known leader of a key terrorist organization would undermine the tough message the US was trying to send in the fight against terrorism.

Given the clear signs that some opening for peace might be in the offing, I began to see the visa request as an opportunity to use Irish-America to press Gerry Adams and the IRA to renounce violence in exchange for engagement with the administration. The burden of proof lay with them, as far as I was concerned. Let them, I thought, make the first move and then we could respond. In the lead up to the joint declaration, we had decided to lay some markers down for Adams, and for his friends in Congress. Conor O'Clery of the *Irish Times* had been pushing for an interview for some time. As he was the most respected of the Irish journalists, we agreed to take some written questions from him and took the opportunity to make a statement on Gerry Adams and his visa request.

Mindful of Clinton's campaign statements and the strong interest of the President's Irish-American supporters in the issue, we wanted to indicate a willingness to engage but also hoped to keep the burden of movement on Adams. Thus, for the first time, the US linked the possibility of giving Adams a visa to progress on the peace process. The President said he would keep the issue of a visa for Adams under review, 'as the developing situation warrants, especially in light of events flowing from the December 15 joint declaration'.

If Adams were to respond positively to the declaration and renounce violence, the President would be prepared to take a new look at the visa. We put the onus on Adams and Irish America. If Irish-America wanted Adams to get the visa, Irish-America would have to press Adams to renounce violence and join the political process.

John Hume's urging to reach out to Adams changed the politics of the issue dramatically. He not only urged me to recommend that President Clinton issue the visa to Adams, he also worked his friends in Congress. Political pressure from Irish-America, Congress, and the political advisers to the President made it clear our hands-off policy was not sustainable. The new dynamic created by the joint declaration required some further gesture on the part of the United States – and John Hume understood that well before we did. We looked at ways short of a visa to engage, such as sending a special envoy or ending the US ban on substantive contacts with Sinn Féin, especially since news of secret British talks with Sinn Féin had recently been leaked. But the issue quickly came down to a visa for Gerry Adams.

Irish-America had no intention of waiting for us to make a decision on how and when to engage. We began to hear Mutual of America's William Flynn was organizing a conference for the parties in Northern Ireland to discuss peace. He planned to invite Gerry Adams and the leaders of the other political parties there. The 'peace' conference was to be organized under the auspices of the respected National Committee on American Foreign Policy (NCAFP), a small, New York-based organization that provides a forum for foreign policy discussions. The group invited Gerry Adams to a conference in New York to start on 31 January as well as John Hume, James Molyneaux, leader of the Ulster Unionist Party, Dr John Alderdice, leader of the Alliance Party, and Dr Ian Paisley, leader of the Democratic Unionist Party. We were now faced with a deadline. Only later did I realize just how right Flynn was to organize this conference.

Added pressure came when, on 6 January, the 'King' of Irish-America and one of the world's most loved men, Tip O'Neill, died. The President described him as 'the Nation's most prominent, powerful, and loyal champion of working people'. Most famous for his line, 'all politics is local', O'Neill was the most loved Irish-American politician. His passing only increased the resolve of Irish-America to get the White House involved in the Northern Ireland peace process and they used the occasion of his passing to intensify the lobby for a visa on behalf of Adams.

Then Irish Prime Minister Albert Reynolds weighed in with a startling new position. He believed Adams was working for peace and he too believed Adams should get a visa. We now had the two leading voices on the Irish side, John Hume and the Irish prime minister, pushing for the visa. Edward Kennedy's sister, Jean, the ambassador in Dublin, was pushing hard too. 'There is no indication you have read my messages and that they have gotten high level attention', she complained to me. In a new twist on the criticism we were getting, that we were too sensitive to pressure from Irish-America, she said, 'the President should be pro-active, not appear to be responding to domestic political pressure'. Later, when she sent in a formal cable recommending the visa following Adams' application on 14 January, four career officers revolted. They sent a 'dissent channel' cable to Washington protesting Smith's recommendation.

On 15 January 1994, Senators Kennedy, Moynihan, Chris Dodd and John Kerry sent a letter to President Clinton echoing John Hume's message that 'granting a visa at this time will enhance, not undermine, the peace process'. The letter noted that the British government was in dialogue with Adams, noted the Downing Street Declaration, and highlighted John Hume's own dialogue with Adams. The fact that Ted Kennedy, having lost two brothers to violence, was now willing to support a visa for a leading proponent of a terrorist organization changed the politics of the issue significantly. 'The United States cannot afford to ignore this possibility and miss this rare opportunity for our country to contribute to peace in Northern Ireland', he argued in the letter.

The Kennedy letter unleashed a flood of support for the visa from a host of Democratic politicians. Within a week of Kennedy's endorsement of the visa request, New York Governor Mario Cuomo and another twenty-two Democratic Senators joined the campaign for the visa. Calls to the President, Vice-President, and various political advisers in the White House, were mounting. It was becoming clear that all of Irish-America and much of the Democratic Party leadership was lining up behind the visa. But while saying 'no' to the visa would cause an uproar among some of the President's closest allies, saying 'yes' would enrage the President's cabinet – including Secretary of State Christopher Warren, FBI Director Louis Freeh, and Attorney-General Janet Reno – and America's closest ally, the UK.

There were now encouraging signs that progress toward peace might be made. Bruce Morrison called me on 11 January to report on his conversations with Adams. Adams, he said, was prepared to say 'his goal is to move the republican movement away from the use of force and to the political process'. He had long since believed the IRA campaign wouldn't lead anywhere and that it had to be replaced by a political process. He didn't want to see another generation of people drawn into a similar situation, and saw himself as the 'guy who'd put his own credibility on the line to make the breakthrough'.

Hume was getting a similar message from Adams. In order for him to support the joint declaration, Adams needed further 'clarifications' from the British, in effect further concessions, including a timetable and a commitment by the British to withdraw from Northern Ireland. He also wanted a commitment to direct talks between the British and Sinn Féin and progress toward allowing Sinn Féin to operate as a normal political party, such as, for instance, lifting the broadcast ban on Sinn Féin officials. If he had a full package, according to Hume, Adams could 'bring it to the IRA'. That meant there was a chance of getting an IRA ceasefire.

After much discussion with the British and the State Department, we decided to use the visa to press for what we thought was achievable: strong statements from Adams renouncing violence and acceptance of the joint declaration. We were linking the visa explicitly to Adams' renunciation of violence and his taking steps to join the political process. National Security Advisor Anthony Lake approved the following language for use with our consulate in Belfast or embassy in Dublin in discussion with Adams: 'In making a decision on whether to grant you a waiver of your ineligibility, it is important for us to have an understanding of your position on achieving peace in Northern Ireland. We therefore must know whether you will state publicly that: You personally renounce violence and will work to that end; and that Sinn Féin and the IRA are committed to ending the conflict on the basis of the Joint Declaration. Our decision on whether to provide you with a visa will depend on whether you are willing to take this important step toward peace'.

We hoped Adams would make a dramatic gesture to justify issuing the visa, but we were beginning to realize he was not in a position to do so. Adams was getting increasingly frustrated over the British failure to reach out to him and over the United States' foot-dragging. In his view, he was already sticking his neck out – and so far, only the Irish government was responding. To prod the White House, he sent a private letter 'To Whom it May Concern' laying out his concerns. Kennedy's office faxed it to me.

The letter was a strong plea for US involvement to break the deadlock in the 'current opportunity for peace'. Arguing that the political climate had 'changed dramatically', a more open and informed climate for debate 'should be encouraged, not discouraged'. Adams argued that the continued denial of a visa would send a 'negative signal to those involved in the risky and difficult business of developing a genuine peace process. Of course, the US administration will be criticized if it takes this progressive step but the risk of such criticism is a small one compared to the risks being taken by people in Ireland'.

By early January 1994, it was increasingly clear to us that Adams was unlikely to meet our own rigid position laid out in the cable to the consul-general in Belfast. But it was also clear that Adams was engaged in a real attempt to promote a peace process and that he and the British were talking past one another. We felt we should be able to find a way to extract *some* initial progress from Adams and grant him the visa. Having received the visa, he would then be in a stronger position to make a significant move toward peace. He would also be under substantial pressure to deliver.

John Hume called me at the White House about recent IRA bombings which, he said, had been ordered by those trying to undermine Adams' more moderate approach. The IRA Army Council was reportedly split on whether Adams should go to the peace conference in New York. If true, that meant Adams had very little room to manoeuvre.

Hume shared the view of Dublin – that the British were handling the peace process 'too starkly. Endorsing the process will take some time'. He argued that the US would have to engage. He believed that giving Adams a visa would impel the peace process forward. But the impact of a 'no' would be significant and, Hume added, 'But it threatens no one if it works'. Hume then harped on one of his constant themes: how best to promote peace. He said that 'it is people who have rights, not territory'. If we could shift the debate to the rights of people, not a discussion of territorial divisions, real and significant progress could be made. 'The key', he argued, 'was changing people's mindset. They have to see that everyone will gain if all rights are guaranteed'.

I had begun to understand that the key problem in Northern Ireland was that each side viewed the conflict as a zero-sum game. If one side gained, the other lost. Real progress would require changing that attitude. Hume had been trying to change that mindset by promoting investment, jobs, visas and economic growth. Now it would be central to Clinton's calculation on engaging in the peace process.

We all were beginning to realize we were likely to give Adams the visa without his first renouncing violence. In late January, Anthony Lake sent a memo to the President recommending that he approve the visa. His memo argued that Adams clearly was reaching out to us, within his own constraints. To turn him down now would be a great set back and humiliation for him – and perhaps could set back the peace process by years. On the other hand, having gotten all of Irish-America to weigh in with the White House in favour of the visa, Adams would be under great pressure to deliver. If we refused, he would be unlikely to move forward anytime soon and might even lose influence with the hardliners. If we gave him the visa and he failed to move, then we might convince Irish-America to isolate him as a fraud. If he did come, and progress was made, obviously everyone would gain. The visa would be as limited as possible, permitting Adams to remain in the US for the duration of the conference only, prohibiting him from travelling further than twenty-five miles from New York and banning any fundraising. While not without risks, the memo argued that it was a win-win situation either way for the President, the United States and the peace process. The memo went to the President four days before Adams needed to get on a plane for the peace conference in New York.

Ultimately, it was the win-win logic – Hume's in fact – that persuaded the President to move forward. His gut instincts had long urged him to take the plunge into Irish politics. Now was his chance to do it. His key supporters in Congress gave him political cover and the fact that his Vice President, Al Gore, a seasoned voice in foreign policy, was for it, reassured him. After throwing our arguments back in our face for about a half-hour, Clinton satisfied himself that issuing the visa was the right thing to do. He ended the phone call with a simple,

'OK, let's do it'. Clinton decided to take the risk for peace. The step would not have happened without John Hume's endorsement and work to gain broad political support for the move. At the time, I had privately hoped we would see a cease-fire by St Patrick's Day. Unfortunately, I would have to wait over six months.

PEACE PROCESS

Hume continued to press behind the scenes for a ceasefire, which finally came in August 1994. Six weeks later, Protestant paramilitaries announced their own cease-fire. Throughout the process of forging peace, John Hume played the key role behind the scenes – and sometimes front and centre – in pushing for his vision of a peaceful and prosperous Northern Ireland. President Clinton visited Ireland in 1995 and made a point of visiting Derry with John Hume. The message was clear – peace would not have occurred without John Hume.

Hume's efforts continued following the end of the IRA ceasefire in 1996, con-stantly reaching out to the White House, Congress, and leaders of both the union-ist and nationalist communities to press for peace. As Adams put it in one of his books, 'John Hume and I met almost immediately after the end of the IRA cessa-tion in February 1996. We had helped to shape the consensus which underpinned a political and diplomatic alternative (to IRA violence)'. Following a meeting between Hume and Adams and the IRA leadership a second ceasefire was declared in July 1997.

The new governments in London led by Labour's Tony Blair and in Dublin led by Fianna Fáil's Bertie Ahern were committed to negotiations. So was Bill Clinton. He and his envoy, Senator George Mitchell, worked tirelessly for a suc-cessful outcome and finally secured the Good Friday Peace Agreement in April 1998. It ended the bloody conflict which had cost over 3500 lives.

The peace in Northern Ireland is now irreversible, but the society is still divided, with great economic disparities between the two communities. The Northern Ireland assembly was suspended and the issue of decommissioning of arms derailed progress. With a strong push from John Hume and his friends in the US, the IRA agreed to disarm in September 2005.

The Nobel Peace Prize Committee recognized Hume's extraordinary contri-bution when it awarded him and the unionist leader David Trimble in 1998 'for their efforts to find a peaceful solution to the conflict in Northern Ireland'. Hume is the only person to also be awarded the other two major peace awards, the Gandhi Peace Prize and the Martin Luther King Award. In 2010, John was voted 'Ireland's Greatest' in a public poll by RTÉ. While his SDLP has been eclipsed by Sinn Féin in the polls, John Hume's contribution to peace will remain in the his-tory books. For three decades, he worked across the US to put Washington on the right side of history. Today, there is an 'Agreed Ireland' where the killing has stopped because of his work.

STILL NOT REALIZED

Nearly more than twenty years after the first IRA ceasefire in August 1994, the peace process has stemmed the violence, but the two communities still have not fully reconciled. Many remain stuck on the injustices of the past and refuse to compromise on parades and flags, and all the while the economy remains under-developed. Today, ninety per cent of children still go to segregated schools and live in segregated neighbourhoods. The so called 'peace' walls that divide the two communities in Belfast still stand. Current leaders on both sides seem incapable of getting past the victim mentality and making the compromises necessary to forge a better future. The way forward is to build an undivided society, with the best schools and expanding economic opportunity.

Only part of John Hume's vision has been realized. While Hume is now retired from politics, that vision remains a key goal for Washington. President Obama has remained engaged, sending envoys, making phone calls, and pushing and prodding for progress. In his acceptance speech of the Nobel Prize in 1998, John Hume said: 'I want to see Ireland as an example to men and women everywhere of what can be achieved by living for ideals, rather than fighting for them, and by viewing each and every person as worthy of respect and honour. I want to see an Ireland of partnership where we wage war on want and poverty, where we reach out to the marginalized and dispossessed, where we build together a future that can be as great as our dreams allow'. His great legacy demands the leaders of Northern Ireland fulfil that dream.

Common Name of Irishman

MARIANNE ELLIOTT

Nationalism in Ireland: how did it start and develop; how did it become so identified with Catholicism; how, if at all, did it adapt to changing circumstances? Like
all 'isms' it is full of contradictions, the most obvious and debilitating the tensions
between its 'constitutional' non-violent and its 'physical force' violent forms, and
the centuries-old inability to reconcile them. This has led to long periods of helplessness and seemed to vindicate opponents' claims that nationalists were all rebels
– a stereotype that romantic nationalism was rarely in any haste to renounce. Has
John Hume – the modern epitome of constitutional nationalism – succeeded in
resolving these contradictions?

   Wolfe Tone was the first to set out the core of both strains of modern nationalism: an Ireland liberated from England, through violent means if necessary, with
the ultimate goal of creating 'the common name of Irishman'. Much of this went
against a number of his past guiding principles and owed a lot to the specific time
and place in which his 'philosophy' was first fully articulated, namely revolutionary France. Even so, this brilliant political writer, with a very special gift for cap-
turing complicated ideas in simple and comprehensible language, bequeathed to
future nationalism its core principles and its inherent contradictions: breaking the
connection with England and developing 'the common name of Irishman'.

> To subvert the tyranny of our execrable Government, to break the connec-
> tion with England, the never-failing source of all our political evils, and to
> assert the independence of my country – these were my objects. To unite the
> whole people of Ireland, to abolish the memory of all past dissensions, and
> to substitute the common name of Irishman in the place of the denomina-
> tions of Protestant, Catholic and Dissenter – these were my means.[1]

---

1 Marianne Elliott, *Wolfe Tone,* 2nd ed. (Liverpool, 2012), p. 300; the whole text is conveniently located in
T.W. Moody, R.B. McDowell and C.J. Woods (eds), *The writings of Theobald Wolfe Tone, 1763–98,* 3 vols
(Oxford, 1997–2007), ii, p. 301.

Tone's emergence as a political writer, to so shape modern nationalism, was one of those occasions highlighting the inherent contradictions of constitutional nationalism: what to do if years of patient effort failed to win reforms. For nearly half a century Catholic leaders had tried but failed to convince government that they were trying to rejoin the political system (from which they were excluded under the penal laws) rather than overthrow it. The history of Ireland was to be littered with concessions granted too late to conciliate. In the 1790s, changed times and the impatience of the young brought about the militant rejection of the moderates. And the process was to be repeated through the next two centuries, each failure providing heroes and martyrs to the militant tradition, as well as feeding a rich tradition of rebel songs. It was a tradition to which all varieties of nationalist unthinkingly subscribed, even though it celebrated a tiny fraction of that tradition and gave hostage to critics who thought Catholics and nationalists were all rebels anyway.

The idea of the romantic rebel transcends national boundaries. Every culture has traditions of the virtuous underdog triumphing against evil, even though the historical reality often does not match up to the myth. Also, as in Ireland, it is very often a case of turning the hostile stereotype of the perceived illegitimate power into the virtuous portrayal of that underdog. In Ireland the twelfth-century Anglo-Norman views of the unruly Irish were transferred to Catholics generally by the Elizabethan reformation in the sixteenth century. They have remained a significant factor in the Protestant psyche ever since. They pervaded the loyalist news-sheets of the early Northern Ireland Troubles and informed the brutal reaction to the civil rights marches of the pre-Troubles. It took many years before unionism gave credit to the overwhelmingly constitutional character of northern nationalism.

For most of nationalism's history the Catholic Church could be found in the constitutional camp, and that in Ulster – attuned to operating in a largely Protestant society – even more so. Militant nationalism was denounced from the altar, and despite the modern sectarian insult of 'Fenian', Fenianism was weaker in Ulster than in the rest of Ireland. Indeed, as the events of 1918 onwards unfolded and partition seemed likely, the Irish Catholic primate, Cardinal Logue, preferred to remain with Britain rather than face partition. Protestant dislike and fear of the Catholic Church deterred any real understanding of its largely moderating role. Though equally, the Church was responsible for squeezing the Protestant voice out of nationalism and cementing the image of nationalism as a Catholic preserve. The misfortune for Northern nationalism is that for those crucial decades pre-and post-partition, the Catholic Church's normally moderate nationalist stance seemed to have disappeared. Logue was followed by the pro-Sinn Féin Joseph MacRory (bishop of Down and Connor from 1915 and then archbishop of Armagh until 1945). He shunned constitutional nationalism's Belfast leader, Joe Devlin, in favour of working through Michael Collins in Dublin, and continued to both oppose Devlin's more pragmatic approach to political realities and to make some very provocative statements against Protestantism itself.[2]

Like northern nationalism generally, the hierarchy's outlook was coloured by the trauma of the birth years of the two new states and the sense of having been abandoned by the rest of Ireland. However, as time passed they were succeeded by a different breed of clerical leadership, whose return to the more traditional non-militant mould of Ulster clerics underpinned the improving relationships that marked the decades after the end of the Second World War. The much more sensitive statements by MacRory's successor, Cardinal John d'Alton (primate 1946–63), were to mark a new realism in nationalism. When he died in 1963, the *Belfast Telegraph* paid tribute in an editorial: he 'regularly used his authority to counsel goodwill and moderation. Thus worthily he won the esteem of all who had anything to do with him … The slow thaw in Catholic opinion here in recent years dates from his coming north'.[3] His funeral took place against the backdrop of the great blizzard of January 1963 and Irish Taoiseach Éamon de Valera paid tribute to the RUC for meeting his cortège at the border and accompanying it to Armagh to ensure it got through for the Cardinal's funeral.[4]

Until then the Nationalist Party was exclusively Catholic and rather old-fashioned, still steeped in the national origin-myth and resentful about how victory had been narrowly snatched from them in 1921. The territory of the new northern state was still provisional until the Boundary Commission (1924–5) was to decide whether majority Catholic areas (Fermanagh, Tyrone, south Down, south Armagh and Derry City) should remain with the rest of Ireland. In the interval those areas proclaimed their allegiance to the Dáil, their spokesmen making some highly provocative and sectarian statements in the process. As the Anglo-Irish war unfolded elsewhere in the country and the IRA attacked RIC barracks in border areas, the Belfast Catholic minority paid the price, as it had done so often in the past and would again in the future. In the so-called 'Belfast pogrom' of 1920–2, Catholic civilians figured disproportionately in the number of deaths, and thousands were expelled from their homes and workplaces. Northern nationalists felt they had been abandoned by the rest of Ireland as the new unionist regime moved quickly to bolster up its own shaky hold on power by removing those electoral procedures that had almost allowed the nationalist counties to break away. Gerrymandering had arrived and the border was left intact.

The Nationalist Party boycotted the new Northern Ireland Parliament and thereby could offer little effective opposition to the early measures that helped

2 Éamon Phoenix, *Northern nationalism. Nationalist politics, partition and the Catholic minority in Northern Ireland, 1890–1940* (Belfast, 1994), pp 25, 111, 374; Marianne Elliott, *When God took sides: religion and identity in Ireland. Unfinished history* (London, 2009), p. 237.   3 *Belfast Telegraph*, 1 Feb. 1963; Daithí Ó Corráin, *Rendering to God and Caesar: the Irish churches and the two states in Ireland, 1949–73* (Manchester, 2006), pp 44–57.   4 *Belfast Telegraph*, 7 Feb. 1963.

install unionist supremacy. But at this stage moderate nationalism's instincts militated against such non-representation and the party had considerable support when it finally took up its parliamentary seats in 1925. There followed several years when unionist concessions might have helped crystallize a more co-operative mood among nationalists. Few came, and the next thirty years were marked by long periods when the elected nationalist politicians simply abstained from parliament. Such high-profile non-recognition of the Northern Ireland state disguised the normal adherence to the laws and co-operation with the state institutions which marked everyday existence of northern nationalists. But it allowed detractors to dismiss them as 'disloyalists', unfit for all manner of public employment. 'It all turns on a question of "loyalty"', wrote J.J. Campbell under the pseudonym 'Ultach', in a famous pamphlet of 1943, 'and it is natural sometimes that "disloyalists" should get hurt ... [and] fail to get jobs. And so on. "Well, they must expect it if they are 'disloyal'," says the outsider. But then the outsider does not know that the words "loyalist" and "disloyalist" have a meaning all their own in Northern Ireland'.[5]

There was an intrinsic inconsistency in post-partition constitutional nationalism. On the one hand nationalists were aggrieved that the unionist regime failed to appoint Catholics to public office. On the other they denounced Catholics who did accept such appointments for joining the enemy. Patrick Shea, one of a very few Catholics to reach the top of the Northern Ireland Civil Service, recalled surprise from his Protestant colleagues at how he had 'got in', and suspicion from fellow Catholics. 'I was probably a "bad Catholic", perhaps secretly a Freemason ... [I] had gone over to "the other side".'[6] Austin Currie, one-time Nationalist Party MP, before co-founding the SDLP, described the dilemma: 'The main problem was the nationalist dilemma since Partition: the need for strong representation to fight discrimination versus the fear of buttressing partition by active participation in its institutions'.

Their representatives became part-time MPs, lacking a party organization, and, after the death of the legendary Joe Devlin in 1934, the party became more closely identified with the Catholic Church, when he had always resisted the idea that he led a Catholic party. The names of his successors as leader have barely scratched the history books. Paddy Devlin, who with John Hume and other new MPs in the 1960s 'had come in as full-time parliamentarians', was critical of the nationalist MPs. 'They were still part-time and poor attenders'. Because of their links to nationalist newspapers, they would put down a question, come in just in time to take the answer, then write 'banner headlines' about how they exposed the evils of

5 'Ultach' [J.J. Campbell], ' "Orange terror": the partition of Ireland', reprinted from the *Capuchin Annual*, 194 (1943), p. 14. 6 Patrick Shea, *Voices and the sound of drums: an Irish autobiography* (Belfast, 1981), p. 197; Nationalist Party leader, T.J.Campbell, 1934–45, was similarly vilified when he was appointed county court judge for Tyrone, the kind of involvement which constitutionalists had traditionally sought. See Brian M. Walker, *A political history of the two Ireland: from partition to peace* (Basingstoke, 2012), p. 68.

the unionist regime. 'It was a pitiful farce that the people reading Catholic news-papers had to put up with such tedious tactics for so many years'.[7] Nor was the Nationalist Party a united block. In its heartlands west of the Bann it often suc-cumbed to the pull exercised by Sinn Féin. Its lengthy periods of abstention from parliament had been a republican rather than a constitutional nationalist policy. The Belfast members were attuned to operating in a largely Protestant milieu; they were more open to compromise and not so clerically aligned. But Belfast was abandoned by the now predominantly rural party after 1946, and Belfast's largely working-class Catholic vote drifted to labour politics.[8]

In fairness to the nationalist politicians of these immediate post-partition decades, they had very little to show for their participation in normal politics and even moderate nationalist voters sometimes turned to Sinn Féin to maintain 'the traditional protest'.[9] Throughout its history, constitutional nationalism recognized that if their people got nothing they would be attracted to the extreme. Yet on the central issue of the re-unification of Ireland and their frequent calls to Dublin to be allowed to sit in the Dáil, nationalists were asking unionists to accept the impossible. And as is so often the way with the underdog, there was no recogni-tion that what they were asking for themselves, recognition of their Catholic-nationalist identity, they were denying to unionists. Nor were things as consistently bleak as portrayed. Monsignor A.H. Ryan, of St Brigid's parish in Belfast, told a meeting at University College Dublin in March 1954, that 'there's a lot more tolerance in Northern Ireland than one would guess from the tone of public controversy'.[10]

Northern Ireland was not a police state, notwithstanding the frequent petty oppressions visited in border areas by the B Specials or the way the Special Powers Act seemed mostly to be used more routinely against the minority.[11] London was very remiss in not intervening more than it did, but it *was* watching. Even union-ist Prime Minister Sir Basil Brooke, so notorious for his sectarian statements at election times, found it necessary in 1951 to remind the Ulster Unionist Council that government could not be seen to discriminate against its citizens (in this case in housing allocation), and hinted at the fact that they were, after all, responsible to a socialist (Labour) government in London.[12] Though it has to be said that those unionists who did argue publicly for a more liberal unionism found little support from their leaders, as evidenced in the interrupted careers of Home Affairs Ministers Brian Maginness and George Hanna. John Hume was to

7 Paddy Devlin, *Straight left: an autobiography* (Belfast, 1993), p. 98. 8 Brendan Lynn, *Holding the ground: the Nationalist Party in Northern Ireland, 1945–72* (Aldershot, 1997), p. 25. 9 Denis P. Barritt and Charles F. Carter, *The Northern Ireland problem: a study in group relations* (Oxford, 1972), p. 51. 10 *Belfast Weekly Telegraph*, 2 Apr. 1954. 11 Marianne Elliott, *The Catholics of Ulster: a history* (London, 2000), pp 382–3; idem, *When God took sides*, pp 242–5: 'Ultach', pp 4–5. 12 Graham Walker, *A history of the Ulster Unionist Party* (Manchester, 2004), pp 116–17.

emerge as a community leader in the more hopeful 1960s, when for nearly two decades things seemed to be improving in Northern Ireland. It is fashionable today to dismiss the years before the outbreak of the Troubles as a false dawn. There was, however, a distinct shift in atmosphere after the war and not just because of the introduction of free education and the welfare state. Investigations into housing largely sustain discrimination charges against councils in Londonderry, Omagh and Dungannon, but also reveal real tensions between such councils and Stormont. The councils certainly could not be trusted to supply the urgent need for public housing revealed in Northern Ireland's first ever housing survey of 1943, so a new body, independent of them, was set up by the government. This was the Housing Trust, which stood up to the age-old attempts at interference from the Orange Order to build 48,000 houses for working people and to allocate them on a mixed-religion basis.[13]

These were also the years that saw the rise of labour politics in Northern Ireland, as bread and butter issues took votes away from the traditionally conservative nationalist and unionist blocks. However, when forced to declare in favour of partition in 1949, the Northern Ireland Labour Party (NILP) lost a lot of nationalist support. But it worked hard on its non-sectarian image and won back many Catholics, particularly the young. In the 1958 general election old nationalism and unionism alike did badly and the NILP broke through to become the Official Opposition in Stormont. Even those Catholics who had been lost to the NILP voted for other anti-partition forms of labour rather than for the Nationalist Party, taking nearly 13% of the total vote against the Nationalist Party's 15%, bringing the overall labour vote to 29%. In 1962 the NILP did even better, taking 26% of votes, with a combined Labour vote of 36.8%.[14] The results prompted a call in the pro-union press for unionism to change.[15]

In the nationalist community also there were calls for a re-think of the old negative nationalist politics. The veteran nationalist MP for Fermanagh-South Tyrone, Cahir Healy, was very critical of a return to abstentionism in the 1950s. The Nationalist Party's failure to contest a number of key constituencies had given Sinn Féin a clear run, just as the militant tradition in nationalism was about the make a dramatic return with a fresh IRA campaign of bombing attacks, mainly on border posts.[16] Such confusion had always cast doubt on the Nationalist Party's non-violence credentials. But this time the IRA received little support from the northern nationalist community, and its thinking was reflected

13 *Northern Ireland Housing Trust Final Report, 1970–71*. HMSO Belfast, 1972, p. 22; my forthcoming book: *Hearthland: the story of a mixed-religion housing in Belfast, 1945–2015*, chapters 2–3; John A. Oliver, *Working at Stormont* (Dublin, 1978), chapters 7–8. 14 Sydney Elliott, *Northern Ireland parliamentary election results, 1921–1972* (Chichester, 1972), p. 97; Aaron Edwards, *A history of the Northern Ireland Labour Party: democratic socialism and sectarianism* (Manchester, 2009), p. 72. 15 *Belfast Telegraph*, 1 and 4 Apr. 1958. 16 Lynn, *Holding the ground*, pp 122–3, 138–43; *Belfast Telegraph*, 8 Aug. 1958.

in the condemnation by the Catholic Church. The Lenten pastoral of Eugene O'Callaghan, bishop of Clogher, in March 1957 was representative:

> That there is obstinate and subtle discrimination against Catholicism and nationalists in the separated counties we are painfully aware. Nevertheless the opposing elements in our nation … constitute the people of one indivisible country, and nothing short of extreme provocation would justify a resort to violence … the border is not merely a geographical division. It is a spiritual division of minds and hearts which physical force cannot heal, but only aggravate.[17]

This was the essence of the more pragmatic nationalism of the 1950s and 60s, and it was in this climate that both the civil rights campaign and John Hume were to emerge. It was of course always there in Tone's 'common name of Irishmen' ideal, but needed considerable reassessment when 'Irishness' had come to presume Catholicism as well as an end to partition.

The more working-class Belfast nationalists had frequently criticized the Nationalist Party's 'bunker mentality'[18] and by the late 1950s and early 60s such irritation was also spreading to its heartlands. There was already a sense among nationalists that the Protestant stereotype of Catholics as 'whinging Micks', always complaining, was the image presented by their representatives and their caution, even hostility, about new ideas was becoming increasingly obvious. Dr Conn McCluskey wrote to the new party leader, Eddie McAteer, about its 'rigid immobility … you are doomed if you do not move on'.[19] Conn and Patricia McCluskey were part of a group of professional Catholics who were demanding equal rights within the existing system and their Campaign for Social Justice (CSJ) would soon produce the Northern Ireland Civil Rights Association (NICRA). They also based their campaign on reliable factual research, the lack of which by the Nationalist Party was painfully exposed in a disastrous televised debate with Brian Faulkner in February 1964. The CSJ's and NICRA's campaigns were, in effect, a return to the essence of constitutional nationalism.

John Hume was to become its most prominent exponent. He was a typical product of the aspirational Catholic working-class family, which respected education as a channel for socio-economic improvement. It was a channel suddenly made easier by the British introduction of free post-primary education. He gained a scholarship to the top Catholic grammar school locally and went on to hold a teaching position there. Later critics often depicted him as the bossy teacher.[20] It

---

17 *Fermanagh Herald*, 9 Mar. 1957.   18 Lynn, *Holding the ground*, p. 143.   19 Ibid., p. 173: Conn McCluskey, *Up off their knees: a commentary on the Civil Rights Movement in Northern Ireland* (Galway, 1989), pp 16–19.   20 See, e.g., *News Letter*, 18 Jan. 1988, cartoon depicting an imposing Hume wagging his

also lay behind what came to be known as 'Hume-speak' and 'the single transferable speech'. 'I keep repeating the same language', he admitted to biographer Paul Routledge. 'That is deliberate. It is the old teacher in me … Not everybody hears or reads a speech. Or even thinks about it. But in public life, if you want to change things you must keep repeating it'.[21]

Derry/Londonderry, with 20% unemployment against a British average of 2.6% and a Northern Ireland one of 8.1%, was a prime example of the non-success of nationalists' culture of complaint against the most gerrymandered unionist council in the province. The Nationalist Party's lack of civic culture – refusing even to attend the bestowal of a civic honour on a Derry industrialist who had brought employment to local Catholics – was singled out for criticism by John Hume in two articles that he wrote for the *Irish Times* in 1964. While recognizing unionist intransigence, these were largely an attack on the ineffective performance of the Nationalist Party, which had offered no constructive opposition and refused to contribute practically to the well-being of people in Northern Ireland.

> Good government depends as much on the opposition as on the party in power … They [nationalist politicians] have – quite rightly – been loud in their demands for rights, but … silent and inactive about their duties. In forty years of opposition they have not produced one constructive contribution on either the social or economics plane to the development of Northern Ireland, which is, after all, a substantial part of the United Ireland for which they strive. … It is this lack of positive contribution and the apparent lack of interest in the general welfare of Northern Ireland that has led many Protestants to believe that the Northern Catholic is politically irresponsible and immature and therefore unfit to rule.

Non-recognition of Northern Ireland was a most unconstitutional stand for a constitutional tradition, he argued, and if they continued such non-recognition they might as well just surrender the nationalist tradition to Sinn Féin. 'If one wishes to create a united Ireland by constitutional means, then one must accept the constitutional position'. Such an acceptance would remove the great 'stumbling block' to normal politics, and allow Catholics to take a part in resolving the problems in Northern Ireland, without the 'fear of recrimination' and name-calling by their own. And he gave specific recent examples of how more constructive suggestions by a number of leading Catholics were denounced in the nationalist press. For the past forty years

finger at Ian Paisley and a diminutive James Molyneux: 'Don't worry boys, you're next in line for a talk.'
21 Paul Routledge, *John Hume: a biography* (London, 1997), p. 39.

> Catholics of all shades of political thought are expected to band together under the unconstructive banner of nationalism. This dangerous equation of nationalism and Catholicism has simply contributed to the postponement of the emergence of normal politics … Worse, it has poisoned the Catholic social climate to the extent that it has become extremely difficult for a Catholic to express publicly any point of view which does not coincide with the narrow nationalist line without bringing on one's head 'a torrent of abuse' and denunciation as 'Castle Catholic' and 'West Briton' among others.

The net effect was to stifle freedom of thought and expression. The association of nationalism with Catholicism was another contradiction, failing to accept that the Protestant tradition was as legitimate as their own. 'The realistic fact that a United Ireland, if it is to come, and if violence, rightly, is to be discounted, must come about by evolution, i.e., by the will of the Northern majority'.[22]

In his second 'Northern Catholic' letter Hume had given credit to the new leader of the Nationalist Party, Eddie McAteer. But the party proved slow to change and in the February 1969 Stormont election John Hume, Austin Currie, Ivan Cooper and Paddy O'Hanlon were elected on manifestos to form a new left-of-centre party, Hume defeating McAteer in the hitherto impregnable nationalist seat of Foyle (which was the greater part of Derry City). With the Belfast Labour MPs, Gerry Fitt and Paddy Devlin, a liberal Protestant senator, Claude Wilton, and Fitt's election agent Senator Paddy Wilson also on board, they launched the SDLP in August 1970 on a manifesto that merged civil rights, labour and nationalist agendas.[23] It promised to be everything the Nationalist Party was not, bringing together a formidable team, perhaps too formidable. 'We were a disparate bunch with a number of strong personalities, used to being big fish in a small pool', recalled Austin Currie.[24] By 1979 Fitt and Devlin had left, largely because of disagreements with Hume. Paddy Wilson too was gone, brutally murdered by loyalist paramilitaries in June 1973.

Some have seen John Hume as one of the 'greener' members of the SDLP, particularly in the Sunningdale and power-sharing executive period 1973–4. This was a different Hume from the one who had so criticized old nationalism. What had happened? The Troubles had happened, internment, Bloody Sunday in Derry, and the return of the IRA – this time with its strength centred in Northern Ireland, with far more power than in the past to take large chunks of nationalism with it. Certainly the faith in unionism delivering reforms – he had opposed the radicals

22 *Irish Times*, 18 May 1964.   23 Currie, *All hell will break loose*, reproduces the draft manifesto in a plate between pp 320–1.   24 Ibid., p. 153.

back in 1968–9 by urging peace so that O'Neill's reforms might be given a chance – was gone, and with it the belief in the internal evolution envisaged back in 1964. The idea of an 'Irish dimension' to any future settlement emerges and was to remain as a crucial element in bringing nationalists and ultimately republicans to accept political participation in Northern Ireland's existing institutions. For a while it looked as if that meant the old nationalist pursuit of 'a United Ireland or nothing', a remark Hume had made to describe feelings of the people of the Bogside the day after Bloody Sunday and one that came to haunt him.[25] Hume certainly did push harder than others on the Council of Ireland and on the Irish dimension in the Sunningdale negotiations. Brian Faulkner found Fitt and Devlin 'less Dublin-orientated than those I called the "countrymen" … which included the Derry representatives'. And yet he came to respect Hume as 'a formidable political thinker with great personal integrity' even if 'a sometimes exasperating dogmatism'.[26]

Yet it was recognized that in the tough negotiations culminating in Sunningdale these were democratic politicians trying to find a way to reconcile nationalists to working within the existing constitutional arrangements, without having to lose sight of the core nationalist aim of re-unification. In Brian Faulkner's account of a particularly difficult moment, when he challenged the Irish Justice Minister to explain what gain might result from the transfer of policing to Council of Ireland control, he was answered by John Hume : 'the identification of the minority with the forces of law and order'. Faulkner knew unionists could never agree; even so he admired the clarity of Hume's assessment.[27] Ultimately, the power-sharing executive of 1974, nationalists' first experience of participatory democracy since 1921, worked well as a team. Faulkner was particularly impressed by Hume's energy as Minister of Commerce, and as mutual understanding developed of each other's difficulties with their particular constituents, compromises were emerging. But the way the men of violence on both sides could render democratic government unworkable was painfully revealed in the Ulster Workers' Council (UWC) strike of May 1974. It was orchestrated by loyalist paramilitaries, but with the support also of anti-Faulkner unionists Ian Paisley, Bill Craig and Harry West. With their grip on the power stations, particularly the Ballylumford station in Craig's East Antrim constituency, the UWC brought Northern Ireland to a standstill and Faulkner resigned.

As a member of the Opsahl Commission in 1993, I was surprised to discover the level of animosity towards John Hume expressed by so many Protestants, given that, above anything, he had remained fervently non-violent throughout his

---

25 P.J.McLaughlin, *John Hume and the revision of Irish nationalism* (Manchester, 2010), pp 25–6. 26 Brian Faulkner, *Memoirs of a statesman* (London, 1978), pp 205, 222, 253; McLoughlin, *Hume and the revision of Irish nationalism*, pp 19–36, 216–19. 27 Faulkner, *Memoirs of a statesman*, p. 232.

career. There was also a sense that he was some kind of Svengali, spinning words
and concepts they did not quite understand. He was seen in the words of the usually generous-minded Ken Bloomfield as one of the SDLP's 'philosopher-kings …
who dreamed grand conceptual dreams'.[28] The 'grand dreams' had by the 1990s
produced Hume's so-called 'new nationalism' of an 'agreed Ireland' based on the
legitimacy of both traditions and with neither sovereign government, Britain or
Ireland, supporting one at the expense of the other. This involved a move away
from the belief in the unitary state as the ultimate expression of nationalism.
Indeed Hume was to argue that the 'agreed Ireland' need not necessarily involve
territorial unification, but a compromise between the two traditions. 'Unity I've
always defined as agreement, not as a takeover bid', he told Fionnuala O'Connor
in 1993. 'Because the moment the two sections of the Irish people actually agree
on how to live together and start working, it will evolve itself … Once people start
working together you grow into a completely new Ireland'.[29] In many ways this is
a return to the 'common name of Irishman' ideal and its weaknesses are the same
as when Tone first coined it: not all the inhabitants of Ireland have considered
themselves 'Irish'.

But what of the militant strand of Irish nationalism, rejected and neutralized
by northern nationalists by the 1960s, but brought back with new vigour in the
Troubles. More emotional, more Catholic, more rooted in the victim psychology
of past and present wrongs, this was far more difficult to challenge than any reasoned and theoretically sophisticated philosophy. Its heartlands were areas that had
not experienced many of the feel-good factors noted above. The SDLP was particularly maligned by republicans with the old and easy put-down of 'Castle
Catholic' – the repertoire extended to 'Uncle Tom' by Gerry Adams, with the old
insinuation of slavish obsequiousness.[30] A particular viciousness was directed
towards Paddy Devlin and Gerry Fitt, as former Catholic working-class heroes.
Hume's efforts to persuade the IRA to stop the violence started early, in 1972.
Fundamental to this was his argument that Britain was no longer the problem.
Republicans had not deviated from Tone's original analysis in their proclamations
that once British withdrawal had occurred, Ulster Protestants might rediscover
their Irishness and re-unite with the rest of Ireland.

The rest of the 1970s and early 1980s were bleak times for constitutional nationalists. Hume himself engineered a long period of the very abstentionism that he had
so criticized in old nationalism. The hunger strikes and swing of the nationalist vote
to Sinn Féin – with another apparent SDLP reversion to old nationalism in not

---

28 Ken Bloomfield, *Stormont in crisis: a memoir* (Belfast, 1994), p. 131; Andy Pollak, et al. (eds), *A citizens'
inquiry: the Opsahl Report on Northern Ireland* (Dublin, 1993), pp 37–8 and Marianne Elliott, 'Religion and
identity in Northern Ireland' in Elliott (ed.), *The long road to peace in Northern Ireland* (Liverpool, 2002),
pp 175–6.   29 Fionnuala O'Connor, *In search of a state: Catholics in Northern Ireland* (Belfast, 1993), p. 94.
30 Gerry Adams, *The politics of Irish freedom* (Cork, 1986), p. 111.

running an election candidate against Bobby Sands – was a very low time for constitutional nationalism. This is when Sinn Féin emerged as a real electoral threat to the SDLP. The hunger strikes had permitted republicanism to pull at the strings of their shared nationalist traditions and to exert 'moral blackmail' on the SDLP. The New Ireland Forum of 1983–4 and the 1985 Anglo-Irish Agreement were recognition by Dublin and London that moderate nationalism needed a lifeline. Despite unionist fury, the modern peace process started then. Constitutional nationalism now had something to show for all its efforts. It was a personal triumph for John Hume, as his two-identities approach was its heart and it restored the SDLP to its position as the main voice of northern nationalism.

Thereafter the Hume-Adams meetings start, with unofficial British and Irish government approval. Hume's challenge to the republicans undermined the very rationale for violence, first set out by Tone and repeated by generations of militant republicans: that Britain's presence in Ireland was the only thing preventing Irish freedom and independence. The very terms of the Anglo-Irish Agreement, he argued, showed that Britain had no strategic reason to remain in Northern Ireland. Irish unity was a matter for the Irish people alone and Britain had undertaken to facilitate that, should a majority so wish. Accordingly, 'the agreement … removes completely the slightest justification for the use of violence in Ireland to achieve political objectives'.[31] Hume was also behind the timely statement by Secretary of State Peter Brooke, in November 1990, that Britain had no selfish or strategic interest in staying in Northern Ireland – an assurance confirmed in the Downing Street Declaration of December 1993 and subsequently by the Framework Document of 1995. In these years, there is no doubt that Sinn Féin was seeking more political participation. It had, after all, been taking its seats on Northern Ireland's local councils since 1983 and it seems that Hume further encouraged this recognition that an 'electoral mandate' would progress their cause further than violence ever would. Violence was simply alienating the unionist people, whose consent was needed to any re-unification.

The Good Friday [or Belfast] Agreement of 1998 ended both the unionist veto, of which old nationalism had complained, as well as Dublin's constitutional claim over Northern Ireland, which had so fed unionist fears. It also guaranteed much of what NICRA had been demanding back in the 1960s. But most of all it incorporated the ideas that Hume had been putting forward for over thirty years: the legitimacy of the two identities within Northern Ireland, their right to decide on their own long-term future, and a guarantee by both British and Irish governments to facilitate the outcome. Sinn Féin were also signatories. Had the two traditions of Irish nationalism been finally re-united? Time will tell, though dissident republicanism has yet to be convinced. But if Britain has ceased to be seen as the

---

31 McLoughlin, *John Hume*, p. 138.

evil genius of Irish wrongs and the two-identity approach to an 'agreed Ireland' accepted, violent republican nationalism ceases to have any rationale. Certainly, as many commentators have pointed out, the language of the 'new' Sinn Féin seems to have stolen John Hume's and the SDLP's clothes.[32] Austin Currie, who had left northern politics in 1989, on meeting Sinn Féin again as part of the 1994 Forum for Peace and Reconciliation, found that they had clearly learned from John Hume. '"Hume-speak" – words and phrases identified with John – poured out of them as if they were their own'.[33]

For two centuries Irish nationalism has oscillated between wanting to join the governing system and seeking to overthrow it. Northern nationalism has usually embraced the former. This is why, as I concluded in a larger study, the SDLP, particularly John Hume, had delivered what most nationalists had wanted.[34] Sinn Féin was brought to recognize the same and has largely shed the 'rebel' image – although its continued abstention from Westminster sits incongruously with its acceptance of Hume's line that Britain is no longer the problem. And what of Tone's other founding philosophy: the common name of Irishman? That was already largely lost in nationalism's identification with Catholicism and both the SDLP and Sinn Féin show no signs of shedding that anytime soon. However, John Hume's 'Agreed Ireland' and the idea that partition is that of the mind rather than territory is in part its re-invention for different times. In this John Hume has succeeded in changing the language of Irish nationalism and helped make constitutionalists of the men of violence.

32 Kevin Bean, 'Defining republicanism: shifting discourses of new nationalism and post-republicanism' in Elliott (ed.), *Long road*, pp 134–41; Kevin Bean, *The new politics of Sinn Féin* (Liverpool, 2007), pp 236–7; Feargal Cochrane, *Northern Ireland: the reluctant peace* (London, 2013), p. 277.   33 Currie, *All hell will break loose*, p. 425.   34 Elliott, *Catholics of Ulster*, p. 428.

Political Leader

CATHY GORMLEY-HEENAN

Understanding political leadership in the context of any conflict or peace process is complicated. It cannot be reduced to a story of heroes and villains, of foxes and lions or of the 'great men' of history. Nor can it be reduced to an overriding normative assumption that to lead is to do the 'right' thing. And yet the more complex and often nuanced realities of political leadership in a conflict and peace process still seem to get lost in the overall narrative thanks to such reductionist approaches. For example, much of the analysis of political leadership during the Northern Ireland conflict and peace process focused on the personalities involved and their perceived leadership style. At various points Gerry Adams was applauded as a statesman, or as a man of warmth and vision;[1] John Hume was given the accolade of 'Saint John' and seen by supporters as 'a man suffused with goodness, shining Gandhi-like in the gloom of local politics';[2] David Trimble was likened to a prophet;[3] Ian Paisley, David Ervine, and Gary McMichael were all described as charismatic, often to reference each individually. Other comments were rather more pejorative. Adams was described as a terrorist;[4] Hume was still called 'Saint John' but the tone had become more wry; Trimble was denounced as 'a hard-line sectarian bigot';[5] and Paisley was still charismatic but the inference was towards the darker side of charisma. In reality, 'charisma' in one community often meant loathing in another. While previous research by the author has suggested that most political leaders in Northern Ireland behaved in an almost 'chameleon-like' fashion, shedding old leadership skin for new when necessity or circumstance dictated,[6] it is certainly not an absolute. This chapter, therefore, reconsiders the overall leadership of John Hume during the Northern Ireland conflict and peace process in terms of his particular role, capacity and over-

1 D. Aitkenhead, 'Time and Gerry', *The Guardian (London)*, 4 Aug. 1997. 2 J. Collins, 'Lessons in the ignoble art of politics', *Irish News*, 21 Aug. 2003. 3 M. Gove, 'Preface' in David Trimble, *To raise up a new Northern Ireland: articles and speeches, 1998–2000* (Belfast, 2001). 4 J. Stevenson, 'Northern Ireland: treating terrorists as statesmen', *Foreign Policy*, 105 (1996), pp 125–40. 5 See R. Dudley-Edwards, 'Trimble and I', *Sunday Independent*, 12 Mar. 2000. 6 C. Gormley-Heenan, *Political leadership and the Northern Ireland peace process* (Basingstoke, 2007).

all effectiveness rather than a consideration of his leadership in more personal terms. Deconstructing the concept of political leadership into the constituent parts of its role, capacity and effect has been useful in previous research to demonstrate that political leadership in Northern Ireland suffered, at times, from confused roles, undermined capacity and negated effects. Applying a similar framework of analysis for Hume's leadership allows the reader to consider this leadership in a rather less beguiling or pejorative manner.

LEADERSHIP PERSONA

While only elected as leader of the SDLP on 28 November 1979, Hume had been the de facto leader of the party in terms of strategic thinking and policy development for some considerable time previously.[7] Before his movement into political leadership, he had been active in community leadership through the establishment of the credit union movement in Ireland in the early 1960s and then through the civil rights campaign. All told, when Hume formally retired from all politics in 2004, he had served in a leadership capacity at community and political levels for more than forty-five years. Such a lengthy tenure has meant that Hume's 'leadership' abilities have been remarked upon often. Some have been kind; others less so. What historians will make of Hume's leadership remains to be seen. They will, of course, scour newspaper clippings and official government records for interviews and analysis which reveal something of the leadership 'traits' of Hume. They will find a mixed bag; Simon Hattenstone, from *The Guardian*, upset that he felt like 'weeping, because this wasn't the John Hume he'd hoped to meet: modest, committed, selfless John Hume';[8] Coleman, from *The Observer*, reflecting on a weariness, a strange paranoia and then a second meeting the following morning in which 'this was not the Hume of the night before. He was a different man'.[9] In both cases these reporters expressed surprise that the person did not reflect the persona that existed around him. This 'image' has been centred on Hume's place in history: for example 'John Hume is a great statesman in Irish history but he cannot be described as a nationalist in the traditional sense because of his post-nationalist ethos. He is perhaps contemporary Ireland's greatest leader. His qualities in bring the Northern Ireland conflict to the international forum have proved his statesmanship';[10] 'One of the finest and most creative political leaders of our generation, a man of extraordinary courage and wisdom and understanding';[11] 'Hume is a great man for setting the vision and has got

7 P.J. McLoughlin, '"Humespeak": the SDLP, political discourse, and the Northern Ireland peace process', *Peace and Conflict Studies*, 15:1 (2008).   8 S. Hattenstone, 'I'm so tired', *The Guardian (London)*, 24 Sept. 2001.   9 T. Coleman, 'Will there be peace in his time?', *The Observer (London)*, 28 July 1996, p. 5.   10 G. Murray, *John Hume and the SDLP: impact and survival in Northern Ireland* (Dublin, 1998), p. 256.   11 Ted Kennedy, as cited in Murray, *John Hume and the SDLP*, p. 223.

massive intellect. He was a visionary …';[12] and 'I have never been among those who put forward John's entitlement to sainthood… However, and I say this without reservation, from the vantage point of history, John Hume will be recognized as a towering figure, in the same league of Irish history as O'Connell and Parnell.'[13] Even those from within unionism have praised his leadership: 'A lot of the successes and prestige of the SDLP is built exclusively on the success and procedures of John Hume'.[14]

The criticisms of his leadership have been directed towards his management style (or lack thereof), his (in) ability to build relationships with unionism and to engage at an intellectual level with them,[15] as well as the rigidity/malleability of his adopted positions irrespective of his perceived magnetism. One senior civil servant commented 'John Hume is normally in his element in the United States, where he is widely regarded as occupying a position somewhere between Charles Stewart Parnell and Mother Teresa. On this occasion, he gave a chilling impression of political bankruptcy, rather like a man who has lost a fortune by backing a particular number consistently at the roulette table and continues to stare at that number even though he no longer has a stake to play'.[16] O'Leary and McGarry saw him as 'less pliant' than his predecessor, Gerry Fitt.[17] Ivan Cooper noted a 'controlling streak' claiming that 'he always delegates to relatively safe lieutenants'.[18] More bluntly put, Cooper said: 'John is not a leader in a divided society. He sticks too closely to the church. He sticks too closely to the traditional line. He doesn't break new ice. He is not a leader'.[19]

This suggests a tale of *two* Humes; the 'saintlike' Hume who was central to the peace process and, without whom, peace in Ireland would never have been possible. Their analysis 'give(s) the impression that Hume almost single-handedly persuaded London, Dublin and the republican movement into the peace process';[20] and the less virtuous Hume, vilified for engaging with Sinn Féin in the Hume-Adams talks in the early 90s and for not engaging sufficiently well with unionists, who declared that he did not give 'two balls of roasted snow' for any of the criticisms levied against him.[21] It is interesting too that the perceptions of the two Humes are not confined to the obvious nationalist versus unionist divide, evidenced in almost all of the political discourse of Northern Ireland, but that the perceptions of Hume was divided within nationalism too, north and south, particularly in the case of Conor Cruise O'Brien who maintained a particularly antagonistic position towards Hume from the 1970s until his death.

12 Eamon Hanna, as cited in Murray, *John Hume and the SDLP*, p. 247.   **13** Currie, as cited in P.J. McLouglin, *John Hume and the revision of Irish nationalism* (Manchester, 2010), p. 235.   **14** Chris McGimpsey, as cited in Murray, *John Hume and the SDLP*, p. 95.   **15** Murray, *John Hume and the SDLP*, p. 256.   **16** Ken Bloomfield, PRONI records.   **17** B. O'Leary & J. McGarry, (1993) *The politics of antagonism: understanding Northern Ireland* (London, 1993).   **18** As cited in Murray, *John Hume and the SDLP*, p. 95.   **19** As cited in Murray, *John Hume and the SDLP*, p. 94.   **20** See S. Wichert, 'The Northern Ireland conflict: new wine in old bottles', *Contemporary European History*, 9:2 (2000), pp 308–9 for a critique of such analysis.   **21** See E. Mallie & D. McKittrick, *The fight for peace: the secret story behind the Irish peace process* (London, 1996), pp 187–8.

It has always been difficult for observers to move beyond this level of analysis lest any critique of Hume's leadership be regarded as small-mindedness in the face of the now accepted 'successes' of the peace process. One reason for such limited analysis has been because most leadership literature has tended to perpetuate the dichotomous constructs of good leaders versus bad leaders;[22] warmongers versus peacemongers;[23] and strong versus weak leaders;[24] while in reality we know that political leadership is neither one diametric nor the other. Instead it is an activity conditioned and motivated by a diverse series of factors and influences within the leader's immediate environment that affect their role, capacity and effect as leaders.[25]

ROLE OF HUME'S LEADERSHIP

Every political leader holds a multiplicity of roles associated with their political positions. However, any mapping of Hume's various roles as leader of the SDLP highlights clear contradictions between the normative understandings of a political leader in a conflict and/or peace process and the more detached behavioural view. The normative view of political leaders in a conflict and/or peace process is that their role is 'to do the right thing'. The more behavioural view suggests that leaders in a conflict and peace process should protect themselves and their followers at the expense of all other things because 'a loss of their followers is a greater threat to party leaders than the collapse of the process'.[26] In either case, this is actioned by convincing party officials, constituents and followers, the media and wider society of the 'plausibility' of their take on the conflict and potential solutions to it. This necessitates a high degree of interaction at the personal level. Henry Mintzberg's lifetime's work on leadership and management has identified three key roles for the leaders of any organization – interpersonal, informational, and decision-making roles, and it is these areas in particular to which we now turn.[27]

Handshakes and historic moments have been used to showcase Hume's interpersonal role and engagements. Images of Hume with Bono from U2 and with Bill Clinton and Ted Kennedy are repeatedly used to underscore the importance of the self-developed networks of contacts most evident in the case of Hume's relationships with influential American congressmen, senators and aide workers. It has been argued, and most would agree, that the eventual US administration's involvement in the Northern Ireland peace process was secured through more than two decades

22 B. Kellerman, *Bad leadership: what it is, how it happens, why it matters* (Harvard, 2004).   23 A.M. Ludwig, *King of the mountain: the nature of political leadership* (Lexington, 2002).   24 M. Colaresi, 'When doves cry: international rivalry, unreciprocated cooeration and leadership turnover', *American Journal of Political Science*, 48:3 (2004), pp 555–70.   25 Gormley-Heenan, *Political leadership and the Northern Ireland peace process*.   26 J. Darby & R. MacGinty, *Contemporary peacemaking: conflict, violence and the peace process* (Basingstoke, 2003).   27 H. Mintzberg, *The nature of managerial work* (New York, 1973).

of Hume's relationship-building with various US administrations and certain individuals within them, not least 'the Four Horsemen' – Tip O'Neill, Hugh Carey, Daniel Moynihan and Ted Kennedy.[28] The informational role of political leadership concerns the monitoring and dissemination of information from others key to the process. How much or how little to disseminate can cause leadership difficulties. The initially secret nature of the Hume-Adams talks, which began first in 1988 and became public knowledge in 1993 following a sighting of Gerry Adams arriving at the home of Hume, meant that many within the SDLP were unaware of the full extent and nature of the talks. Hume did not extend his informational role towards disseminating the content of these talks to the party, leading to a degree of uneasiness within the party because they simply did not know enough about the process.[29] Of course, Hume-Adams signalled a third leadership role for Hume – a primary decision-making role. Decisions taken, as evidenced through the initiation of the Hume-Adams talks, were not necessarily collective decisions within the overall party leadership but rather were Hume's decisions in his capacity as individual party leader. The converse became true, however, as the process moved onto a subsequent phase. During the talks process which culminated in the Good Friday Agreement in 1998, it was said that Hume had taken a back seat in much of the actual negotiations in the multi-party talks, and had been there only 'physically but not mentally',[30] leaving the negotiations themselves to Séamus Mallon, Seán Farren, Denis Haughey, Mark Durkan and Alex Attwood. Hume's leadership role changed over the course of the peace process from front stage to back stage. In part this might be explained as Hume's conditioning by the normative expectations of leaders – to win the peace at all costs – in the words of Horowitz this would have meant Hume accepting the position: 'I shall do the right thing, no matter what its effect on me and the parochial interests I represent, even if the effect on us is adverse'.[31] The benefit of hindsight has shown that Hume's sustained and successful attempts at engaging Adams in the process were undertaken at the expense of the SDLP's electoral successes in later years, with the party eventually eclipsed by Sinn Féin as the main nationalist party in Northern Ireland.

CAPACITY OF HUME'S LEADERSHIP

Hume's role in the peace process was, of course, inextricably linked to the capacity that he had to fulfil that role. While an examination of Hume's leadership roles can focus on a variety of actions and activities expected of them, any examination

28 McLaughlin, *John Hume and the SDLP*, pp 107–11. 29 Murray, *John Hume and the SDLP*, p. 198.
30 F. O'Connor, *Breaking the bonds: making peace in Northern Ireland* (Edinburgh, 2001), p. 31. 31 D. Horowitz, 'Explaining the Northern Ireland agreement: the source of an unlikely constitutional consensus', *British Journal of Political Studies*, 32:2 (2002), pp 193–220.

of his capacity must focus on his ability and aptitude to deliver on the same. In short, what capacity did Hume have to influence the shape and direction of the peace process? Various spheres of influence are always available to political leaders which can be utilized as they undertake their roles and can be distilled into three main areas: the influence of office, the influence of events and the influence of the personal.[32] The influence of office can be related to the attitude of a party leader towards that office. Many in Northern Ireland displayed traits of 'reluctant leadership'. For example, Gerry Adams claimed not to have wanted to become President of Sinn Féin.[33] David Trimble had a fairly ambivalent attitude to becoming leader of the UUP when the leadership contest for office first got underway.[34] But while Hume, as leader of the SDLP, did not face any overt challenges to his leadership of the party during his tenure of office, it has been suggested that he was subject to significant dissension from the collective party leadership of the SDLP in relation to the strategy and approach that Hume had adopted during the peace process. At the very early stages of the peace process, when negotiations had begun with Adams, several in Hume's own party were expressing disquiet. The SDLP leader was reported to have said: 'If it's a choice between the party and peace, do you think I give a f*** for the party?'[35] Indeed, the influence of office was not something that was alleged to have appealed to Hume anyway. Instead, Hume saw his office of leadership as a practical tool that he used to promote influence with other political players when necessary. It was often reported that during the peace process Hume operated outside of the confines of his office and in some instances without the knowledge of other leaders within the party's elite. This led to considerable tensions within the SDLP. As a consequence, the political triumph of the first IRA ceasefire for Hume was marred by the critics who accused him of being 'too autocratic, of holding too much power in his own hands, [and] of failing to bring his party colleagues along with him'.[36] Such criticisms were indicative of a slight loss of influence for Hume as a consequence of his earlier Hume-Adams dialogue. And yet, there was still no challenge to his office of leadership. Perhaps an unintended consequence of Hume's lack of interest in the organization and structure of the party was that no new blood was apparent in the ranks of the party and therefore no hungry would-be leadership challengers awaited.[37] Hume, himself, believed strongly in the influence of events, noting that: 'There are serious limitations to political leadership in Northern Ireland; people can only be led as far as they want to be led. There is ample evidence to demonstrate the truth of that, and therefore a great deal of what happened has been the inevitability of

---

32 H. Elcock, *Political leadership* (Cheltenham, 2001).   33 G. Adams, *Hope and history: making peace in Ireland* (Dingle, 2004).   34 D. Godson, *Himself alone: David Trimble and the ordeal of unionism* (London, 2004).   35 O'Connor, *Breaking the bonds*, p. 25.   36 A. Cadwallader, 'A political triumph for the Derryman', *Irish Press*, 1 Sept. 1994.   37 McLaughlin, *John Hume and the SDLP*.

events rather than being particularly shaped by anyone'.[38] That said, personalities have mattered as much as events during the conflict and peace process in Northern Ireland. As noted already, it was Hume's near 'iconic' status in the US that allowed him to use his 'personal' influence to press the US administration into helping Northern Ireland during the peace process. Indeed, McKittrick and McVea claim that: 'by the early 1990s he was, in sum, the most influential nationalist politician in Northern Ireland'.[39]

There are, however, contradictions to be noted in understanding the power and influence of the personal and the capacity that such power and influence afforded the political leaders at different points in the peace process. Perception and reality are two issues at the heart of the seeming contradictions. For example, John Hume had, on the one hand, 'managed to develop the power of influence and has walked with more useful people than princes'. On the other, it was clear that, while he was turning into an icon outside of his party, the party itself effectively lacked leadership during critical stages of the peace process.[40] The perception was that Hume had the capacity to lead his own party towards a peace process as well as the capacity to influence other actors at the international level. The reality, at least for many senior political actors within the SDLP, was that Hume was better at the latter than the former. What is most critical to any understanding of the capacity of political leadership to affect the overall peace process through their personal influence is that the perception of their personal influence often mattered as much, if not more, than the reality. In this respect, it is clear that the most potent source of influence during the peace process was personal rather than structural.

EFFECT OF HUME'S LEADERSHIP ON OTHER LEADERS

Personal stories and anecdotes from political leaders suggested a tale of two peace processes: one was a story of hope and humour and the other a story of hardened attitudes and self-importance.[41] The nature of the relationship between many of the political leaders involved in the peace process was rather poor. Relations between the leadership of Sinn Féin and the leadership of the SDLP barely stretched beyond the fledgling association with John Hume. Adams' recall of their first meetings with the SDLP in 1989 was that 'apart from John Hume, they were hostile, confrontational, on occasion arrogant ... right up to the end of the discussions, Séamus Mallon, Austin Currie and Seán Farren lectured and hectored

---

38 J. Hume, *Belfast Telegraph*, 27 Oct. 1974. 39 D. McKittrick and D. McVea, *Making sense of the Troubles* (Belfast, 2000), p. 186. 40 O'Connor, *Breaking the bonds.* 41 Gormley-Heenan, *Political leadership and the Northern Ireland peace process.*

us'.[42] Gerard Murray's work also details the opposition among senior SDLP personnel towards the Hume-Adams dialogue.[43] And yet the fledgling relationship between Hume and Sinn Féin was acknowledged as something special by those within SF: 'Hume was the first political leaders to respond … the first that agreed to meet and started the process … I would give him his due credit, and I do generously, because he was the only one that had the backbone … he was the only one at that time'.[44] This undoubtedly weakened any prospect of a positive relationship within unionism. Suspicious of Hume's relationship with Sinn Féin, unionists saw this as a 'fearful alliance of nationalist forces'.[45]

That said, relations between Hume and mainstream unionism were often sour with many unionists holding Hume in decidedly low esteem, even before news of Hume-Adams came to light. Accusing him of using contradictory rhetoric, one unionist claimed that Hume's was not a coherent political philosophy and that 'Teeth across Northern Ireland grate when they hear the awkward sound bites about a divided people, flag-eating and agreements which threaten nobody'[46] and 'verbal camouflage, beneath which hides his true objective: a united Ireland'.[47] It was, eventually, Hume's alleged reference to 'the unionist boil [that] had to be lanced' that would appear to vindicate unionist hostility towards Hume and their reluctance to buy into 'Hume-speak'.[48] This suspicion of Hume's language or 'Hume-speak' continued far beyond the eventual Good Friday Agreement.[49] It was, at least for some, subtly attacked by David Trimble as he collected his Nobel Peace Prize along with Hume in 1998:

> The tradition from which I come, but by which I am not confined, produced the first vernacular bible in the language of the common people, and contributed much to the scientific language of the enlightenment. It puts a great price on the precise use of words, and uses them with circumspection, so much so that our passion for precision is often confused with an indifference to idealism. Not so. But I am personally and perhaps culturally conditioned to be sceptical of speeches which are full of sound and fury, idealistic in intention, but impossible of implementation; and I resist the kind of rhetoric which substitutes vapour for vision. Instinctively, I identify with the person who said that when he heard a politician talk of his vision, he recommended him to consult an optician.[50]

42 Adams, *Hope and history*, pp 78–9.   43 Murray, *John Hume and the SDLP*.   44 Mitchell McLaughlin, as cited in McLoughlin, *John Hume and the SDLP*, p. 221.   45 McLoughlin, *John Hume and the SDLP*, p. 222.   46 S. King, 'The tragedy of Hume', *Ulster Review*, 22 (Spring 1997).   47 McLaughlin, *John Hume and the SDLP*, p. 224.   48 P. Bew and H. Patterson, 'The new stalemate: unionism and the Anglo-Irish Agreement' in Paul Teague (ed.), *Beyond the rhetoric: politics, the economy and social policy in Northern Ireland* (London, 1987).   49 McLoughlin, ' "Humespeak"'.   50 D. Trimble, *Nobel Lecture*, 10 Dec. 2008. Available online at: http://www.nobelprize.org/nobel_prizes/peace/laureates/1998/trimble-lecture.html.

Deconstructing Hume's leadership into that of its role, capacity and effect has merely further illustrated the complicated and sometimes contradictory nature of political leadership during the conflict and peace process in Northern Ireland. This means that there is a very limited value to classifying individual leaders as either one 'type' of leader or another since it runs the risk of being disproved as a consequence of changing behaviours dictated by changing political circumstances. This is true to a point, but not for Hume.

CHAMELEONS, CONSISTENCY AND HUME'S LEADERSHIP

Anthropomorphism is used as a way of explaining the behaviour or characteristics of humans by representing these behaviours as something else. Previous research on the cohort of political leaders during the Northern Ireland conflict and peace process revealed enough contradictions and inconsistencies in their roles, capacities and effects as leaders to warrant anthropomorphisizing their particular motivations, characteristics and behaviours. The multiple contradictions and inconsistencies were expressed as a form of 'chameleon-like leaders': an inconstant political leadership that shifted according to the opinion of others and the climate in which it existed, just as a chameleon can change its colour to blend with its background.'[51] In practice, this meant that the majority practiced a type of chameleonic politics where they said one thing but did something different, or where they said different things to different audiences at different times for different effect. Hume, however, had always been something of an outlier in this regard. Other than a detected change in attitude towards the British government, which varied slightly at time from applauding to chiding their efforts on Northern Ireland, Hume maintained continuity of thought and action throughout his time as leader of the SDLP and afterwards. His oft-repeated view was that the conflict was as a consequence of the division of the people on the island of Ireland and not the territory of the island of Ireland and he 'never for one moment departed from a complete insistence on the non-violent approach, despite all the pressure on him, his family and his electorate'.[52] Hume himself saw political leadership as needing consistency (more than the more commonly sought characteristic of pragmatism). He said: 'It's about changing the language of others. I say it and go on saying it until I hear the man in the pub saying my words back to me'.[53] While some may have used the term 'Hume-speak' in a derogatory way, there is no doubt that it was Hume's phraseology upon which much of the peace process was

51 Gormley-Heenan, *Political leadership and the Northern Ireland peace process*, pp 144–5. 52 Currie, as cited in McLoughlin, *John Hume and the SDLP*, p. 235. 53 J. Hume, 'Quote, unquote', *The Independent* (London), 21 Dec. 1996.

built.[54] When Good Friday 1998 came, Hume's ideological sentiments were peppered throughout the agreement and the three structural strands of the agreement were underpinned by the thinking of Hume.[55] Consistency of language and steadfastness of purpose were key. Chameleonic leadership therefore, captured so well through the leadership of many others among Northern Ireland's political elite, cannot explain Hume.

CONCLUSION

And yet it is important that an analysis of Hume's leadership is not simply reduced either to the personalized accounts, offered in the various biographies, or to mainstream media analysis, which often focused on who shook hands with whom, and where, and the significance of this for the broader political environment. Though the chameleon-like behaviours of his erstwhile political colleagues from right across the spectrum do not define Hume, perhaps the use of another creature might allow us to explain Hume's leadership here. The salmon is best known for its steadfast endurance and its ability to swim upstream, against the current, in order to return to its birthplace to reproduce. With steadfastness, endurance and in swimming against the tide of his own party at times, Hume's leadership journey through the conflict and peace process has been much like that of the salmon. An apt analogy for the tale of two Humes since supporters will say that the salmon holds a special place in Irish mythology, associated most with stories of wisdom and knowledge. Critics will point out that in their haste to get upstream (returning to their place of birth in order to spawn) the salmon can 'miss', with fatal consequences, some of the obstacles that stand in their journey's way such as predators, dangerous currents and pollution. Heroes and villains, foxes and lions, power wielders and power seekers when used as labels of leadership all ignore the difficulty in assigning villainy or sainthood in matters of politics. The salmon perhaps offers us an 'out' from the perpetuation of such false dichotomies that are used to explain political leadership and have, in the tales of *two* Humes, been used to explain Hume's leadership.

---

54 McLoughlin, "'Humespeak'".   55 McLaughlin, *John Hume and the SDLP.*

Married to John

PAT HUME

EARLY DAYS

When I married John in December 1960, I had only heard him speak in public once. It was at the Colmcille Debating Society and the motion was 'Ireland should join the Common Market'. Needless to say he was ardently in favour of the motion! At that stage he didn't have any great interest in politics and spent his free time either following Derry City Football Club or playing cricket for City of Derry (he was a left-hand spin bowler). I first met John during the Easter holidays in 1958 when he was doing substitute teaching before sitting the finals for his degree in French and history at St Patrick's College, Maynooth, where he had been studying to be a priest. He had been hospitalized for several weeks in May and June the previous year with severe stomach inflammation when the exams were taking place, and so had to postpone taking them for a year. During his time in hospital, John had reflected at length on his vocation. After much soul search-ing, he had decided not to continue training for the priesthood.

Like many of his peers he was deeply appreciative of the opportunities that the education reforms of 1947 had given him, and he strongly believed in the eman-cipatory power of education. When he graduated, he began teaching in the new secondary school in Strabane, St Colman's. He was a natural teacher with a real love of his subjects and a passion for education as everyone's right.

John's students got excellent results through the use of teaching methods that were innovative at the time, such as only allowing the minimum of English to be spoken in his French language classes, and fostering knowledge of French culture in after school groups. These innovations were acknowledged by the French consul in Belfast, who awarded him a month in a French university, which he spent in Paris. When teaching history, he asked his students, many of whom were from remote rural areas, to search their barns and sheds for old implements that were no longer used and together they set up a museum. In addition, the students pro-duced a quarterly newsletter on the many agricultural changes that were taking place in those years. When he subsequently began teaching in St Columb's College, he organized the college's first debating society and took the group to Stormont to meet Prime Minister Terence O'Neill, and to Áras an Uachtaráin to meet President de Valera.

In that first cohort of people to benefit from educational reform, there was a strong desire to give back to the community. Throughout the sixties, John was part of a very active network of energetic and committed people, who could see the enormous resources which existed in the community and were determined to allow them to flourish. With Fr Anthony Mulvey, the indomitable Paddy (Bogside) Doherty, a local businessman Michael Canavan and many other generous and gifted people they established the first credit union in Northern Ireland, and the Derry Housing Association among other projects, with a strong focus on self-help. The credit union provided a place where less well-off people who had no access to bank loans, and thus were dependent on loan sharks at demanding financial times, could pool their savings and then borrow when they needed. Great emphasis was put on their common bond; all those involved were neighbours, so there were very few delinquent loans. In those years all the administrative work was voluntary. John was the first treasurer of Derry Credit Union and travelled throughout Ireland helping to set up new branches. In 1964 he was elected President of the Credit Union League of Ireland. John loved this idea of self-help and of people being able to have the dignity of going to make their purchases with the cash in their hands and without usurious interest rates in the background.

This interest in self-help extended to entrepreneurship, and in 1966, he left teaching with the aim of setting up a business that would create local employment. For a long time, he had been singing the praises of the River Foyle which was then one of the best salmon rivers in Europe. Michael Canavan had bought a former bakery which needed a tenant, so with financial help from Michael, the smoked salmon premises – Atlantic Harvest – was opened. John went to Scotland to learn the secrets of smoking salmon and for a short while the family lived like lords while this great delicacy (which it was in those years) was tested. Now he needed gourmet markets, so trips to London followed where he secured orders from Sawers (one of the biggest chains of delicatessens at the time). Armed with samples of his product he also went to Southampton where he got orders from the prestigious Cunard Line. He had a great advertisement that he used to put in *The Times* in the month before Christmas in which he wrote of the marriage of the shavings from the famous Derry oak trees and the Foyle salmon which resulted in a unique product which could be airmailed to customers. The enterprise was very successful and some jobs were created.

John was tireless during these years and on coming back from whatever part of the country he had been in, he would work on his MA thesis 'The economic and social development of Derry between 1825 and 1850 – the growth of the city outside the walls'. Based on it he wrote the script for a half-hour documentary, *A City Solitary*. With the help of a local art teacher, Terry Mc Donald, who was a wizard with a camera, a post office engineer named Charlie Gallagher and a Church of Ireland clergyman with a magnificent speaking voice, Brian Hannon, the film was completed for the princely sum of ninety-one pounds. The film was shown on BBC and RTÉ and caused quite a stir at the time. Talking about the city's bridges he stressed how important it was to build bridges in the community and to unite the two traditions. He examined the word Londonderry – London (the Celtic derivation is 'The Fort of the Ships'), the siege tradition, and Derry (Doire meaning oak grove), the Colmcille tradition, and he advocated acceptance of both names. Interestingly, that is the situation in the city now.

In 1964, following the showing of the film, he was invited by the *Irish Times* to write an opinion piece on what he thought of the political situation in the North. This resulted in two lengthy articles that were to provide the foundation for his later work. Everyone thought he was contemplating going into politics in 1965, but he was critical of the abstentionist policy of the Nationalist Party and to go as an independent didn't appeal to him at the time. He enjoyed teaching in St Columb's College and preferred to continue with his work in the credit union movement and the housing association.

However, the events of the next few years were to change his mind, when a series of injustices underlined the inescapable need for political change. People in the north-west had some hope of life improving when Terence O' Neill replaced Lord Brookeborough in 1963, especially after his meetings with Taoiseach Seán Lemass, in Belfast and Dublin. Unfortunately, the reverse was to happen. In a short period Derry lost out in terms of its infrastructural development. The Derry-Glasgow shipping link ceased operating, the second rail link to Belfast was withdrawn and with it the rail link to Dublin ended, a new city for the North was being planned for the eastern counties, to be named Craigavon, just twenty miles from Belfast. New motorways were also being planned for the eastern counties and not for Derry or the western counties. Compounding this absence of investment in Derry and the west was the publication of the Lockwood Report recommending that a new university for Northern Ireland be situated in Coleraine, with Derry's Magee College to be downgraded. This decision was supported by a few officials (the so-called 'faceless men') from Derry Corporation who were afraid that a prosperous Derry could disturb the gerrymandered status quo. It is hard to capture the depth of the frustration and anger felt across the entire city at this time, not least because all the protests were in vain.

These unjust decisions were symptomatic of the structural discrimination that was built into the heart of Northern Ireland. The unrest caused by these decisions was felt by many, but for John it came to a personal head when a petition from the Derry Housing Association to build 500 houses in the Duncreggan Road was refused (the new houses would have upset the carefully gerrymandered constituency demographics). The city had the worst housing record in the North – ten per cent of the entire population were living either in one room or in Nissen huts which had been used by the American Navy during the war. Between 1966 and 1967 the Derry Housing Association had housed 100 families and had built 27 new houses; Derry Corporation had built none. John had hoped that if the really stark figures were presented, that justice rather than politics would prevail, but it was not to be. These realizations, together with inspiration from international leaders such as Martin Luther King who were engaged in similar struggles, led him to become involved in the emerging civil rights campaign.

FAMILY LIFE, 1960–72

During this time, the Hume family was growing – Therese, Áine, Aidan and John were born in the 1960s, our youngest daughter, Mo, was born in 1972. I was able to continue teaching, thanks to the invaluable help of a neighbour of John's mother, Molly Doherty, whom we all called Nana. Nana stayed with us for twenty years and didn't miss one day, arriving at 8.30 and leaving when I came home from school. It would be impossible to write about those years without including Nana's role in keeping all of us afloat. She had a sense of humour and energy that helped get all of us through many of the times of exhaustion and uncertainty which were to follow. She was practical, warm and welcoming, and managed to find something to laugh about in the most trying of situations. While I was teaching, I knew that Nana would manage the unpredictabilities of life in our house, which grew ever more demanding as those years passed.

In those early years, although life was very busy, we had no sense of what was ahead. When I look back, those days were chaotic but very happy. We didn't have a television until 1965; John was out a lot as he got increasingly involved in local politics, but I had good friends who visited often and the house was always full of life. Every year we rented a house in Gweedore and everybody looked forward to that. Our second daughter, Áine, wrote an essay for her Irish exam at the time describing the annual trip to Gweedore as our very own Tír na nÓg – Land of Youth. Friends from the previous year were reunited; children had competitions on the beach; there were picnics and evening walks to smell the honeysuckle, eat the unripe gooseberries and see the salmon boats sail out. There was the annual climb of Errigal mountain and the 'voyage' to Gola Island. The weather in July was never brilliant, but it's amazing how a group of mammies can enjoy sitting on the beach chatting while the children entertain each other. When the weather was really bad, the children congregated in Mrs Stratford's garage (Brid Rodger's mother); and then there was the odd really beautiful day when the area became paradise. John rarely enjoyed the full break especially after 1968 as there was always something going on at home. However, Gweedore also provided a backdrop for a range of significant meetings, such as those leading to the formation of the SDLP.

ELECTORAL POLITICS AND ESCALATING CONFLICT

When John eventually left Atlantic Harvest to go into electoral politics in February 1969, Michael was able to get another manager. John also gave up all his interests to devote his time totally to what was to be thirty-six years of non-stop pressure. Our bungalow in Beechwood Avenue had become too small for the growing family and so we moved to a Victorian terrace house between Creggan and Bogside where we still live. Derry Corporation had been disbanded as one of Terence O'Neill's reforms and a commission put in its place. This meant that there were no other public representatives for the city at the outbreak of the Troubles except John and he became the main contact for all kinds of representations.

When I look back I wonder how we all survived the years that followed. There was the ever-increasing cycle of rioting and arrests. Young people coming from a disco or just going down town for a message could be taken for questioning by security forces to one of the five interrogation centres in the city. Worried parents were constantly at the house or on the phone as we tried to trace their offspring. John often put out statements on how counter-productive violence was and these usually resulted in protests outside our house. The irony was that the next day the same protesters could arrive at the door but this time looking to convey a partic-ular problem alongside the other distraught families. Over those years, intimida-tion affected the atmosphere throughout the whole community across the North. We received daily telephone calls threatening violence and we had an ongoing stream of abusive letters and bullets in the post; the house was attacked several times. We had to leave on a number of occasions and relied on the hospitality of kind friends who provided shelter for myself and the five children whenever we were warned by the police that things were too dangerous to stay at home.

After the introduction of internment in 1971 the pressures became immense. John led a march against internment on Magilligan beach close to the prison where some internees were being held on 23 January 1972 and when he returned, he was very deeply worried. The march had been met by soldiers of the Paratroop Regiment and he had seen that these men were not responsive to reason and had used unnecessary violence towards the marchers. He was aware of the level of frus-tration and emotion among people who were being forced to live under a very abused rule of law, but he was so distressed about the risk of serious violence that he pleaded with NICRA that the march planned for the following Sunday in Derry should be cancelled. He announced at a meeting in the Ardowen Hotel that he would not be taking part, but emotions were high and the march went ahead without him. The consequences of what became Bloody Sunday devastated him and he spent the night of 30 January and subsequent days between the A&E department in the city's Altnagelvin hospital, visiting families, and trying to trace those who were missing.

As violence grew in severity, the chaos increased for the whole population. Our house became a place where people came with so many desperate stories and the phone went at all hours. Throughout this time, I continued teaching full-time and I also became more involved in working with the constant stream of people calling to our home. We were sustained by the many friends who came often and stayed to drink tea and to help. The children and I will forever be grateful to those people who became the local activists of the early SDLP – who not only provided a kind and reassuring presence to all of us, but they consoled, reflected, listened, planned and also found something to laugh about in the darkest times. Here I make special mention of our next-door neighbours – Nellie and Jack Crumlish – and other neighbours for their unfailing support and kindness.

Then in 1974 there was the power-sharing government that had so much potential. I remember 1 January and John returning from Stormont in a ministerial car. He asked me to go out to talk to the driver who was feeling quite ill. I introduced myself to Tony (not his real name) and invited him in for a cup of tea. He looked so bad that I suggested that he rest on the spare bed upstairs and John phoned our friend Dr Jim Cosgrove. Jim talked to Tony for a while and then asked him to roll up his sleeve for an injection. His arm was covered with tattoos 'Ulster shall fight and Ulster shall be right', 'For God and Ulster' etc., and Tony was protesting he had got them when he was young and foolish. Whatever Jim did for him he had the tea and something to eat and slept very soundly. He came every day for the duration of the executive and our children loved him. We heard afterwards that no driver had been willing to take John because of where he lived and all the names had to be put into a hat. Poor Tony had picked the short straw and the nearer he came to Derry the more petrified he became. It saddened me so much that the blinkered perceptions we can have of each other can damage what should be open, warm, neighbourly relationships.

John really enjoyed his time as Minister of Commerce and was forging links with some big American companies for investment before the collapse. He and Brian Faulkner opened the Northern Ireland Office in Brussels. Brian officially opened it in English, and John opened it in Irish and French. Brian told me afterwards that he was very proud on that day – all their identities were represented – British, Irish and European. The mayhem of the Ulster Workers' strike and the continuing violence of the IRA were a source of great heartbreak and frustration to all the courageous men who continued to run the gauntlet every day and to get themselves to Stormont in spite of road blocks and threats. Loyalists, anti-

Sunningdale unionists and the IRA were jubilant with their success and, as a result, all efforts to repeat the Sunningdale Agreement were to be off the table for the next twenty-four years.

After the end of the power-sharing executive, I received a letter from Lady Lucy Faulkner. In it she said that her own attitudes had changed greatly during the executive's short five months. She said 'One of the minor miracles was being able to watch John Hume on television! Fury gave way to fear (maybe he'll say the wrong thing) and fear to respect and respect to very genuine admiration'. I have treasured this letter since, as an example of how, as John so often said, working together ('spilling sweat not blood') allows prejudices to be challenged and real trust, which, tragically, is in such short supply in Northern Ireland, to develop.

THE US DIMENSION

In November 1972 John had a phone call from Senator Edward Kennedy. He said he would be in Bonn in a few weeks time and would appreciate a meeting with him. John assured him he would be there. It was when he put the phone down that he remembered that he was unemployed, Stormont having been prorogued in March, and even though my salary was adequate for running the house, it didn't permit luxuries like a trip to Germany. It was for unexpected expenses like this that being a member of the credit union was so useful. Loan in place, what was to be the first of many important meetings took place between Edward Kennedy and John. The Irish Ambassador to Germany Seán Ronan and his wife Brigid (very gracious, hospitable people) provided the venue and also accommodation for John.

This lengthy exchange of views helped steady the statements which were emanating from the US in the aftermath of internment and Bloody Sunday. Further work was done by John when he was awarded a fellowship in Harvard in 1976. He and Michael Lillis from the Department of Foreign Affairs became close friends of the group called 'the Four Horsemen' – Senators Kennedy and Moynihan, Speaker Tip O' Neill and Governor Hugh Carey. They issued a very important St Patrick's Day Declaration in 1977. This was followed by a statement from President Carter asking the Irish and British governments to work together to facilitate agreement. If their work were to be successful, he promised that the US would provide economic help. This crucial assistance came after the Anglo-Irish Agreement in 1985 when President Reagan, Tip O'Neill and Senator Kennedy helped initiate the International Fund for Ireland which has created over 60,000 jobs. Later, the search for peace absorbed a great deal of President Clinton's time in office and he and his wife Hillary were tireless in cajoling and encouraging our politicians to reach agreement.

EUROPE AND WESTMINSTER

John was elected to the European Parliament in 1979. I set up and ran his office and remained in this role until 2005 when John retired. John was attracted to the practice of consensus politics and the high level of debate that characterized the parliament in Strasbourg and he felt that this offered a model for Northern Ireland. He had also realized during his time in the US that it was vital to see local problems from an international perspective. As a historian, he was passionate about the EU as a model of peace building, and he welcomed the diversity of views and the breadth which this forum allowed. From the beginning, John saw in Europe a blueprint for a structure capable of accommodating the various sets of relationships that were needed to foster progress, in cooperation and not with antagonism.

The seventies in Northern Ireland had been a bleak and violent decade when views hardened and narrowed. During those years, direct rule, in particular during the extremely sterile time of Roy Mason's tenure as Secretary of State, provided ever-diminishing opportunities for creative approaches. John was elected to Westminster in 1983, and even though he didn't enjoy the adversarial style of politics practised there, he made some great friends in all parties, in particular Kevin McNamara and Stan Orme who had visited us after the huge march on 16 November 1968 and had slept on our floor. They were invaluable friends to John during his time in Westminster. While John never embraced the Westminster style of politics with the same passion as he did Europe, he was pragmatic about his time there and found it invaluable in communicating the complexities of the political situation in the North to the various parties and the need for a comprehensive solution.

It is difficult still to recall the tragedy of the hunger strikes and all of the emotion and violence that ensued. John had tried very hard to negotiate a settlement and was heartbroken when ten young men eventually died. There was enormous pressure on the SDLP to withdraw all councillors from public office. They didn't withdraw, knowing that there was a real need to maintain some coherence in the midst of the potential disintegration of society. The dangers of high emotion on all sides were repeated at many stages during those tragic years. For the SDLP, the inviolate values of non-violence and mutual human respect sustained their vision.

TAKING A CHANCE FOR PEACE

The 1985 Anglo-Irish Agreement began to change the dynamic when the British government gave a formal role to the Irish government in northern affairs, and by formally acknowledging that Irish unity is a matter for those who want it persuading those who don't, thereby removing the core justification given by the IRA for their use of violence. This led to debate and re-appraisal within the IRA and was something John saw as an opportunity. Perhaps the next visible signs of movement began with talks in 1988 between the SDLP and Sinn Féin, facilitated by Fr Alec Reid at Clonard. Those talks discussed the use of force and whether or not it was justified. They ended inconclusively, but John continued to meet and debate with Sinn Féin leader Gerry Adams privately. Violence was continuing to wreak havoc and people were being killed every day. John remained committed to doing anything possible to break that cycle of violence. It is difficult to explain the complexities of this time when so many people felt that hope of a solution was almost exhausted. It was clear that engaging with those whose methods he completely opposed was a difficult and high-risk strategy. John made the decision that he would carry personal responsibility for this strategy, and for its potential failure.

When the word of the talks was leaked to the media, John was vilified in many sections of the press. The effects on his health and well-being were very visible. He lost a lot of weight, his sleep was fitful, and he was deeply exhausted. The ever-present death threats became much more intense and extended to many colleagues in the SDLP. After a particularly grim fire-bombing of our house and my car in 1987 we purchased a second home in Donegal, just thirty-five minutes from Derry. This weekend retreat was essential for all the family during these days. The thing that sustained John and his colleagues most through these huge pressures were the letters, cards and assurances of prayers from thousands of people who wanted peace to prevail.

CONCLUSION

Good Friday 1998 was an amazing day. All of the parties that participated and contributed to the success on Good Friday have been highly praised for their courage and foresight and rightly so. We all wanted our grandchildren to grow up in a peaceful society and in spite of ups and downs, life is now so much better. Behind the scenes, the people who played a major part in the negotiations were the highly talented small group of officials from the Department of Foreign Affairs in Dublin. From 1969 they were indefatigable in seeking a solution to our conflict. They worked weekends and evenings, meeting political representatives to discuss and listen to ideas for a way forward. Both John and I and all the family appreciate their help and friendship during those years.

The SDLP group of public representatives was a very skilled and visionary group of people – people of great courage who survived unrelenting threats and intimidation. I remember well the horror we all felt when the Currie house was broken into and UVF scratched on Annita's body. Séamus Mallon lived in the so-called 'murder triangle', but he was fearless in his condemnation of violence regardless of where it came from. He was a rock of honesty and courage and his clarity sustained the SDLP through many difficult times. In the years when John was travelling, Séamus was the beacon of reason that maintained the party's morale. At a local level, each election was overseen with immense skill by Berna McIvor, a woman of exceptional erudition, warmth and, of course, humour. She was one of a group of local people who provided heart, friendship, generosity and limitless courage, and this pattern was repeated across the whole party. None of what the SDLP achieved would have happened without their insistence on maintaining the party's core vision and values. John's five European elections were superbly organized from Belfast by our friend Tom Connolly who succeeded in increasing the vote substantially each time.

From his earliest writing John's vision was of a society that embraced diversity, where traditions of belief and identity were given equal respect and where violence was not tolerated. His father's political views remained his touchstone. While he paraphrased these as 'You can't eat a flag', he was passionate in believing that respect for diversity and economic justice were essential components of any self-respecting society. He told the story of Northern Ireland repeatedly to anyone whom he thought could provide help. His efforts bore economic fruit, through the work of Tip O Neill and others in the US and through Jaques Delors (head of the European Commission) and others from Europe whom he brought to the streets of Derry and Belfast. He organized exchange visits between local businesses and the US (Derry–Boston Ventures) which opened many much needed markets. He worked very closely and successfully in Europe with his fellow MEPs, Ian Paisley, John Taylor and Jim Nicholson to highlight the needs of Northern Ireland and bring about the resultant economic benefits. From the beginning John believed that the creation of a peaceful society had an economic as well as a political aspect. Despite an already frenetic schedule, John would go to any corner of the globe if he thought it might create one job at home.

When I ask the kids about the experience of growing up in the chaos that was our life, they all agree that – in spite of the madness – it was a privilege to be surrounded by the huge network of very diverse people who passed through our house every day, and they deeply appreciate the integrity and huge dedication that John demonstrated throughout his political career. John's health has suffered somewhat as the cumulative pressures of those years took a toll. The natural landscape of Donegal has been our haven and the support and love of many friends, our privileged sustenance. Life has been at times relentless in its pressures, but always generous in its gifts.

Contributors

PAUL ARTHUR is Distinguished Visiting Professor of Peace Studies at Chapman University, California, and Honorary Professor of Peace Studies at Ulster University. He has been a Senior Fellow at the United States Institute of Peace and a Fulbright Scholar at Stanford University. He has published widely on unofficial diplomacy, political violence and British-Irish relations.

ARTHUR AUGHEY is Professor of Politics at the Ulster University, Senior Fellow at the Centre for British Politics at the University of Hull, Fellow of the Academy of Social Sciences and Leverhulme Senior Research Fellow 2009–11. He has published widely on Northern Ireland politics, British Conservatism and constitutional change in the United Kingdom.

AUSTIN CURRIE graduated from Queen's University Belfast in 1963, and was elected to the Northern Ireland Parliament for East Tyrone in 1964. A leading civil rights campaigner and founder member of the SDLP, he became Minister for Housing in the power-sharing executive in 1974. In 1989 he was invited to join Fine Gael, and was elected to Dáil Éireann for Dublin West. He was Fine Gael's presidential candidate in 1990, and a minister of state in the departments of Justice, Education and Health, 1994–7. Now retired from politics he lives in County Kildare.

SEÁN DONLON spent thirty years in the Irish Civil Service including periods as Ambassador to the US, Secretary General of the Department of Foreign Affairs and Special Adviser to the Taoiseach. Thereafter he has been involved in the aviation financing and insurance sectors. He has also been Chancellor of the University of Limerick and is currently a resident director of the London-based European Bank for Reconstruction and Development.

MARK DURKAN was educated at St Columb's College, Derry, Queen's University Belfast and the Ulster University. A member of the SDLP, he was Westminster assistant to John Hume from 1981, and elected chair of the SDLP, 1990–5. A key member of the party's negotiating team for the Good Friday Agreement, he served in the Northern Ireland Assembly, 1998–2009, where he was Minister for Finance and Personnel and later Deputy First Minister. He was elected leader of the SDLP in 2001. He resigned his Assembly seat and party leadership in 2009 to concentrate on Westminster to which he was elected in 2005.

MARIANNE ELLIOTT is from Belfast; she is Professor Emeritus of Irish Studies at Liverpool University and a Fellow of the British Academy. She was a member of the international Opsahl Commission on Northern Ireland, 1993 and co-author of its report. Among her books are *Partners in revolution: the United Irishmen and France*, *Wolfe Tone*, *The Catholics of Ulster*, *When God took sides: religion and identity in Ireland*. She is currently completing a book on mixed religion housing in Belfast, 1945–2015. She was awarded an OBE in 2000 for services to Irish Studies and the Northern Ireland peace process.

CATHY GORMLEY-HEENAN is the Director of the Institute for Research in Social Sciences (IRISS) and a Professor of Politics in the School of Criminology, Politics & Social Policy at the Ulster University. Her primary research interests lie in the areas of political elites, peace processes, public policy and the politics of divided societies. She is author of *Political leadership in the Northern Ireland peace process*.

MAURICE HAYES was Assistant Secretary in the Office of the Northern Ireland Executive in 1974, and subsequently acted as adviser to the Chairman of the Constitutional Convention. He had previously been Town Clerk in Downpatrick and first Chair of the Community Relations Commission. Subsequently he served as Head of Personnel in the Northern Ireland Civil Service and as Permanent Secretary, Department of Health and Social Services. He was Northern Ireland Ombudsman and Boundary Commissioner and a member of the Patten Commission on policing. He served two terms in Seanad Éireann-Irish Senate as the Taoiseach's nominee and was Chair of the National Forum on Europe. A memoir of his civil service career, *Minority verdict*, was published in 1995.

PAT HUME is John Hume's wife and a former teacher. She managed John Hume's constituency office from his election to the European Parliament in 1979 until he retired from elected politics in 2005. She was a member of the Northern Ireland Memorial Fund, the RTÉ Authority and the Spirit of Ireland Awards. She holds honorary doctorates from Misericordia University, Pennsylvania, Iona College, New York, the National University of Ireland and Magee College, Ulster University.

BRIGID LAFFAN is Director and Professor at the Robert Schuman Centre for Advanced Studies, European University Institute, Florence. She was Vice-President of UCD and Principal of the College of Human Sciences from 2004 to 2011. She was the founding director of the Dublin European Institute UCD from 1999 and in March 2004 she was elected as a member of the Royal Irish Academy.

In September 2014 Professor Laffan was awarded the Lifetime Achievement Award of the Academic Association for Contemporary European Studies.

DAVID McKITTRICK has reported on the Troubles in Northern Ireland since the early 1970s, first for the *Irish Times* and latterly with the *London Independent.* He is author and co-author of a number of books including *Lost lives* which records all deaths of the Troubles. Awards include the Orwell prize and Ewart-Biggs prize for promoting peace and reconciliation.

SEÁN O'HUIGINN was a career diplomat in the Irish Department of Foreign Affairs between 1968 and 2009. He served as Consul-General in New York, and as Ambassador in Saudi Arabia, Copenhagen, Washington, Berlin and Rome. He was closely involved with Northern Ireland issues as Irish Joint Secretary of the British-Irish Intergovernmental Conference (1987–90), and with the peace process as Head of the Anglo-Irish Division of the Department (1991–7), and subsequently as Ambassador in Washington (1997–2002).

ÉAMON PHOENIX is Principal Lecturer in History and Head of Lifelong Learning at Stranmillis University College, Queen's University, Belfast His books include *Northern nationalism: nationalist politics, partition and the Catholic minority in Northern Ireland 1890–1940* (Belfast, 1994) and he is co-editor of *Conflicts in the North of Ireland, 1900–2000* (Dublin, 2010). He is a daily columnist for the *Irish News* and a regular broadcaster and commentator on Irish history. He is member of the Irish government's Advisory Committee on Centenaries.

NANCY SODERBERG served in the White House as Deputy National Security Adviser, as ambassador at the United Nations, as adviser to Senator Edward Kennedy, and on four presidential campaigns. She was President Clinton's adviser on Northern Ireland. She is President and CEO of Soderberg Global Solutions and a Distinguished Visiting Scholar and Director of the Public Service Leadership Programme at the University of North Florida. Appointed by President Obama as Chair of the Public Interest Declassification Board in 2011, she previously served as President of Connect US Fund and as Vice-President of the International Crisis Group. She publishes and speaks regularly on national security policy and is the author of two books on American foreign policy.

EDITORS

SEÁN FARREN hails from Dublin and has been a member of the SDLP since 1972. He has served on the party's executive, and was chair, 1980–4. A former councillor on Coleraine Borough Council, and MLA for the constituency of North

Antrim, he served on the New Ireland Forum, 1983–4 and the Forum for Peace and Reconciliation, 1994–6. In November 1999 he was appointed minister in the new power-sharing executive and served until its suspension in October 2002. He retired from the Assembly in 2007. Currently he is a Visiting Professor at the Ulster University where for many years he was a member of faculty in the School of Education. He is the author of *Paths to a settlement in Northern Ireland* and *The SDLP – the struggle for agreement in Northern Ireland.* He is married to Patricia and lives in Portstewart, Co. Derry.

DENIS HAUGHEY hails from Coalisland, Co. Tyrone. He graduated from Queen's University Belfast in 1967, and was a leading civil rights campaigner in the East Tyrone area. A member of the SDLP from its foundation, he served as party vice-chair, and chair, 1973–8. In 1980 he became a full-time adviser on European affairs to SDLP leader John Hume. In 1982 he was elected to the Northern Ireland Assembly for the constituency of Mid-Ulster and served on the New Ireland Forum. He was a member of the SDLP negotiating team in the Brooke/Mayhew talks, and in the talks leading to the Good Friday Agreement. Elected to the Northern Ireland Assembly in 1998, again for the constituency of Mid-Ulster, he was appointed junior minister in the Office of the First Minister and Deputy First Minister, 1999–2002. He is married to Maureen and is now retired from politics.

Index

Numbers in italics refer to plate numbers.